CW00408292

Ayatul Kursi

The Verse of the Throne

THE IMPENETRABLE ARMAMENT

Written by Muhammad Ibrahim Nasrullah Burujerdi

Translated by Saleem Bhimji

Edited by Arifa Hudda

Foreword by Tahera Kassamali

ISBN: 978-1-927930-14-4
Āyatul Kursī: The Verse of the Throne - The Impenetrable Armament

FOR FREE DISTRIBUTION - NOT FOR SALE

Written by Muhammad Ibrahim Nasrullah Burujerdi
Translated by Saleem Bhimji
Edited by Arifa Hudda
Foreword by Tahera Kassamali

Published by Islamic Publishing House

www.iph.ca · iph@iph.ca

Islamic Publishing House
The_IPH
TheIPH

Cover Design and Layout by Saleem Bhimji for the Islamic Publishing House

Printed in Canada by Marquis Book Printing (www.marquisbook.com/en/)

Dedication

The publication of this book was made possible through the generous support of our donors.

Please recite *Sūrah al-Fātiḥa* and ask Allāh for the Divine reward (*thawāb*) to be conferred upon the donors and also the souls of all the deceased in whose memory their loved ones have contributed graciously towards the publication of *Āyatul Kursī: The Impenetrable Armament.*

اللهم كن لوليك الحجة بن الحسن صلواتك
عليه وعلى آبائه في هذه الساعة وفي كل
ساعة وليا وحافظا وقائدا وناصرا ودليلا
وعينا حتى تسكنه أرضك طوعا وتمتعه فيها طويلا

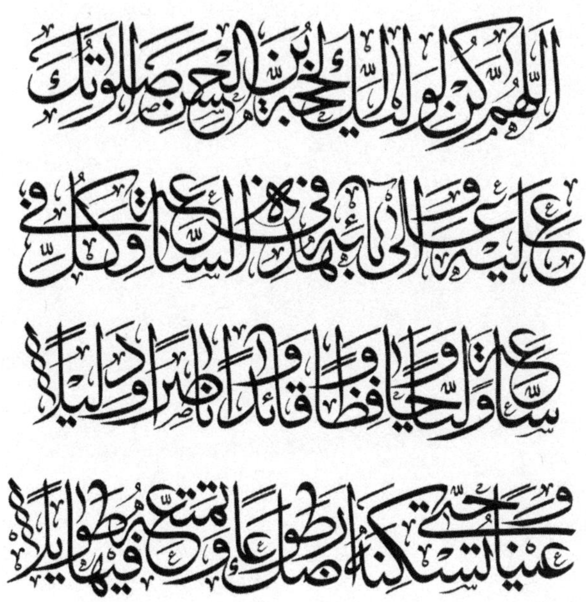

O Allah, be, for Your representative, the Hujjat (proof), son of al-Hasan, Your blessings be upon him and his forefathers, in this hour and in every hour: a guardian, a protector, a leader, a helper, a proof, and an eye - until You make him live on the Earth, in obedience (to You), and cause him to live in it for a long time.

Contents

Transliteration Table

The method of transliteration of Islamic terminology from the Arabic language has been carried out according to the standard transliteration table mentioned below.

ء	ʾ	ر	r	ف	f
ا	a	ز	z	ق	q
ب	b	س	s	ك	k
ت	t	ش	sh	ل	l
ث	th	ص	ṣ	م	m
ج	j	ض	ḍ	ن	n
ح	ḥ	ط	ṭ	و	w
خ	kh	ظ	ẓ	ه	h
د	d	ع	ʿ	ي	y
ذ	dh	غ	gh		
Long Vowels					
ا	ā	و	ū	ي	ī
Short Vowels					
ـَ	a	ـُ	u	ـِ	i

Terms of Respect

The following Arabic phrases have been used throughout this book in their respective places to show the reverence which the noble personalities deserve.

Used for Allāh (God) meaning:
Exalted and Sublime (Perfect) is He

Used for Prophet Muḥammad meaning:
Blessings from Allāh be upon him and his family

Used for a man of high status (singular) meaning:
Peace be upon him

Used for woman of a high status (singular) meaning:
Peace be upon her

Used for men/women of a high status (dual) meaning:
Peace be upon them both

Used for men and/or women of a high status (plural) meaning:
Peace be upon them all

Used for a deceased scholar meaning:
May his resting [burial] place remain pure

Introduction by the Author

In the Name of Allāh, the Most Gracious, the Most Merciful

Turning one's full attention towards Allāh ﷻ and engrossing oneself in the remembrance of the Beloved is an act which holds a special significance within the teachings of Islam; and fundamentally, the essence of obedience, worship and one's spiritual worth stems from being in the constant remembrance of Allāh ﷻ.

The religion of Islam believes that the source of a human being's spiritual power and strength, and the only factor which can lead one to success and perfection is found in the unremitting remembrance of Allāh ﷻ; and that all of the tribulations which a person goes through, the negative ethical traits which someone may display, and the spiritual defects and sicknesses which one may be plagued with all stem from one's heedlessness of Allāh ﷻ.

Various practical guidelines have been laid down within the teachings of Islam which every Muslim needs to follow to be in the constant remembrance of Allāh ﷻ so that in one's day to day life, one can remember the Creator in a complete fashion and not fall into the pits of negligence of the Almighty. Among these acts, the most important one which leads to the remembrance of Allāh ﷻ is the five daily prayers - as it disengages a person's thoughts [and actions] from the monotony of the transient world and reunites one with the Beloved.

Keeping in mind the spiritual life giving effects which the remembrance of Allāh ﷻ has, we see that there are many instances in the Noble Quran in which the believers have been told to continuously think about Allāh ﷻ, and are told that through this, the source of life of the hearts of the believers is quenched. The Noble Quran states:

﴿يَا أَيُّهَا الَّذِينَ آمَنُوا اذْكُرُوا اللَّهَ ذِكْراً كَثِيراً ﴿٤١﴾﴾

> O you who believe! Remember Allāh – a frequent remembering![1]

In addition, the Noble Prophet of Islam ﷺ stated: "The similitude of those who remember Allāh to those who are heedless (of Him) is like the living among the dead, or a green tree among a forest of dried up trees. Such a person [who remembers Allāh ﷻ] is like one who stands in combat among those who are fleeing the battlefield."[2]

In regards to the importance of the remembrance of Allāh ﷻ, the Noble Prophet ﷺ has also stated:

إِنَّ أَهْلَ الْجَنَّةِ لاَ يَتَحَسَّرُونَ عَلىٰ شَيْءٍ فَاتَهُمْ مِنَ الدُّنْيَا كَتَحَسُّرِهِمْ عَلَىٰ سَاعَةٍ مَرَّتْ مِنْ غَيْرِ ذِكْرِ اللّٰهِ

> Indeed the people of Paradise shall not regret anything which passed from them in the transient world as much as the grief that they will feel in regards to the time which passed [while in the transient world] in which they were not occupied in the remembrance of

---

[1] *Quran*, Sūrah al-Aḥzāb (33), verse 41.

[2] *The Alchemy of Happiness*, vol. 1, p. 253.

Allāh.[3]

Among all types of the remembrance of Allāh ﷻ, the one which is the greatest manifestation of the remembrance of Allāh ﷻ is the recitation of Āyatul Kursī – the Verse of The Throne, which has been described in the books of the Muslims as being 'the pinnacle of the Noble Quran', and it also holds the loftiest status from among all of the verses of the Quran.

In addition, there are numerous traditions which encourage us to recite Āyatul Kursī. In one narration, Imām ʿAli ؑ stated that after he heard the merits of this verse, not a single night passed without him reciting Āyatul Kursī!

Indeed, just as the breath of Prophet ʿIsā (Jesus) ؑ brought forth miracles, Āyatul Kursī can also produce miracles and extraordinary occurances for a person who recites it, which we will speak about later on [in this book].

Our discussions in regards to Āyatul Kursī will be divided into the following sections[4]:

1. A concise and easy to understand commentary of Āyatul Kursī.
2. Is Āyatul Kursī one verse or three verses?
3. The merits of Āyatul Kursī.

During my research, I was not able to find any books which discussed the topics mentioned above and realized that many people have been deprived of the blessings of this magnificent verse of the Quran, and thus it was my desire that this insignificant

---

[3] *Mustadrak al-Wasāʾil wa Mustanbit al-Masāʾil*, vol. 5, p. 288, trad. 5878

[4] In order to allow the readers a greater appreciation and understanding of Āyatul Kursī, we have added the commentary of the late ʿAllāmah Sayyid Muḥammad Ḥusayn Ṭabāʾṭabāʾī as translated by the Late ʿAllāmah Sayyid Saeed Akthar Rizvi, as well as excerpts from *Tafsīr-e Nūr* of Shaykh Mohsin Qaraʾati on lessons which can be learnt from this passage. (Tr.)

service of mine serves as a stepping stone for people to gain a better understanding of Allāh ﷻ and that this work gains the pleasure of the Most High, God Willing.

Muḥammad Ibrahim Nasrullah Burujerdi

Thursday, 12th of Muḥarram al-Ḥarām 1425 AH[5]
Martyrdom anniversary of Imam al-Sajjād ؑ
Qum, Iran

[5] There are differences of opinion in the books of history as to the death date of the 4th Imām and some scholars also narrate the 25th of Muḥarram as being the martyrdom anniversary of Imām al-Sajjād ؑ.

Introduction by the Translator

Devout Muslims around the world are continually surrounded – both spiritually and physically – with the Noble Quran. Not only do they recite it themselves, but they also hear it being recited - either in the Islamic centres or via an app on their smartphone; some use its calligraphy as a wallpaper on their personal digital devices, and others also decorate their homes with its beautiful verses. In addition, occasionally Muslims will also hang Quranic verses on the rear-view mirror in their cars with the hope of being protected by Allāh ﷻ through its verses.

However with all of this physical attachment to the Quran, what is more important is that we also need to understand the contents of the verses which Allāh ﷻ revealed to Prophet Muḥammad ﷺ.

One of the first steps in understanding the Quran is to constantly recite it in the original ʿArabic, with the aim of attaining guidance from Allāh ﷻ; while at the same time, trying our best to learn enough ʿArabic which will facilitate an understanding of the Quran in the original language that it was revealed in. Although translations of the Quran are now available in almost every language, with tens of translations available in English alone, however once a person begins to study the Quran in ʿArabic, they will come to realize how deficient any translation is, no matter how authoritative or accurate it may be.

From there comes the next step which is to read the translation – and not only one translation, but numerous translations – keeping in mind that the rendition into the host language can never fully cover the depth and beauty of the original ʿArabic; however it is a start in being able to understand the message. In this field, there are countless acceptable translations[6] of the Quran in English which will allow the reader an entry into the world of the Quran.

Once we have understood its general meaning via a translation, we then need to devote time to study and read the commentaries which the scholars of Islam have spent hundreds of years and thousands of hours in preparing – through their meticulous study of the Quran and *aḥādīth* of the Prophet ﷺ and his noble family ﷺ - researching each and every word contained in the Quran, along with the history behind the verses - seeking to provide a comprehensive understanding of the Book of Allāh ﷻ for us to be able to read and ponder upon. Some of these commentaries are now available in English to facilitate the layman a glimpse into the deeper meanings and messages of the Quran.

Once we are able to make our way through these stages while seeking assistance from Allāh ﷻ we will then be able to better appreciate the Noble Quran and seek to implement its teachings in our day to day lives.

All of the verses and chapters of the Quran must be looked at in this fashion, and we owe it to the legacy of Prophet Muḥammad ﷺ to devote some of our time to that Book of guidance which he spent his entire life in working for, as a means to get closer to Allāh ﷻ and be better human beings.

It gives us great pleasure to present this book which takes an in-

[6] A useful site with over 15 English translations of the Quran can be found at: http://2pm.co/demo/2500/. (Last accessed on January 20, 2017).

depth look at one of the most popular passages of the Quran – commonly known as Āyatul Kursī - The Verse of the Throne - to the seekers of knowledge of the Quran.

Contained in the largest chapter of the Quran, Sūrah al-Baqarah (chapter 2), the 255th verse of this chapter holds a unique distinction within the tradition of Islam. First and foremost is its designation as The Verse of the Throne.

It is a verse which is rather unique, not only due to the brevity of it, but at the same time, maintaining the Quranic elegance of containing profound and multi-layered meanings. Even the actual make-up of the passage – and how the balance of the words and statements present us with an equilibrium. The verse reads as follows:

﴿ٱللَّهُ لَآ إِلَٰهَ إِلَّا هُوَ ٱلْحَىُّ ٱلْقَيُّومُ لَا تَأْخُذُهُۥ سِنَةٌ وَلَا
نَوْمٌ لَّهُۥ مَا فِى ٱلسَّمَٰوَٰتِ وَمَا فِى ٱلْأَرْضِ مَن ذَا ٱلَّذِى
يَشْفَعُ عِندَهُۥٓ إِلَّا بِإِذْنِهِۦ يَعْلَمُ مَا بَيْنَ أَيْدِيهِمْ وَمَا
خَلْفَهُمْ وَلَا يُحِيطُونَ بِشَىْءٍ مِّنْ عِلْمِهِۦٓ إِلَّا بِمَا شَآءَ
وَسِعَ كُرْسِيُّهُ ٱلسَّمَٰوَٰتِ وَٱلْأَرْضَ وَلَا يَـُٔودُهُۥ حِفْظُهُمَا
وَهُوَ ٱلْعَلِىُّ ٱلْعَظِيمُ ﴿٢٥٥﴾﴾

Allāh - there is no god except Him – He is the Living One, the All-Sustainer. Neither drowsiness befalls Him nor sleep. To Him belongs whatever is in the heavens and whatever is on the earth. Who is it that may intercede with Him except by His permission? He knows that which is before them and that which is behind them, and they do not comprehend anything of His knowledge except what He wishes. His throne embraces the heavens and the earth, and He is not wearied by their preservation, and He is the All-Exalted, the All-Supreme.

When we analyze Āyatul Kursī piece by piece, and decode it into its individual and distinctive constituents, we see that each portion or 'sentence' is actually contingent upon that which comes before it, and therefore:

1. When we say that Allāh ﷻ is ﴾the Ever-Living One, the All Sustainer﴿ - ﴾الْحَيُّ الْقَيُّومُ﴿, then we must understand that this is reliant upon His absolute Lordship over everything in creation which is manifest in what came before it in this passage where we say ﴾Allāh - there is no god except Him﴿ - ﴾ٱللَّهُ لَآ إِلَٰهَ إِلَّا هُوَ﴿.

2. Moving on, when we affirm that ﴾To Him belongs whatever is in the heavens and whatever is on the earth﴿ - ﴾لَّهُۥ مَا فِى ٱلسَّمَٰوَٰتِ وَمَا فِى ٱلْأَرْضِ﴿ we do so knowing and understanding that for such power, authority and dominion to continue, He must never become lethargic or sleepy and so it is mentioned that ﴾Neither drowsiness befalls Him nor sleep.﴿ - ﴾لَا تَأْخُذُهُۥ سِنَةٌ وَلَا نَوْمٌ﴿.

3. We are then told that ﴾He knows everything that which is before them and that which is behind them﴿ - ﴾يَعْلَمُ مَا بَيْنَ أَيْدِيهِمْ وَمَا خَلْفَهُمْ﴿ and as such, when it comes to the topic of intercession and advocating on behalf of others, it is not possible to delude or trick Him as His knowledge covers everything, and so we read ﴾Who is it that may intercede with Him except by His permission?﴿ - ﴾مَن ذَا ٱلَّذِى يَشْفَعُ عِندَهُۥٓ إِلَّا بِإِذْنِهِۦ﴿.

4. Penultimately, when we read that His dominion covers the entire scope of creation – that which we as human beings have discovered, and that which is waiting to be found as we say that ﴾His seat embraces the heavens and the earth﴿ - ﴾وَسِعَ كُرْسِيُّهُ ٱلسَّمَٰوَٰتِ وَٱلْأَرْضَ﴿ then we are drawn to the natural conclusion that what we as His creations know about Him, His power,

authority and dominion, is limited and conditional upon what He wants us to know and we attest to this by stating ❬And they do not comprehend anything of His knowledge except what He wishes.❭ - ❬وَلَا يُحِيطُونَ بِشَيْءٍ مِنْ عِلْمِهِ إِلَّا بِمَا شَاءَ❭.

5. Finally, to conclude this passage of Āyatul Kursī and which is in reality a summary of the entire text of The Verse of the Throne, the synopsis is encapsulated in the final lines which show us that ❬And He is the All-Exalted, the All-Supreme❭ - ❬وَهُوَ الْعَلِيُّ الْعَظِيمُ❭ - the power, authority and maintenance of the entire cosmos and all that He has created is not a difficult thing for Him ❬and He is not wearied by their preservation,❭ - ❬وَلَا يَئُودُهُ حِفْظُهُمَا❭.

In this way, The Verse of the Throne comes to a close[7] and can be compared to a building in which the foundation is first laid (which in this case is the last portion of the verse, ❬and He is the All-Exalted, the All-Supreme❭ - ❬وَهُوَ الْعَلِيُّ الْعَظِيمُ❭, and each subsequent layer or level adds to the majesty and splendor of that building until it reaches to the apex of the building – the top of the magnificent structure, which in this case is ❬Allāh - there is no god except Him❭ - ❬اَللَّهُ لَا إِلَٰهَ إِلَّا هُوَ❭.

Thus, both the foundation of Āyatul Kursī is Allāh ﷻ and the pinnacle of Āyatul Kursī is also Allāh ﷻ - and everything in between is nothing other than the description of The Most High.

The leader of all verses

Amongst the prophets and messengers of Allāh ﷻ, some have a greater status than others and they are not all on one equal level,

[7] Keep in mind, as we will later on mention, that Āyatul Kursī is actually only ONE verse, (thus the word *āyat* is the singular) however in many of the traditions from Prophet Muḥammad ﷺ and his noble family ؑ, they have advised that in many circumstances and supplications, one should also recite verse 256 and 257 to 'complete' this passage.

just like Allāh ﷻ says in the Quran:

﴿تِلْكَ الرُّسُلُ فَضَّلْنَا بَعْضَهُمْ عَلَىٰ بَعْضٍ مِنْهُمْ مَنْ كَلَّمَ اللَّهُ وَرَفَعَ بَعْضَهُمْ دَرَجَاتٍ وَآتَيْنَا عِيسَى ابْنَ مَرْيَمَ الْبَيِّنَاتِ وَأَيَّدْنَاهُ بِرُوحِ الْقُدُسِ ﴿٢٥٣﴾﴾

> From these messengers, We preferred some above others. There are some to whom Allāh spoke; and We have exalted some of them by degrees; and We gave Jesus, the son of Mary, manifest signs, and strengthened him with the Holy Spirit...[8]

Similiarly the chapters and verses of the Quran are also not all equal and the same – some chapters and verses have a higher degree of importance over other ones.

The secret to why this is the case lies in the fact that the contents of certain passages is of greater depths and profundity than the other ones – and this is based on many factors including the method of composition of that passage (by Allāh ﷻ), including the individual sentences, words and letters and how they are combined together.

Therefore in the case of Āyatul Kursī, which is referred to as The Verse of the Throne due to the usage of the word throne (*kursī*) within it, in addition to it starting with the name of Allāh ﷻ, and the possibility of the passage containing The Greatest Name of Allāh ﷻ – what is known as *al-ism al-aʿḍham*, this verse has also been referred to in the traditions as the leader (*sayyid*) of all verses, and we see that Allāh ﷻ is referred to within it on thirteen occasions. By reviewing the Quran, we see that there is not a single other verse which makes reference to Allāh ﷻ so many times in one verse.

---

[8] *Quran*, Sūrah al-Baqarah (2), verse 253.

There are five visible citations of Allāh ﷻ through His proper name, in addition to the four attributes of His in this verse; there are also nine uses of the apparent pronoun to refer to Allāh ﷻ, and two hidden pronouns in the verbs used which relate back to Him. This is further explained below:

The five names of Allāh ﷻ which are mentioned in Āyatul Kursī are:

- *Allāh* (أَللهُ) – God
- *Al-Ḥayy* (أَلْحَيُّ) – The Ever-Living
- *Al-Qayyūm* (أَلْقَيُّومُ) – The All Sustainer
- *Al-ʿAlī* (أَلْعَلِيُّ) – The All Exalted
- *Al-ʿAḍhīm* (أَلْعَظِيمُ) – The All Supreme

The nine pronouns relating to Allāh ﷻ which are mentioned in Āyatul Kursī are:

- **He** (هُوَ)
- Does not over take **Him** (لَا تَأْخُذُهُ)
- For **Him** (لَهُ)
- With **Him** (عِنْدَهُ)
- With **His** permission (بِإِذْنِهِ)
- **His** knowledge (عِلْمِهِ)
- **His** Chair (كُرْسِيُّهُ)
- Fatigue **Him** (يَؤُودُهُ)
- **He** (هُوَ)

The two hidden pronouns contained in the verbs used which relate back to Allāh ﷻ and found in Āyatul Kursī are:

- **He** knows (يَعْلَمُ)
- **He** wills (شَآءَ)

Another beauty and phenomenon of this passage is the "negating and affirming" nature of each pair of 'sentences' in this passage, which is seen in the following pattern:

1	**Affirming**	أَللّٰـهُ Allāh
2	**Negating**	لَا إِلٰه إِلَّا هُوَ There is no god except Him
3	**Affirming**	الْحَىُّ الْقَيُّومُ He is the Ever-Living One, the All Sustainer.
4	**Negating**	لَا تَأْخُذُهُ سِنَةٌ وَلَا نَوْمٌ Neither drowsiness befalls Him nor sleep.
5	**Affirming**	لَهُ مَا فِى السَّمٰوَاتِ وَمَا فِى الأَرْضِ To Him belongs whatever is in the heavens and whatever is on the earth.
6	**Negating**	مَنْ ذَا الَّذِى يَشْفَعُ عِنْدَهُ إِلاَّ بِإِذْنِهِ Who is it that may intercede with Him except by His permission?
7	**Affirming**	يَعْلَمُ مَا بَيْنَ أَيْدِيهِمْ وَمَا خَلْفَهُمْ He knows that which is before them and that which is behind them,

8	**Negating**	وَلاَ يُحِيطُونَ بِشَيْءٍ مِنْ عِلْمِهِ إِلاَّ بِمَا شَآءَ and they do not comprehend anything of His knowledge except what He wishes.
9	**Affirming**	وَسِعَ كُرْسِيُّهُ السَّمٰوَاتِ وَالأَرْضَ His seat embraces the heavens and the earth,
10	**Negating**	وَلاَ يَئُودُهُ حِفْظُهُمَا and He is not wearied by their preservation,
11	**Affirming**	وَهُوَ الْعَلِيُّ الْعَظِيمُ and He is the All-Exalted, the All-Supreme.

A third and yet another unique, and miraculous aspect of the composition of Āyatul Kursī lies in the fact that there is a pattern of correlation which exists between the nine sentences which make up this verse.

With this "symmetry," we see that there is harmony between the first and ninth part of Āyatul Kursī; second and eighth part of this verse; third and seventh part; fourth and sixth part; with the fifth portion of the verse standing on its own.

The following chart further explains this incomparable concept with greater clarity:

<table>
<tr><th>9th Sentence</th><th>1st Sentence</th></tr>
<tr><td>وَهُوَ ٱلْعَلِىُّ ٱلْعَظِيمُ</td><td>ٱللَّهُ لَآ إِلَـٰهَ إِلَّا هُوَ ٱلْحَىُّ ٱلْقَيُّومُ</td></tr>
<tr><td>and He is the All-Exalted, the All-Supreme.</td><td>Allāh - there is no god except Him – He is the Living One, the All-Sustainer.</td></tr>
<tr><th>8th Sentence</th><th>2nd Sentence</th></tr>
<tr><td>وَلَا يَـُٔودُهُۥ حِفْظُهُمَا</td><td>لَا تَأْخُذُهُۥ سِنَةٌ وَلَا نَوْمٌ</td></tr>
<tr><td>and He is not wearied by their preservation,</td><td>Neither drowsiness befalls Him nor sleep.</td></tr>
<tr><th colspan="2">5th Sentence</th></tr>
<tr><td colspan="2">يَعْلَمُ مَا بَيْنَ أَيْدِيهِمْ وَمَا خَلْفَهُمْ</td></tr>
<tr><td colspan="2">He knows that which is before them and that which is behind them,</td></tr>
<tr><th>7th Sentence</th><th>3rd Sentence</th></tr>
<tr><td>وَسِعَ كُرْسِيُّهُ ٱلسَّمَاوَاتِ وَٱلْأَرْضَ</td><td>لَّهُۥ مَا فِى ٱلسَّمَاوَاتِ وَمَا فِى ٱلْأَرْضِ</td></tr>
<tr><td>His seat embraces the heavens and the earth,</td><td>To Him belongs whatever is in the heavens and whatever is on the earth.</td></tr>
<tr><th>6th Sentence</th><th>4th Sentence</th></tr>
<tr><td>وَ لَا يُحِيطُونَ بِشَىْءٍ مِّنْ عِلْمِهِۦٓ إِلَّا بِمَا شَآءَ</td><td>مَن ذَا ٱلَّذِى يَشْفَعُ عِنْدَهُۥٓ إِلَّا بِإِذْنِهِۦ</td></tr>
<tr><td>and they do not comprehend anything of His knowledge except what He wishes.</td><td>Who is it that may intercede with Him except by His permission?</td></tr>
</table>

Thus we see the eloquent nature of this passage and the subtle nuances with which Allāh ﷻ not only conveys a clear meaning to us, but also how He uses the power of the ʿArabic language to depict such a marvel of literature.

Although the final portion of this book focuses on various traditions about the importance of Āyatul Kursī, however to conclude our introduction, and to stir the hearts to want to study and reflect deeper on this beautiful passage of the Quran, we present some traditions on the merits and worth of The Verse of the Throne.

The Best Verse

It has been narrated from Abī ʿAbdillāh ؑ that he said:

قَالَ أَبُو ذَرٍّ: يَا رَسُولَ اللّهِ! مَا أَفْضَلُ مَا أُنْزِلَ عَلَيْكَ؟ قَالَ: آيَةُ الْكُرْسِيِّ

Abū Dharr said: 'O Messenger of Allāh! What is the best of that which was revealed upon you?' He (the Messenger of Allāh ﷺ) replied: 'Āyatul Kursī.'[9]

Leader (*Sayyid*) of all Verses

It has been narrated from [Imām] ʿAli ؑ that he said:

سَمِعْتُ رَسُولَ اللّهِ ﷺ يَقُولُ: وَ الْقُرْآنُ سَيِّدُ الْكَلَامِ وَ سُورَةُ الْبَقَرَةِ سَيِّدُ الْقُرْآنِ وَ آيَةُ الْكُرْسِيِّ سَيِّدُ سُورَةِ الْبَقَرَةِ فِيهَا خَمْسُونَ كَلِمَةً فِي كُلِّ كَلِمَةٍ بَرَكَة

I heard the Messenger of Allāh ﷺ say: 'The Quran is the leader of all speech; and Sūrah al-Baqarah is the

[9] *Tafsīr* of al-ʿAyyāshī, vol.1, p. 137.

leader of the Quran; and Āyatul Kursī is the leader of Sūrah al-Baqarah and contained within it [Āyatul Kursī] are fifty words and in each word are contained blessings.'[10]

The Greatest Verse

It has been narrated from Abī Amāmah that he said:

قُلْتُ: يَا رَسُولَ اللّٰهِ أَيُّمَا أُنْزِلَ عَلَيْكَ أَعْظَمُ؟ قَالَ: ﴿اَللّٰهُ لاَ إِلٰهَ إِلاَّ هُوَ الْحَيُّ الْقَيُّومُ﴾ - آيَةُ الْكُرْسِيِّ

I asked: 'O Messenger of Allāh! What is the greatest thing which has been revealed to you?' He [the Messenger of Allāh ﷺ] replied: '﴾Allāh! There is no god other than Him, the Ever-Living, the All Sustaining﴿ - Āyatul Kursī.'[11]

Peak of the Quran

It has been narrated from Jaʿfar b. Muḥammad ؑ that he said:

قَالَتِ الْجِنُّ: إِنَّ لِكُلِّ شَيْءٍ ذُرْوَةٌ وَ ذُرْوَةُ الْقُرآنِ آيَةُ الْكُرْسِيِّ

The Jinn had said: 'There is a summit to everything and the summit of the Quran is Āyatul Kursī.'[12]

A Special Gift to the Prophet ﷺ

It has been narrated from Sudayy b. Amāmah al-Bāhilī that he had heard ʿAlī b. Abī Ṭālib ؑ say:

إِنَّ رَسُولَ اللّٰهِ ﷺ أَخْبَرَنِي قَالَ: أُعْطِيتُ آيَةَ الْكُرْسِيِّ مِنْ كَنْزٍ

[10] *Mustadrak al-Wasāiʾil wa Mustanbiṭ al-Masāʾil*, vol. 4, p. 337, trad. 4825.

[11] *Al-Durr al-Manthūr*, vol. 2, p. 12.

[12] *Tafsīr* of al-ʿAyyāshī, vol. 1, p. 136.

تَحْـتَ الْعَـرْشِ وَ لَـمْ يُؤْتَهَـا نَبِـيٌّ كَانَ قَبْـلِي. قَـالَ عَـلِيٌّ عليه السلام: فَـمَا بِـتُّ لَيْلَـةً قَـطُّ مُنْـذُ سَـمِعْتُهَا مِـنْ رَسُـولِ اللَّـهِ صلى الله عليه وآله حَتَّـى أَقْرَأَهَـا.

Indeed the Messenger of Allāh ﷺ informed me, saying: 'I have been given Āyatul Kursī which is a treasure from beneath the Divine emperion (*'arsh*) and no prophet before me has ever been given such a thing.' 'Alī ؑ then said: 'After hearing this statement from the Messenger of Allāh ﷺ, I never went to sleep without reciting it (Āyatul Kursī).'[13]

Some Rewards for Reciting Āyatul Kursī

It has been narrated from the Commander of the Faithful [Imām 'Alī] ؑ that he said:

سَـمِعْتُ نَبِيَّكُـمْ عَـلَى أَعْـوَادِ الْمِنْـبَرِ وَ هُـوَ يَقُـولُ مَـنْ قَـرَأَ آيَـةَ الْكُـرْسِيِّ فِي دُبُـرِ كُلِّ صَـلَاةٍ مَكْتُوبَـةٍ لَـمْ يَمْنَعْـهُ مِـنْ دُخُـولِ الْجَنَّـةِ إِلَّا الْمَـوْتُ وَ لَا يُوَاظِـبُ عَلَيْهَـا إِلَّا صِدِّيـقٌ أَوْ عَابِـدٌ وَ مَـنْ قَرَأَهَـا إِذَا أَخَـذَ مَضْجَعَـهُ آمَنَـهُ اللَّـهُ عَـلَى نَفْسِـهِ وَ جَـارِهِ وَ جَـارِ جَـارِهِ وَ الْأَبْيَـاتِ حَوْلَـه

I heard your Prophet say the following while he was on the pulpit (*mimbar*) that: 'Whoever recites Āyatul Kursī after every obligatory *ṣalāt* will find that nothing will prevent that person from entering into paradise except death, and no one will be steadfast in this [in the recitation of Āyatul Kursī] except those who are the truthful ones or the true worshippers. In addition, a person who recites it [Āyatul Kursī], when one is taken from one's bed [as one dies], Allāh Himself

---

[13] *Al-Amālī* of Shaykh al-Ṭusī, pp. 508-509; *Al-Burhān*, vol. 1, p. 541.

> will look after that individual, his neighbour and the neighbour of his neighbour and [the people who live in the] houses around him.'[14]

In another tradition it is narrated from ʿAmrū b. Abī al-Miqdām that he said: I heard Abā Jaʿfar al-Bāqir ﷺ say:

> مَنْ قَرَأَ آيَةَ الْكُرْسِيِّ مَرَّةً صَرَفَ اللَّهُ عَنْهُ أَلْفَ مَكْرُوهٍ مِنْ مَكْرُوهِ الدُّنْيَا وَ أَلْفَ مَكْرُوهٍ مِنْ مَكْرُوهِ الْآخِرَةِ أَيْسَرُ مَكْرُوهِ الدُّنْيَا الْفَقْرُ وَ أَيْسَرُ مَكْرُوهِ الْآخِرَةِ عَذَابُ الْقَبْرِ.
>
> A person who recites Āyatul Kursī one time will find that Allāh removes 1,000 detestable things from the detestable things of this world from that individual, and 1,000 detestable things from the detestable things of the world to come – and the most simplest of those detestable things from this world will be indigence, and the most simplest of those detestable things of the world to come will be the punishment in the grave.[15]

In a final tradition on this topic, which we quote, it has been narrated from Ṣuday Abi Umāmah al-Bāhilī that he heard ʿAlī b. Abī Ṭālib ﷺ say:

> مَا أَرَى رَجُلًا أَدْرَكَ عَقْلُهُ الْإِسْلَامَ وَ وُلِدَ فِي الْإِسْلَامِ يَبِيتُ لَيْلَةً سَوَادَهَا- قُلْتُ: وَ مَا سَوَادُهَا، يَا أَبَا أُمَامَةَ قَالَ: جَمِيعَهَا- حَتَّى يَقْرَأَ هَذِهِ الْآيَةَ ﴿اللَّهُ لا إِلَهَ إِلَّا هُوَ الْحَيُّ الْقَيُّومُ﴾ فَقَرَأَ الْآيَةَ إِلَى قَوْلِهِ: ﴿الْعَلِيُّ الْعَظِيمُ﴾، ثُمَّ قَالَ: فَلَوْ تَعْلَمُونَ مَا هِيَ- أَوْ قَالَ: مَا فِيهَا- لَمَا تَرَكْتُمُوهَا عَلَى حَالٍ، إِنَّ رَسُولَ

---

[14] *Al-Tawḥīd,* p. 18.

[15] Ibid., pp. 625-626.

اللَّـهِ ﷺ أَخْـبَرَنِي قَـالَ: أُعْطِيـتُ آيَـةَ الْكُـرْسِيِّ مِـنْ كَنْـزٍ تَحْـتَ الْعَـرْشِ وَ لَـمْ يُؤْتَهَـا نَبِـيٌّ كَانَ قَبْـلِي. قَـالَ عَـلِّي : فَـمَا بِـتُّ لَيْلَـةً قَـطُّ مُنْـذُ سَـمِعْتُهَا مِـنْ رَسُـولِ اللَّـهِ ﷺ حَتَّـى أَقْرَأَهَـا.

I don't see a person [meaning that I don't expect a person] who understands Islam and was born into it, to pass the night in its darkness (he sleeps all of the night) unless he recites the following verse ❨Allāh – there is no God except for Him – the Ever-Living, the All Subsisting. He then read the verse until he reached to, ❨The All-Exalted, the All-Supreme❩. Then he (ʿAlī) said: 'If you knew what this verse was or what was in it, then you would not abandon it in any situation. Indeed the Messenger of Allāh ﷺ informed me saying: 'I was given The Verse of the Throne from a treasure under the Throne (dominion of Allāh ﷻ) which no Prophet ﷺ before me was given.' Then ʿAlī ؑ said: 'I haven't passed any night since I heard that from the Messenger of Allāh ﷺ unless I recited this verse.''[16]

☙

This book seeks to delve into the beautiful verse [and the two which follow it in order to "complete" Āyatul Kursī] in a number of ways:

1. First, for us to read and understand its basic English translation;
2. From there, we look at a brief explanation of some key phrases and terms used in it;
3. We then delve into one of the most detailed explanations written on this collection of verses as authored by the late ʿAllāmah Sayyid Muḥammad Ḥusayn Ṭabā'ṭabā'ī from his

[16] Ibid., p. 626.

monumental 20 volume exegesis of the Noble Quran, *al-Mizān fī Tafsīr al-Quran*, as translated by the Late Allāmah Sayyid Saeed Akthar Rizvi ﷶ. Although this portion was not a part of the original book, however since we wanted to ensure that the readers have a clear understanding of The Verse of the Throne, we decided to include this commentary in this work.

4. The question as to whether Āyatul Kursī is one verse or three verses (verses 255, 256 and 257) is then answered by a review of some of the traditions which speak about this topic.

5. We then present a summary of the lessons which we can learn from Āyatul Kursī as mentioned in *Tafsīr-e Nūr* authored by the contemporary scholar, Shaykh Mohsin Qara'ati. Although not a part of the original work, as it was found to add value to this discussion and to make Āyatul Kursī even more practical and relevant to our lives, we translated and have included it in this book.

6. After that, we then return back to the original text of the book and continue to delve into the beauty, power and potency of Āyatul Kursī by reviewing the various traditions that are included in the books of *aḥādīth* which speak about the worth of this passage and what can be achieved by its recitation – obviously with reflection and understanding the contents of it.

☙

Along the way of the publication of this book, I have benefitted from the constant assistance and support of our editor and my wife, Sister Arifa Hudda, who accepted our request to edit this book and offer valuable suggestions and comments to bring this project to fruition. We are eternally indebted to her for all of her services. In addition, our daughter, Muhadditha Fatema Saleem also read over the entire book and offered her own proofreading changes to the text.

It is due to the generous financial contributions of our well-wishers and donors around the world who supported this project financially by contributing directly to us and via our crowd-sourcing campaign on **Taha Funder (www.tahafunder.com)** for which we are extremely grateful.

In addition, we would be amiss if we did not expressly acknowledge the two extraordinary anonymous donors in Ontario, Canada and London, UK whose extremely generous donations greatly helped us to publish this book and ensure its complimentary distribution – indeed their rewards are solely with Allāh ﷻ.

We are also indebted to **The World Federation of KSIMC (www.world-federation.org)** in general, and in particular the Islamic Education department for their generous contribution towards the printing of this book and for all of their support in the distribution of this book throughout the United Kingdom.

Finally, we are indebted to the **Academy for Learning Islam (www.academyforislam.com)** for their continuous support of our projects and their specific contribution towards the publishing of this work.

We ask Allāh ﷻ to reward all of the donors and institutions, and to bless their family and loved ones and to shower their deceased family and friends with His special mercy.

As you read through this work, we ask that you overlook any typographical errors and to inform us via e-mail if you find any of the same, so that these may be corrected for an online version or future printings.

Finally, when you – the reader – make your way through this book and become habituated to a continuous recitation of Āyatul Kursī, we would humbly request that you remember everyone who was instrumental in completing this project – including the author, translator, editor, donors and their families, and everyone else.

We are hopeful that Allāh ﷻ accepts all of our prayers, and grants us that which we have prayed for others – with no reduction in what anyone is given, for surely with Him are the treasures of the heavens and the earth, and He does not tire in giving to His servants in abundance, nor do His bounties ever decrease by Him bestowing upon His creations.

May Allāh ﷻ hasten the advent of our awaited saviour, Imām al-Ḥujjah (aj) and may He enable us to increase in our knowledge and practice of the faith of Islam – such that we are worthy of being amongst his adherents, supporters and helpers who are able to sacrifice everything that we have in his way.

"The achievement of my aim depends on God alone."
Surah Hud (11), verse 88

Saleem Bhimji
20th of Jumādī al-Thānī, 1438 AH
Birth Anniversary of Fāṭima al-Zahrā the daughter of Prophet Muhammad ﷺ
March 19th, 2017
Kitchener, Ontario, Canada

Foreword

by Tahera Kassamali

The Holy Quran is a gift from God to human beings to guide them towards achieving the main purpose of life; reaching perfection and closeness to Allah ﷻ.

The verses are a source of joy and happiness for the believer as they connect him to His creator. He learns about Allah ﷻ and His expectations of him which he would not otherwise have known. It is thus that the Quran says about itself:

﴿فَبِذَٰلِكَ فَلْيَفْرَحُوا هُوَ خَيْرٌ مِّمَّا يَجْمَعُونَ ۝٥٨﴾

Let them rejoice in that! It is better than what they amass.[17]

Many people do not experience that sense of joy when reciting the Quran. This could stem from not understanding the depth of the message of the verses. A ritualistic reading of the holy book does not spark a love of Quran in the heart. It is upon reflecting and understanding that the Quran opens up many new doors to the reader and becomes exciting and pleasurable. The insights gained become a light through which believers walk on the true path in life.

---

[17] *Quran*, Sūrah Yūnus (10), verse 58.

In every era, the Quran reveals new insights and guidance for its readers. People are able to gain strength and inspiration from it to face the challenges of their times. A person once came to Imam Jaʿfar al-Ṣādiq ﷺ and asked why the Quran only increased in freshness the more it was propagated and studied. Imam replied that it was because God had sent it for all times to come and for all people, so it would remain new and fresh till the Day of Judgement.[18]

To study and understand the messages of the Quran we need the interpretations of experts on these verses.

The Holy Prophet of Islam and his purified household are the guides who explain the verses correctly. It is they who are the walking Qurans, the ones who will never be separated from it until the Day of Judgement (*Ḥadīth al-Thaqalayn*). Shia commentators of the Quran have always referred directly or indirectly to the Imams.

The verses of the Quran known as the Āyatul Kursī are among the most exalted and treasured verses of the Quran. The Holy Prophet ﷺ told Imam Ali ﷺ:

> عَنْ عَلِيٍّ عليه السلام قَالَ :سَمِعْتُ رَسُولَ اللّهِ ﷺ يَقُولُ: وَ الْقُرْآنُ سَيِّدُ الْكَلَامِ وَ سُورَةُ الْبَقَرَةِ سَيِّدُ الْقُرْآنِ وَ آيَةُ الْكُرْسِيِّ سَيِّدُ سُورَةِ الْبَقَرَةِ فِيهَا خَمْسُونَ كَلِمَةً فِي كُلِّ كَلِمَةٍ بَرَكَةً
>
> The chief of the Quran is Sūrah al-Baqarah, and the chief of Sūrah al-Baqarah is Āyatul Kursī. O Ali, it has fifty words and each word has fifty blessings.[19]

Many other *aḥādīth* expound on the great significance of these verses. The profound description of the qualities of Allah in sublime and rhythmic language make these verses outstanding.

This book will, Inshā-Allāh, allow readers to reflect on the depth of the messages of Āyatul Kursī.

---

[18] *Mīzān al-Ḥikmah*, tradition 16135.

[19] *Tafsīr-e Nimūneh.*

It will help create joy and enthusiasm for reciting it often, as has been recommended in the *aḥādīth*. It is a noble venture by the author and translator and will reap a manifold reward.

Tahera Kassamali
July 20th, 2017
Toronto, Ontario, Canada

Section 1

ʿArabic Text and Translation of Āyatul Kursī[20]

أَللّٰـهُ لاَ إِلٰهَ إِلاَّ هُوَ الْحَىُّ الْقَيُّومُ

Allāh - there is no god except Him – He is the Ever-Living, the All-Sustainer.

لاَ تَأْخُذُهُ سِنَةٌ وَلاَ نَوْمٌ

Neither drowsiness befalls Him nor sleep.

لَهُ مَا فِى السَّمٰوَاتِ وَمَا فِى الأَرْضِ

To Him belongs whatever is in the heavens and whatever is on the earth.

مَنْ ذَا الَّذِى يَشْفَعُ عِنْدَهُ إِلاَّ بِإِذْنِهِ

Who is it that may intercede with Him except by His permission?

---

[20] We include the ʿArabic text of Āyatul Kursī (verse 255) and the two verses which follow it. For a better understanding on whether Āyatul Kursī is only verse 255 or also includes verses 256 and 257, refer to section four of this book. (Tr.)

يَعْلَمُ مَا بَيْنَ أَيْدِيهِمْ وَمَا خَلْفَهُمْ

He knows that which is before them and that which is behind them,

وَلاَ يُحِيطُونَ بِشَيْءٍ مِنْ عِلْمِهِ إِلاَّ بِمَا شَآءَ

and they do not comprehend anything of His knowledge except what He wishes.

وَسِعَ كُرْسِيُّهُ السَّمٰوَاتِ وَالأَرْضَ

His throne embraces the heavens and the earth,

وَلاَ يَئُودُهُ حِفْظُهُمَا

and He is not wearied by their preservation,

وَهُوَ الْعَلِيُّ الْعَظِيمُ ﴿٢٥٥﴾

and He is the All-Exalted, the All-Supreme.

لاَ إِكْرَاهَ فِي الدِّينِ

There is no compulsion in religion:

قَدْ تَبَيَّنَ الرُّشْدُ مِنَ الغَيِّ

rectitude has become distinct from error.

فَمَنْ يَكْفُرْ بِالطَّاغُوتِ وَيُؤْمِنْ بِاللهِ

So one who disavows the rebels and has faith in Allāh

فَقَدِ اسْتَمْسَكَ بِالْعُرْوَةِ الْوُثْقَى

has held fast to the firmest handle

لاَ انْفِصَامَ لَهَا

for which there is no breaking;

وَاللَّهُ سَمِيعٌ عَلِيمٌ ﴿٢٥٦﴾

and Allāh is All-Hearing, All-Knowing.

اللَّهُ وَلِيُّ الَّذِينَ آمَنُوا

Allāh is the Master of the faithful:

يُخْرِجُهُمْ مِنَ الظُّلُمَاتِ إِلَى النُّورِ

He brings them out of the darknesses into the light.

وَالَّذِينَ كَفَرُوا أَوْلِيَاؤُهُمُ الطَّاغُوتُ

And as for the faithless, their patrons are the rebels,

يُخْرِجُونَهُمْ مِنَ النُّورِ إِلَى الظُّلُمَاتِ

who drive them out of the light into the darknesses.

أُولَٰئِكَ أَصْحَابُ النَّارِ

They shall be the inmates of the Fire,

هُمْ فِيهَا خَالِدُونَ ﴿٢٥٧﴾

in it they shall remain [forever].

Section 2

Concise Commentary

﴿أَللّـهُ لاَ إِلَهَ إِلاَّ هُوَ الْحَىُّ الْقَيُّومُ﴾

Allāh - there is no god except Him – He is the Living One, the All-Sustainer.

Allāh ﷻ is that Essence and the One who possesses all of the attributes of perfection. In addition, He is the Originator of the entire universe of existence, and thus in the world of creation, nothing else is worthy of being worshipped except for Him – and this is noted in the phrase: 'لاَ إِلَـهَ إِلاَّ هُـوَ' - '*la ilāha illa huwa*' – 'There is no creature worthy of worship except for Him' - which the Noble Quran has used [many times] to express the Oneness and Uniqueness of the Almighty Creator of the Universe, and this phrase also forms the core belief of Islam.

The word 'اَللّـهُ' – '*Allāh*' - also conveys this same meaning and thus, the sentence 'لاَ إِلَـهَ إِلاَّ هُـوَ' - '*la ilāha illa huwa*' – 'There is no creature worthy of worship except for Him' - is yet a further emphasis to this reality.

The meaning of the word 'اَلْحَـيُّ' – '*al-Ḥayy*' - is 'living' and its understanding in relation to Allāh ﷻ is just as His other characteristics – it denotes a perpetual and continuous trait which only He possesses.

The 'life' which Allāh ﷻ possesses is the 'true' meaning of life because His 'life' is a part of His Essence and is not accidental, nor has it come to Him from another source. However in relation to the human being, 'life' is not a part of their essence, rather it has been gifted to them by another source – namely Allāh ﷻ.

The meaning of Allāh ﷻ being 'alive' is not the same as the life which human beings or other creations possess in which they are nourished, grow, procreate, attract and repel things and have the power of sense and movement. Rather, the meaning of 'living' in relation to Allāh ﷻ is an extensive and true meaning which includes His knowledge and the faculty of ability [to perform an action], since in reality, it is through knowledge and the faculty of ability that we are able to differentiate the living from the dead. However, as for the traits of growth, movement and other such things, these are all effects of creations which are imperfect and limited, and it is for this reason that they possess these traits to make up for their own shortcomings - since that entity which does not have such limitations and shortcomings has no need for these traits (growth, nourishment, etc...) – meaning Allāh ﷻ.

The word 'اَلْقَيُّوم' – '*al-Qayyum*' or 'The All-Sustainer' - is built upon the ʿArabic pattern of the hyperbolic noun and comes from the root word 'قِيَام' – '*qiyām*'. Based on the origin of this word, it denotes an entity which possesses the trait of being the 'All-Sustaining' and it is a trait which is part of its essence. It also shows us that all creations who are sustained are done so through Allāh ﷻ - in other words, all creations in the world of existence rely solely upon Him for their requirements.

In daily conversation, the word 'قِيَام' – '*qiyām*' is used in the meaning of 'standing up', however we know that this meaning has no basis when used in relation to Allāh ﷻ as He has no physical body or physical traits. Therefore, when we use this word in relation to Allāh ﷻ, it refers to His power of creation, maintenance (of the creations) and His over-seeing of everything, and it is only Allāh ﷻ who possesses all of these traits. In addition, He performs these actions on a continuous basis without any cessation.

﴿لَا تَأْخُذُهُ سِنَةٌ وَلَا نَوْمٌ﴾

Neither drowsiness befalls Him nor sleep.

The word 'سِنَةٌ' – '*sinah*' - is a specific type of slackness which comes about just before a person falls asleep and it can also be referred to as a light sleep or dosing off; the word 'نَـوْمٌ' – '*nawm*' - means sleep and this is a state which a person falls into in which his [five] bodily senses [sight, smell, touch, taste and hearing] come to a standstill - due to the natural effect of sleeping.

In reality, the sentence 'لَا تَأْخُذُهُ سِـنَةٌ وَ لَا نَـوْمٌ' - '*la takhuduhu sinatun wa lā nawm*' - 'Neither drowsiness befalls Him nor sleep' - is another emphasis on the fact that Allāh ﷻ - being the All-Sustainer - has a complete maintenance over the entire world of creation and this necessitates that the one who is looking over the system does not fall into heedlessness even for an instant of time.

Therefore, in His sole authority over the affairs of the entire world of creation, Allāh ﷻ does not fall into inattention or negligence at all. Thus, anything which would detract from the principle of His Over-Seeing is on its own, not a part of Him. Indeed, even the smallest of things which may lead to the slightest inattention such as a light sleep or drowsiness are not a part of Allāh's ﷻ essence!

﴿لَهُ مَا فِي السَّمٰوَاتِ وَمَا فِي الأَرْضِ﴾

To Him belongs whatever is in the heavens and
whatever is on the earth.

Due to the fact that directing all of the affairs of the entire universe is not possible without absolute ownership of the heavens and the earth and all that is within them, it is for this reason that after mentioning that Allāh ﷻ is the All-Sustainer, we are then clearly told that the absolute ownership of everything in creation is also Allāh's ﷻ and any sort of intervention in the world of existence comes about solely by Him.

Therefore, whatever humanity has at their discretion or they make use of, is in actuality not their own property; rather, it has been given to them as a loan for a time period to make use of by observing certain conditions from the True Owner.

﴿مَنْ ذَا الَّذِى يَشْفَعُ عِنْدَهُ إِلاَّ بِإِذْنِهِ﴾

Who is it that may intercede with Him except by His permission?

The form of this sentence is, in the terminology of the ʿArabic grammarians, an interrogative denial form or what is referred to [in English] as a rhetorical question – the understanding of this portion of the verse is that no one has the power to intercede for others without the permission of Allāh ﷻ. In reality, this sentence completes the understanding of the *'qāyyumiyyah'* – 'the power of creation and maintenance' – of Allāh ﷻ and His sole ownership over everything in the world of existence.

Therefore, if we see that a person is interceding for others in the presence of Allāh ﷻ, then we must understand that this does not mean that that individual has an independent power to do so, or that one is completely free in one's actions; rather they have been given the station of intercession from Allāh ﷻ. Thus, since a person's power of intercession for others is through the permission of Allāh ﷻ, this becomes yet another proof for the maintenance (*qāyyumiyyah*) and sovereignty (*mālikyyah'*) of Allāh ﷻ.

﴿يَعْلَمُ مَا بَيْنَ أَيْدِيهِمْ وَمَا خَلْفَهُمْ﴾

He knows that which is before them and that which is behind them.

After discussing the issue of intercession, albeit in brief, at this point, we see one of the reasons why intercession has been mentioned as is. The line under review explains to us that, "Allāh ﷻ has complete knowledge of the past and the future of those who are intercessors and He even knows what has been kept hidden from them. Therefore, they are not able to bring up some new issue in His presence for those whom they wish to intercede for such that through this, Allāh ﷻ would change His opinion in regards to those people (who need the intercession)."

When it comes to the standard forms of intercession, a person who is interceding would use one of two ways to shape the person whom he is going towards to seek intercession for:

1. The first way is that an intercessor would present some information in regards to why that person whom one is trying to intercede for is worthy and deserving of this blessing, such that the person who has the authority to intercede may change one's opinion.

2. The other way is that a person who is interceding will explain the relationship which one has with the person who needs intercession, so that through the explanation of the close ties which exist between the individuals, the one who has the power to intercede may change one's opinion.

It is clear that both of these forms of intercession rely upon the fact that the one who is acting as an intermediary has information in regards to the one whom he is trying to intercede for, which the person whom he is going to for the intercession may not necessarily have. However, if the individual whom the interceder is going to has a complete awareness and knowledge over all things and all creations [such as Allāh ﷻ], then there is no one who can ever enter into His presence to intercede for another, since it is He and He alone who must confirm and validate the worthiness of those who are seeking intercession and then grant it to them.

﴿وَلاَ يُحِيطُونَ بِشَيْءٍ مِنْ عِلْمِهِ إِلاَّ بِمَا شَآءَ﴾

And they do not comprehend anything of His knowledge except what He wishes.

This portion of the verse reinforces the previous sentence and alludes to the limited knowledge of the person who is trying to intercede for others in the presence of the All-Knowing Allāh ﷻ, and that those individuals do not possess the same sphere of knowledge that Allāh ﷻ has because they have been granted only a small amount of knowledge and that too whatever He has conferred upon them.

Thus, from this portion of the verse we can deduce that there is not a single individual who possesses knowledge on his own and everything which a human being knows, has been granted to him by Allāh ﷻ.

As time passes, we see that gradually, the curtains are being lifted from the secrets of the astonishing aspects of creation of the universe and a new set of truths are being presented to humanity and their knowledge and awareness of the universe is expanding – however as we have to emphasize, all of this comes to us from Allāh ﷻ.

﴿وَسِعَ كُرْسِيُّهُ السَّمٰوَاتِ وَالأَرْضَ﴾

His Chair (dominion) extends over the heavens and the earth.

The root of the word 'كُرْسِي' – '*kursī*' or 'throne' is 'كِرسٌ' – '*kirs*' - and its initial meaning is 'original' and 'fundamental'.

In addition, sometimes this word is used to refer to multiple things which are joined together; and it is for this reason that a short chair-like throne is referred to as *'kursī'*, while the opposite of this, a large throne, is referred to as an 'عَرْش' – *"arsh'* - or something which has a canopy over it, or even a canopy itself is referred to with this word, or a throne which has tall legs (is also referred to with this word).

When a teacher is instructing a class and at times sits on a chair, we see that occasionally, the word 'chair' is used metaphorically for knowledge. In addition, due to the fact that a person who is in authority often sits on a chair in his official role in government, we see that sometimes, the word 'chair' is also used metaphorically for power and authority.

In the above quoted verse we read that the 'Chair' of Allāh ﷻ covers the entire expanse of the heavens and the earth – and in this verse, the meaning of 'Chair' can be any of the following:

1. **Realm of His Governance**

By this we mean that Allāh ﷻ governs over the entire domain of the heavens and the earth and his realm of authority extends everywhere and thus, the 'Chair' of Allāh ﷻ comprises the entire material world – the earth, stars, galaxies, nebula, etc...

Naturally, according to this definition, the meaning of the 'Throne' of Allāh ﷻ must be something even greater and loftier than this material world, and thus the meaning of the 'Throne' is the universe, the souls, the angels and the supernatural world. Of course, this is the meaning if we accept that the 'Throne' and the 'Chair' are two opposite things – one which refers to the 'material and natural world'; while the other is the 'supernatural world'.

2. **The Domain of His Knowledge**

The knowledge of Allāh ﷻ encompasses the entire realm of the heavens and the earth and there is nothing which is out of the sphere of His knowledge; just as was previously mentioned that sometimes the word 'chair' is an allegorical term used for knowledge.

We see this same point mentioned in numerous traditions, such as in the narration from Ḥafṣ b. Ghayāth from Imām Ja'far al-Ṣādiq ﷺ in which he is reported to have asked the Imām ﷺ in regards to this verse (under review) and the Imām ﷺ replied, "The meaning of it is His (comprehensive) knowledge."

3. His Essence which encompasses all things

Another meaning of 'Chair' is the essence of Allāh ﷻ which encompasses everything in existence. With this interpretation, the meaning of this (section of the verse) would be: The 'Chair' of Allāh ﷻ is the area which encompasses the entire expanse of the heavens and the earth.

In a tradition from Imām 'Alī ﷺ in regards to the commentary of this section, he has stated:

أَلْكُـرْسِيُّ مُحِيـطٌ بِالسَّـمٰوَاتِ وَ الأَرْضِ وَ مَـا بَيْنَهُـمَا وَ مَـا تَحْـتَ الـثَّرىٰ

> The 'Chair' is the surroundings of the skies and the earth and that which is between them and that which is under it (the earth).

In addition, from some of the traditions, we can deduce that the 'Chair' is even more expansive than the heavens and the earth - such that the sum of these two in relation to the 'Chair' can be compared to a ring which is in the middle of a desert; and in this regards, there is a tradition from Imām al-Ṣādiq ﷺ in which he has stated:

وَ مَـا السَّـمٰوَاتِ وَ الأَرْضِ عِنْـدَ الْكُـرْسِيِّ إِلاَّ كَحَلْقَـةِ خَاتِـمٍ فِي فَـلاَةٍ

وَ مَـا الْكُـرْسِيِّ عِنْـدَ الْعَـرْشِ إِلاَّ كَحَلَقَـةٍ فِي فَـلاَةٍ

And what is the expanse of the heavens and the earth in relation to the 'Chair' - except like the relationship of a ring in the middle of a desert; and what is the expanse of the 'Chair' in relation to the 'Throne' except like the example of the ring in the middle of a desert!

The first and second meaning mentioned are completely clear and understandable, however the third meaning is something which up until today, science has yet to discover - since the existence of such a universe which is made up of heavens and the earth, but is much greater in size to this world of ours, has yet to be scientifically proven to exist.

In any case, there is no proof to reject such a thing existing - rather, the scientists believe that with the continued progress in the development of instruments capable of measuring the solar system and beyond, the expansion of the heavens and the earth is actually taking place. Indeed, no one claims that the expanse of the world of existence is only the amount that has been discovered today. Rather, there is a strong belief that there are unlimited worlds in existence which are out of the range of our viewing ability with today's instruments.

It goes without saying that the discussion up until this point in the three commentaries mentioned do not contradict one another, and thus in summary we can state that: The entire expanse of the heavens and the earth falls under the governance and authority of Allāh ﷻ, and the 'Chair' of His knowledge encompasses the entire universe and there is nothing which is outside the sphere of His governance and awareness.

﴿وَلَا يَـُٔودُهُ حِفْظُهُمَا﴾

And He is not wearied by their preservation.

The source of the word 'يَؤُودُهُ' - '*yaūduhu*' or 'wearied' is 'أود' - '*awd*' which literally means heavy or weighty – and in this verse, the meaning being conveyed is that the preservation of the heavens and the earth is not something which is at all difficult for Allāh ﷻ, since He is in no way like His creations whose power is limited, and sometimes we see that creations may fall tired or are unable to perform certain tasks.

His power is unlimited and in the face of an unlimited power, there is no such thing as 'difficult or easy'; 'challenging or simple' - these are all terms which hold true for creations who are limited in their power and ability.

﴿وَهُوَ الْعَلِيُّ الْعَظِيمُ﴾

And He is the All-Exalted, the All-Supreme.

This portion of the verse confirms the previous segment and tells us that there is nothing which is difficult for Allāh ﷻ - as He is greater than having any entity similar to Him, nor does He have a partner, and He does not possess any deficiency or shortcomings. Allāh ﷻ, the supreme and grand, whose Essence is never-ending and who never gets tired, never loses power, nor does He ever become unattentive or unaware of His responsibility of maintaining and over-seeing the entire world of creation - and indeed, His knowledge encompasses all things.

﴿لَا إِكْرَاهَ فِي الدِّينِ﴾

There is no compulsion in religion.

In commenting on the history of revelation of this verse, the well-known commentator of the Quran, al-Ṭabrasī, in his work, *Majma' al-Bayān* has related the following event:

> A man from [the city of] Medina, named Ḥaṣīn, had two sons. There were merchants who would come from distant lands, bringing their goods to sell in Medina and from among these traders, some of them met his two sons and invited them to [leave Islam and accept] Christianity. After being put under extreme pressures to leave their faith (and enter into Christianity), they succumbed and left Islam.
>
> Once their trading was complete, the caravan of traders decided to travel back to the Levant and Ḥaṣīn's two sons accompanied them.
>
> Ḥaṣīn became extremely upset (at his sons leaving Islam and embracing Christianity) and conveyed his displeasure to the Noble Messenger ﷺ and wanted the Prophet ﷺ to [forcefully] bring his two sons back to the faith of Islam, and so he asked the Prophet ﷺ: "Am I permitted to force the two of them to come back to the faith of Islam?"
>
> At this point, the above portion of the verse was revealed to the Prophet ﷺ explaining that: "In terms of accepting the faith – there is no compulsion or force."

In *Tafsīr al-Manār* it has been narrated that Ḥaṣīn wanted to force his two sons to come back to Islam. The two young men (the sons of Ḥaṣīn came to the Prophet ﷺ to complain to him [about the pressures being put on them to return to Islam]). Ḥaṣīn protested to the Prophet ﷺ and said: "How can I allow my children to enter into the fire of hell while I see all of this!?" It was at this point in time, that the verse under discussion was revealed to the Prophet.

﴿قَدْ تَبَيَّنَ الرُّشْدُ مِنَ الغَيِّ﴾

Rectitude has become distinct from error.

The lexical meaning of the word 'رُشْد' – *'rushd'* is 'to find the path' and to 'reach to a stage' and it is the opposite of 'غَيّ' – *'ghayy'* which means 'becoming misguided from the truths' and 'being distanced from reality.' Since religion is concerned with the heart and mind of people and the foundations of religion are built upon faith and certainty, one must follow the path of logic and reason.

However, as we understand from the history of revelation of this verse, some people came to the Messenger of Allāh ﷺ and asked him for permission to compel others, such as Ḥukkām b. Jābir, to change the people's mind set [and force them into the religion of Islam]. This verse of the Quran quoted above clearly answered them that beliefs are not something which can be imposed upon people. This verse also gave a powerful response to those who thought that in certain aspects, Islam was intrusive and imposing and that it was spread by the sword and through coercion [which is far from the truth].

[Within the religious teachings] we see that Islam does not even permit a father to compel his own children to revert back to the faith of Islam (if they have left Islam), and thus through this, the right of others [to remain on their own faith] becomes explicitly clear.

Indeed, if it was possible to compel a person through force to change their religion, then it would have been necessary that before anyone else, a father would have had the right to force his children - however we see that even he does not have such consent!

﴿اللَّهُ وَلِيُّ الَّذِينَ آمَنُوا يُخْرِجُهُم مِّنَ الظُّلُمَاتِ إِلَى النُّورِ وَالَّذِينَ كَفَرُوا أَوْلِيَاؤُهُمُ الطَّاغُوتُ يُخْرِجُونَهُم مِّنَ النُّورِ إِلَى الظُّلُمَاتِ أُولَٰئِكَ أَصْحَابُ النَّارِ هُمْ فِيهَا خَالِدُونَ﴾

> Allāh is the Master of the faithful: He brings them out of the darknesses into the light. And as for the faithless, their patrons are the rebels, who drive them out of the light into the darknesses. They shall be the inmates of the Fire, they shall remain in it [forever].

The lexical meaning of the word 'وَلِيّ' – '*walī*' is 'close' and 'without separation' and it is for this reason that a person's guardian who fulfills the nurturing and supervision is referred to as a *walī*. In addition, close and dear friends are also referred to as being the *walī* (singular) and *awliyā'* (plural) of one another – however it is clear that the meaning of this verse is contained in the first definition given.

After the clarification of the fact that disbelief (*kufr*) and belief (*īmān*), and truth (*ḥaqq*) and falsehood (*bāṭil*) are apparent for all and the correct path (of life) has been made distinct from the road which leads towards misguidance, the verse then goes on to conclude that every single person – believer or disbeliever – has a leader and guide who takes them on their own specific path. The leader and guide of the believers is Allāh ﷻ and their path is one of leaving multiple darknesses and progressing towards the [one] light; however the leader of the disbelievers and oppressors will strive to take them on the opposite path in which they will go from the [one] light to the various [types of] darknesses. Their eventual outcome is expressly mentioned - such people will remain in the fire of hell for perpetuity.

Section 3

Commentary from Tafsīr al-Mizān[21]

﴿أَللّٰـهُ لاَ إِلٰهَ إِلاَّ هُوَ الْحَيُّ الْقَيُّومُ﴾

﴿Allāh is He besides Whom there is no god, the Ever-Living, the Self-Subsisting by Whom all subsist.﴾

In the first chapter of the Quran (Sūrah al-Fātiḥa), some explanation was given about the name "Allāh" and it was mentioned that it ultimately means "The Being Who concentrates in Himself all of the attributes of perfection". It makes no difference whether the name Allāh ﷻ is derived from *alaha* [as in the phrase] *alaha al-rajul* (the man was bewildered; yearned for) or from [the word] *alaha* (worshipped).

"Allāh" (the Divine name) was originally *al-Ilāh* and the "I" in the middle was omitted because of frequent use. The word *al-Ilāh* is

[21] Taken from the World Organization For Islamic Service (WOFIS) translation of the late ʿAllāmah Sayyid Saeed Akhtar Rizvi available online at http://www.wofis.com/Publications.aspx?bookID=8. Last accessed on August 30, 2016. In the original commentary, ʿAllāmah Ṭabāṭabā'ī references his own commentary of other verses in explaning passages within Āyatul Kursī – we have also brought these explanations into this section. (Tr.)

derived from *alaha* (he worshipped) or from *aliha* or *waliha* (he was bewildered) and is on the paradigm of the ʿArabic pattern of *al-fiʿāl* in the meaning of the *al-mafʿūl* (the object-noun). For example, *al-kitāb* (the book) means *al-maktūb* (the written); likewise *al-Ilāh* means *al-malūh* that is, 'the One who is worshipped', or 'the One about whom minds are bewildered'.

Quite clearly it has become the proper name of God and was commonly used in this meaning in ʿArabic long before the Quran was revealed. The fact that even pre-Islamic ʿArabs used this name for God, may be inferred from the following verses of the Quran:

﴿وَلَئِن سَأَلْتَهُم مَّنْ خَلَقَهُمْ لَيَقُولُنَّ ٱللَّهُ فَأَنَّىٰ يُؤْفَكُونَ ٨٧﴾

And if you should ask them who created them, they would certainly say: Allāh...[22]

﴿فَقَالُواْ هَـٰذَا لِلَّهِ بِزَعْمِهِمْ وَهَـٰذَا لِشُرَكَآئِنَا ٣٦﴾

And they say: This is for Allāh - so they assert - and this is for our associates.[23]

Other Divine names may be used as adjectives for this name; for example, "the Beneficent and the Merciful Allāh"; also, this name is used as a subject of the verbs derived from other Divine names; for example, "Allāh knew", "Allāh had mercy", "Allāh gave sustenance" etc. However the word "Allāh" is never used as an adjective to any other name, nor is the verb derived from it used to describe other names, and therefore this is a clear proof that it is the proper name of God.

The Divine existence, in as much as Allāh ﷻ is the God of everything, presupposes that He should have all of the attributes of perfection; and as a result, this name points to all of the perfect attributes. That is why it is said that the name, "Allāh", means "the

---

[22] *Quran*, Sūrah al-Zukhruf (43), verse 87.

[23] *Quran*, Sūrah al-Anʿām (6), verse 36.

One Who is the Essential Being, and Who encompasses all of the attributes of perfection." But the fact is that it is the proper name of God and no other meaning (except that related to worship or bewilderment) can be taken into consideration here.

﴾He besides Whom there is no god﴿

This phrase has been explained under the commentary of verse 2:163 [and it is mentioned within this section] and its literal translation is, "there is no god except He."

We have explained the meaning of *al-Ilāh* (The God) was explained in the commentary of the first verse of the first chapter, Sūrah al-Fātiḥa, [however to sum up that discussion, we mention that] oneness is a self-evident idea, which needs no explanation. A thing is called one in view of one of its attributes. For example, one man, one scholar or one poet. These words show that the related attribute is indivisible, and not subject to plurality. For example, the manhood of one man, Zayd, is not shared between him and someone else. It is in contrast with manhood of two men - Zayd and ʿAmr, for example which is shared by the two, and is therefore numerous. Thus Zayd, in context of his attribute of manhood, is one and indivisible and not subject to plurality. But when he is looked at in this very context combined with his other attributes - like his knowledge, power, life, etc. - then he is not one but he is a multiple in reality.

Allāh ﷻ is One, in view of His attributes, like His Divinity, which is not shared by anyone else. He is One in His Divinity as well as in His knowledge, power and life. He has knowledge, unlike other knowledge, and power and life unlike others' powers and lives. Also, He is One because His attributes are not multiple, they are not separate from one another except in their verbal meanings; His knowledge, His power and His life, are all one thing, all are His very being and none of them are separate from the other. Allāh ﷻ knows everything by His power, and has power by His life, and is alive by His knowledge. He is not like other things where attributes are multiple and numerous - not only in meaning but in reality also.

Sometimes a thing possesses the characteristic of oneness in its personality, that is by its very nature and essence, it cannot accept multiplication or division in its self; it cannot be divided into various parts or into its person and name etc. This oneness is called the oneness of a person, and it is referred to with the word *al-aḥad* (one); this word is never used except as the first construct of a genitive construction or in a negative, prohibitive or similar sentences, in the meaning of no one, any one, etc. For example, we say: "No one came to me." This sentence negates the personality itself, irrespective of its oneness or plurality, because this oneness is related to its nature and essence, and not to its attribute. This connotation will be lost if we were to say, "One man did not come to me." This sentence does not imply that two or more men did not come; it is because "oneness" in this sentence is an attribute of the comer, not of his person.

The reader should keep in mind this short explanation until we write about it in detail - Allāh willing, under the verse: "Say: 'He, Allāh, is One.'"[24]

The word *aḥad* (unique) is an attribute which is derived from the word *wāḥid* (one), but the word *aḥad* is used about something which cannot be counted or numbered and something that does not accept numerousness (from all aspects) - not evidently or imagined. Therefore, the word *aḥad* does not mean one, unlike the word *wāḥid*, so that we may start counting two, three and so on.

In the (usage of the) word *aḥad*, whatever is followed by a second is that very same thing. For example if someone says: "No

[24] *Quran*, Sūrah al-Ikhlāṣ (112), verse 1. This has been extracted from the on-line translation of *Tafsīr al-Mizān* found at www.almizan.org and is presented in this section. (Tr.)

one (from the people) came to me" (*mā jā'anī min al-qawmī aḥad*), it negates the coming of one, two or more; but if someone says "one (from the people) did not come to me" (*mā jā'anī wāḥidu minhum*) it negates the coming of only one - but not two, three or more.

In this backdrop, the word *aḥad* (in the verse under discussion) is used in a positive sentence and it has a connotation that in His essence, Allāh ﷻ is such as no one like unto Him can even be imagined - be it one or more. Therefore, regardless of its condition in actuality, it is impossible even to imagine it properly.

The words, "And your God is one God," imply that Divinity is exclusively reserved for Allāh ﷻ, and that His Oneness in Divinity is such as becomes His sublime status.

The word *al-wāḥid* (The One), as understood by the audience of the Quran gives the idea of oneness, on a general type. That meaning may be applied to various kinds of oneness, however only a few of those connotations may be applied to Allāh ﷻ. The word "one" may show oneness of number, of species, or of genes, etc, and people were bound to take it in the meaning best suited to their beliefs and ideas. This is why the Quran did not say: "And Allāh is one God", because this sentence does not establish monotheism; even the polytheists say that He is one God, in the same way as each of their deities is one god. Nor would the sentence, "And your God is one", have established monotheism, because it could be imagined that He is one in the species of Divinity. People say, when they enumerate the species of animals: The horse is one; the mule is one - although horse and mule are manifold in number. That is why the Quran said: "And your God is one God." In this statement, "One God" (in contrast to two or more gods) is made the predicate of "Your God." In this form, the sentence clearly establishes the belief of monotheism, by restricting the godhead to one of the gods in which they believed.

﴾There is no god but He.﴿

This sentence further emphasizes the clear declaration of the preceding sentence about monotheism and negates every possible misinterpretation or superstition. The negating particle "*lā*" (no) is used here to negate the genes; *ilāh* (god) denotes here the real and actual God. The sentence has an implied predicate "existent," and the meaning will be as follows: There is no real and actual god existing "but He". The pronoun "He," used in place of the proper name, Allāh ﷻ, is in the nominative, not subjunctive case. Therefore, the word "but" is not used here as a particle of exception; rather it is an adjective in the sense of "other than." The complete sentence, thus means: "There is no real god, other than Allāh, existing."

The sentence therefore aims at the repudiation of gods other than Allāh ﷻ - the deities which has no real existence outside the imagination of their worshippers. It does not aim at refuting other deities and proving the existence of Allāh ﷻ, as many scholars have thought.

Our explanation is supported by the fact that the sentence needs only a negative mode, and not a negative followed by an affirmative. Only repudiation of other imaginary deities is enough to confirm the Oneness of Allāh ﷻ in His godhead. Moreover, the Quran treats the existence of Allāh ﷻ as a self-evident truth which needs no proof or argument. The Quran only cares to affirm and prove His attributes; for example, it only proves that Allāh ﷻ is One; that He is the Creator, the Knower, the Powerful and so on.

Question: You say that the sentence has an implied predicate existent (or some other word of the same meaning). If so, then it would only negate the actual existence of other deities but not the "possibility" of their existence.

Reply: First, it is meaningless to suppose that there could be a "possible" or transient being (having equal relation with existence and non-existence), which would be the ultimate cause of all of the existing things and their affairs. Secondly, we could change the predicate to "true" or "actual"; then the meaning would be: "There is no god in reality other than He." This would show that other deities worshipped besides Allāh ﷻ, in fact have no existence at all.

﴾The Ever-Living﴿

The ʿArabic word "*al-ḥayy*" is on an ʿArabic pattern which denotes perpetuity, and therefore the word means not only living, but Ever-Living.

From the very beginning, humanity realized that there are two kinds of things around them: first, those things whose condition does not change as long as they exist, like stones and other such materials; second, those things which do change - like trees, animals and human beings themselves. One also finds that after some time, such things start to deteriorate and even lose consciousness, however they still exist until they reach a certain point at which time, their existence comes to an end. Thus one realizes that there is something else, besides the senses, which keeps one alive and it is the source of all things and their perceptions and it is called "life;" and its absence is named "death." It is life which is the source of knowledge (perception) and power.

Allāh ﷻ has mentioned this life in many places as an accepted fact:

﴿ٱعْلَمُوٓا۟ أَنَّ ٱللَّهَ يُحْيِى ٱلْأَرْضَ بَعْدَ مَوْتِهَا ١٧﴾

Know that Allāh gives life to the earth after its death.[25]

﴿وَمِنْ آيَاتِهِ أَنَّكَ تَرَى الْأَرْضَ خَاشِعَةً فَإِذَا أَنْزَلْنَا عَلَيْهَا الْمَاءَ اهْتَزَّتْ وَرَبَتْ إِنَّ الَّذِي أَحْيَاهَا لَمُحْيِي الْمَوْتَىٰ ٣٩﴾

And among His signs is this, that you see the earth still, but when We send down on it the water, it stirs

[25] *Quran*, Sūrah al-Ḥadīd (57), verse 17.

and swells; most surely He who gives it life is the Giver of life to the dead.[26]

﴿وَمَا يَسْتَوِي الْأَحْيَاءُ وَلَا الْأَمْوَاتُ ٢٢﴾

And neither are the living nor the dead alike.[27]

﴿وَجَعَلْنَا مِنَ الْمَاءِ كُلَّ شَيْءٍ حَيٍّ ٣٠﴾

And We have made of water every living thing.[28]

These verses describe all three kinds of living things, the vegetable, the animal and the human being.

Likewise, Allāh ﷻ describes various types of life:

﴿وَرَضُوا بِالْحَيَاةِ الدُّنْيَا وَاطْمَأَنُّوا بِهَا ٧﴾

And they are pleased with this world's life and are content with it[29]

﴿قَالُوا رَبَّنَا أَمَتَّنَا اثْنَتَيْنِ وَأَحْيَيْتَنَا اثْنَتَيْنِ ١١﴾

They shall say: Our Lord! You made us subject to death twice, and twice have You given us life...[30]

The two lives referred to in this verse are: the life of *al-barzakh* - the period after death in this world before the Day of Resurrection; and the life on the Day of Resurrection. Thus, there are various types of life, just as there are various types of living things.

Although Allāh ﷻ mentions the life of this world as an accepted fact, in various other verses of the Quran, He describes it as an unsound, imperfect and insignificant thing, such as when He says:

﴿وَمَا الْحَيَاةُ الدُّنْيَا فِي الْآخِرَةِ إِلَّا مَتَاعٌ ٢٦﴾

---

[26] *Quran*, Sūrah Fuṣṣilat (41), verse 39.

[27] *Quran*, Sūrah Fātir (35), verse 22.

[28] *Quran*, Sūrah al-Anbiyā' (21), verse 30.

[29] *Quran*, Sūrah Hūd (10), verse 7.

[30] *Quran*, Sūrah al-Mo'min (40), verse 11.

And this world's life is nothing compared to the hereafter, but it is (only a) means.[31]

﴿تَبْتَغُونَ عَرَضَ الْحَيَاةِ الدُّنْيَا﴾

...coveting the (transitory) goods of this world's life...[32]

﴿تُرِيدُ زِينَةَ الْحَيَاةِ الدُّنْيَا﴾

Desiring the adornments of this world's life...[33]

﴿وَمَا الْحَيَاةُ الدُّنْيَا إِلَّا لَعِبٌ وَلَهْوٌ﴾

And this world's life is nothing but a play and an idle sport...[34]

﴿وَمَا الْحَيَاةُ الدُّنْيَا إِلَّا مَتَاعُ الْغُرُورِ﴾

And this world's life is nothing but a means of deception.[35]

Summarizing the above verses, the attributes used for this world's life include:

1. It is a means, and a means is sought to obtain an end and to reach a goal, it is not an end in itself.
2. It is a transitory thing, and transitory things go away quickly.
3. It is an adornment, and an adornment is used to attract eyes towards the things which are adorned. In other words, what catches the eyes is not the real thing, and the real thing does not attract the eyes.
4. It is a play, and a play keeps a person oblivious of really

---

[31] *Quran*, Sūrah Ibrāhīm (13), verse 26.

[32] *Quran*, Sūrah al-Nisā' (4), verse 94.

[33] *Quran*, Sūrah al-Kahf (18), verse 28.

[34] *Quran*, Sūrah al-An'ām (6), verse 32.

[35] *Quran*, Sūrah Āle 'Imrān (3), verse 185.

important responsibilities.

5. It is a vain sport, and a vain sport is indulged in for imaginary reasons – not real ones.
6. Finally, it is a means of deception, and such things deceive the human beings.

A comprehensive verse which explains all of the above mentioned points, is the following one:

﴿وَمَا هَٰذِهِ الْحَيَاةُ الدُّنْيَا إِلَّا لَهْوٌ وَلَعِبٌ وَإِنَّ الدَّارَ الْآخِرَةَ لَهِيَ الْحَيَوَانُ لَوْ كَانُوا يَعْلَمُونَ ﴿٦٤﴾﴾

And this life of the world is nothing but a sport and a play; and as for the next abode, that most surely is the [real] life - did they but know![36]

The life of this world in comparison to the life of the hereafter is not a real life, as the previous verse shows. It is transitory, while the life of the hereafter is the real life because it will not end and death will not reach it. Allāh ﷻ says:

﴿آمِنِينَ ﴿٥٥﴾ لَا يَذُوقُونَ فِيهَا الْمَوْتَ إِلَّا الْمَوْتَةَ الْأُولَىٰ ﴿٥٦﴾﴾

...in security; they shall not taste therein death except the first death.[37]

﴿لَهُم مَّا يَشَاءُونَ فِيهَا وَلَدَيْنَا مَزِيدٌ ﴿٣٥﴾﴾

They shall have therein what they wish and with Us yet is even more.[38]

Thus, there will be no death in the life hereafter and there will be no deficiency in that life, nor will there be any annoyance for anyone there. But the first factor — security — is the basic characteristic of

---

[36] *Quran*, Sūrah al-Furqān (25), verse 64.

[37] *Quran*, Sūrah al-Dukhān (44), verses 55-56.

[38] *Quran*, Sūrah Qāf (50), verse 35.

that real life.

Therefore, the life of the hereafter is the real life because there is no death in it; and as Allāh ﷻ Himself has declared in many other verses, it is He Who will control it. Obviously, the life of the hereafter is also dependent and not independent. It has not received this characteristic of eternity by itself - it is a gift given by Allāh ﷻ.

Going a step further, it will be realized that the real life is only that which 'cannot' be overtaken by death. The life of the hereafter 'will not' be overtaken by death; but it 'can' be overtaken if Allāh ﷻ pleases; but then that also is not "real" life. Real life is that in which non-existence at any stage is impossible and this is what is an essential being - in other words, where life is not acquired by a person, but a person is life itself and life is the person himself. Allāh ﷻ says:

﴿وَتَوَكَّلْ عَلَى ٱلْحَيِّ ٱلَّذِى لَا يَمُوتُ ٥٨﴾

And rely on the Ever-Living Who does not die.[39]

Thus, the only real life is Divine Life - the Essential Being.

The above discourse shows that the exclusiveness in the verse:

﴿هُوَ الْحَيُّ لَا إِلَٰهَ إِلَّا هُوَ ٦٦﴾

He is the Ever-Living, there is no god but He.[40]

is real, not relative; and in reality, He is the **only** Living One, because real life, unconquered by death or deterioration, is His alone.

In the verse under discussion, as in a similar verse:

﴿اللَّهُ لَا إِلَٰهَ إِلَّا هُوَ الْحَيُّ الْقَيُّومُ﴾

Allāh there is no god but He, the Ever-Living, the Self-

[39] *Quran*, Sūrah al-Furqān (25), verse 58.

[40] *Quran*, Sūrah al-Mo'min (40), verse 66.

Subsisting...[41]

the word 'Allāh' is the subject, 'there is no god but He' is its first predicate, the 'Ever-Living' is the second and the 'Self-Subsisting' is the third predicate. Accordingly, the meaning would be "Allāh is the Ever-Living;" and life is reserved for Allāh ﷻ only; and others will only get life **if** and **when** He bestows it upon them.

❴The Self-Subsisting by Whom all subsist)

This word is on the paradigm of *fay'ūl* (from the verb *al-qiyām* which means to stand); as is *al-qayyam* on the paradigm of *fay'al*, in the same meaning and is a paradigm which is used to show the maximum degree of a quality. The original meaning of the verb (to stand) has, by association, been extended and now it is used for protecting a thing, or accomplishing a task and managing it, bringing up a thing, looking after it and having power over it. Allāh ﷻ clearly says that He "stands" with the affairs of all of His creations, that is He watches them, looks after them, and brings them up and has all power over them. He says:

﴿أَفَمَنْ هُوَ قَآئِمٌ عَلَىٰ كُلِّ نَفْسٍ بِمَا كَسَبَتْ ﴿٣٣﴾﴾

How shall He Who stands (watchful) over each and every soul as to what it accomplishes (let them go unpunished inspite of His knowledge)?42

Another verse is more comprehensive and states:

﴿شَهِدَ اللَّهُ أَنَّهُ لَا إِلَٰهَ إِلَّا هُوَ وَالْمَلَائِكَةُ وَأُولُو الْعِلْمِ قَآئِمًا بِالْقِسْطِ لَا إِلَٰهَ إِلَّا هُوَ الْعَزِيزُ الْحَكِيمُ ﴿١٨﴾﴾

Allāh bears witness that there is no god but He and so do the angels and those possessed of knowledge,

[41] *Quran*, Sūrah al-Baqarah (2), verse 255.
[42] *Quran*, Sūrah al-Ra'd (13), verse 33.

> standing with (maintaining) justice, there is no god but He, the Mighty, the Wise.[43]

He maintains His creation with justice; He does not give nor does He withhold but with justice - and existence is nothing except giving and withholding; He gives to everything what it deserves; and lastly He declares that this maintaining with justice is according to His two great names, the Mighty and the Wise: by His Might He maintains everything; and by His Wisdom He does justice to all things.

Allāh ﷻ is the origin of everything. Existence as well as all attributes, qualities and the effects of everything begin from Him and all other "origins" originate from Him. He stands over everything in the real and comprehensive sense of "standing," as explained above. There is no weakness or flaw in His "standing," and other things cannot stand except by Him.

This attribute is reserved for Him in both ways: "standing" cannot be found except in Allāh ﷻ, and Allāh ﷻ is never anything but standing. The former is understood by the syntax of the sentence: Allāh ﷻ is the "standing." The latter is understood by the next sentence: "Slumber does not overtake Him nor sleep."

This discourse leads us to believe that the name *al-Qayyūm* (the Standing) is the basis for all of the Divine names which refer to His attributes of action in any way, like the Creator, the Sustainer, the Originator, the Resurrector, the Bestowal of life, the Giver of Death, the Forgiver, the Compassionate, the Affectionate and so on.

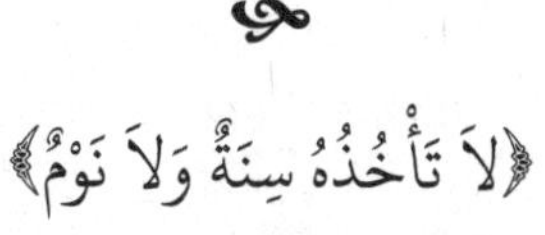

﴿Slumber does not overtake Him nor sleep.﴾

---

[43] *Quran*, Sūrah Āle ʿImrān (3), verse 18.

The word "*al-sinah*" means drowsiness and the word "*al-nawm*" is sleep, an inert condition in which the muscles are relaxed and the consciousness is suppressed by natural factors in the body of an animal or a human being; while "*al-ru'ya*" (dream) is something else - it is the vision which passes through the mind in one's sleep.

A criticism has been leveled against this sentence that it is contrary to the sequence demanded by rhetoric: when two things are thus mentioned in an affirmative sentence - the weaker point is mentioned first and then one progresses to the stronger one; for example we say, "Zayd can carry a load of fifty kilograms - even a hundred." But in a negative sentence the sequence is reversed: it goes from a stronger to a weaker point: for example, "he cannot carry a load of a hundred kilograms, let alone fifty" or "he does not spend hundreds of dollars on himself, let alone tens.'' According to this rule, as the sentence here is in the negative, it should have been written thus: "Sleep does not overtake Him, nor slumber."

REPLY: A sequence does not always follow the affirmativeness or negativeness of a sentence. For example look at the sentence, "he is too weak to carry a load of twenty kilograms, or even ten." It is an affirmative sentence, but still the stronger point comes first. It would be against the norms of rhetoric, if the weaker point, that is, ten kilograms was mentioned first. In fact, the only correct procedure is to look at the context and see what it demands.

Now, look at the Quranic sentence. Sleep is more contrary to the attribute of "standing" in comparison to slumber. Therefore, eloquence demands that first slumber must be denied, and then the stronger point – sleep will be negated. The meaning thus will be: The weaker factor (slumber) has no effect on His power and standing, nor does the stronger one (sleep) have any effect.

﴿لَهُ مَا فِي السَّمٰوَاتِ وَمَا فِي الأَرْضِ مَنْ ذَا الَّذِى يَشْفَعُ

﴿عِنْدَهُ إِلَّا بِإِذْنِهِ﴾

﴾Whatever is in the heavens and whatever is in the earth is His, who is there that can intercede with Him except by His Permission?﴿

The perfect and comprehensive "standing" of Allāh ﷻ means that He owns, in real ownership, the heavens and the earth and what is in them. That is why His attribute of "standing" is followed here by a declaration of that ownership. It was for the same reason that the attribute of "standing" was joined with the declaration of His Oneness: His Oneness would not be complete if He was not "standing."

There are two sentences here, both of which are followed by other sentences which remove the possibility of any misunderstanding. The sentence, ﴾whatever is in the heavens and whatever is in the earth is His﴿, is followed by the sentence, ﴾who is there that can intercede with Him except by His permission?﴿ Then the next sentence, ﴾He knows what is before them and what is behind them﴿, is followed by the words, ﴾and they cannot comprehend anything of His Knowledge except what He pleases.﴿

In the sentence, ﴾Whatever is in the heavens and whatever is in the earth is His﴿: Allāh ﷻ owns everything, and He has authority over them all; things and all of their attributes, properties and traits exist because of God and only Him.

The verse, from the word ﴾the Self-Subsisting﴿ up to this sentence proves that the total authority is Allāh's ﷻ alone - there is no work connected with anything, right from its existence up to its ultimate end that is not done by Him and does not proceed by His permission.

On realizing this eternal truth, one might wonder about the system of "cause and effect" prevalent in the world. What is the significance of these causes then? How can they have any influence or any effect when nothing has any effect or power except for

Allāh ﷻ?

The sentence, ﴾who is he that can intercede with Him except by His permission﴿?, answers this speculation - for these causes are intermediaries in such affairs. In other words, they are intercessors who cause the bringing of a thing or effect into being, but only by the permission of Allāh ﷻ, and intercession means being an intermediary in bringing about a good thing or averting something evil.

There is no doubt that an intercessor has some influence on the affairs of a certain thing for which one intercedes, and such influence can be contrary to the complete authority and total sovereignty of Allāh ﷻ, had it not been based on the permission of Allāh ﷻ Himself. But every cause draws its effectiveness only from the decree of Allāh ﷻ Himself, and there is no cause and no instrument which is independent from the will of Allāh ﷻ. Every cause is a cause, because Allāh ﷻ has made it so. Therefore, whatever effect and influence it has on anything is in fact "done" by Allāh ﷻ. Ultimately, there is no authority except that of Allāh ﷻ, and no "standing" except His.

As already explained, intercession means being an intermediary in the world of cause and effect - it may be a creative intercession, that is, being an intermediary cause of creation; or a legislative intercession, that is, interceding in the award of recompense on the Day of Judgement, as is clearly mentioned in the Quran and *Sunnah* (as was described in the commentary on Sūrah al-Baqarah, verse 48).[44] The sentence, ﴾who is he that can intercede with Him...﴿ is preceded by a description of His "standing" and total authority; these two attributes cover His power and authority in both creation and legislation. Therefore, the intercession mentioned in this sentence must cover both creative and legislative intercessions.

[44] This section is presented here. (Tr.)

Intercession

Commentary on Verse 2:48

﴿وَاتَّقُوا يَوْمًا لاَ تَجْزِى نَفْسٌ عَنْ نَّفْسٍ شَيْئًا وَلاَ يُقْبَلُ مِنْهَا شَفَاعَةٌ وَلاَ يُؤْخَذُ مِنْهَا عَدْلٌ وَلاَ هُمْ يُنصَرُونَ﴿٤٨﴾﴾

> And guard yourselves against the day when no soul shall serve as a substitute for another soul at all, nor shall intercession be accepted for it, nor shall ransom be taken from it, nor shall they be helped.

The temporal power and authority, with all of its various systems and varying conditions, is based on the necessity of life. The only justification of this institution is that it fulfills this need in the framework of the prevailing factors of society. It sometimes exchanges a commodity for another, or it gives up a benefit for another, at times it substitutes an order with another - without any hard and fast criterion to regulate such dispensations.

The same phenomenon is observed in their judiciary. Logically, a crime must be recompensed with punishment. Yet sometimes a judge, because of some extraneous reasons, decides not to punish a criminal. Sometimes the criminal arouses in the judge an overwhelming feeling of pity by his passionate appeal for mercy; or he wins him over by bribe which induces him to deliver an unjust verdict. At other times, an influential person intercedes with the judge on behalf of the said criminal and the judge cannot ignore that intercession; or the said criminal becomes a state witness leading to the conviction of even more depraved criminals, and is then released without any punishment. It is also possible that his clan or colleagues get him freed from the clutches of the authorities. Whatever the case may be, it is a well established custom in the governments of the world and human society on a whole to sometimes let the wrong-doers go free in different circumstances.

The ancient tribes and the idol-worshippers believed that the life hereafter was an extension of this one; that the customs of this world were valid for that world as well; and that the next world was permeated by the same actions and reactions which prevailed in this one.

Thus they offered sacrifices and offerings to their deities seeking forgiveness for their sins or assistance in their needs. The offerings were given as a means of being used to intercede on their behalf. Sometimes a sin was expiated or help was sought by even offering a human sacrifice!

These ancient tribes carried this idea of continuation of the life in the world to come to such an extent that they would even bury a person with all types of necessities of life, not forgetting things such as their ornaments and weapons in order that the individual may make use of them on their onward journey. Sometimes, they would even bury the person's concubines and soldiers with him to keep him company – but they would be buried alive.

These sorts of things can be seen in archaeological museums around the world, and indeed some of these types of ideas have persisted even among the Muslims - with all of their diverse cultures and languages, albeit in modified forms.

In no uncertain terms, the Quran has rejected all such superstitious beliefs and baseless ideas and has stated:

﴿وَالْأَمْرُ يَوْمَئِذٍ لِلَّهِ ١٩﴾

And the command on that day shall be entirely Allāh's.[45]

The Quran also states:

---

[45] *Quran*, Sūrah al-Infitār, (82), verse 19.

﴿وَتَقَطَّعَتْ بِهِمُ الْأَسْبَابُ ﴿١٦٦﴾﴾

...and their ties [with others] will be severed.[46]

In yet another passage, the Quran states:

﴿وَلَقَدْ جِئْتُمُونَا فُرَادَىٰ كَمَا خَلَقْنَاكُمْ أَوَّلَ مَرَّةٍ وَتَرَكْتُمْ مَا خَوَّلْنَاكُمْ وَرَاءَ ظُهُورِكُمْ ۖ وَمَا نَرَىٰ مَعَكُمْ شُفَعَاءَكُمُ الَّذِينَ زَعَمْتُمْ أَنَّهُمْ فِيكُمْ شُرَكَاءُ ۚ لَقَدْ تَقَطَّعَ بَيْنَكُمْ وَضَلَّ عَنْكُمْ مَا كُنْتُمْ تَزْعُمُونَ ﴿٩٤﴾﴾

And certainly you have come to Us alone as We created you at first, and you have left behind your backs the things which We gave you, and We do not see with you your intercessors about whom you asserted that they were (Allāh's) associates in respect to you; certainly the ties between you are now cut off and what you asserted is gone from you.[47]

Another verse of the Quran states:

﴿هُنَالِكَ تَبْلُو كُلُّ نَفْسٍ مَا أَسْلَفَتْ ۚ وَرُدُّوا إِلَى اللَّهِ مَوْلَاهُمُ الْحَقِّ ۖ وَضَلَّ عَنْهُمْ مَا كَانُوا يَفْتَرُونَ ﴿٣٠﴾﴾

There shall every soul become acquainted with what it sent before, and they shall be brought back to Allāh, their true Master and what they did fabricate shall escape from them.[48]

There are many similar verses in the Quran and they show that the life of the hereafter is cut off from the natural causes which govern

---

[46] *Quran*, Sūrah al-Baqarah (2), verse 166.

[47] *Quran*, Sūrah al-Anʿām (6), verse 94.

[48] *Quran*, Sūrah Yūnus (10), verse 30.

this life, and it is quite separate from the material connections [which we see in this world].

Once this principle is understood, then all of the above mentioned myths will automatically be cleared up, however the Quran is not content with this general declaration, rather, it refutes each and every myth and superstition described above:

﴿وَاتَّقُوا يَوْمًا لاَ تَجْزِى نَفْسٌ عَنْ نَفْسٍ شَيْئًا وَلاَ يُقْبَلُ مِنْهَا شَفَاعَةٌ وَلاَ يُؤْخَذُ مِنْهَا عَدْلٌ وَلاَ هُمْ يُنصَرُونَ ﴿٤٨﴾﴾

And be on your guard against the day when no soul shall avail another in the least - neither shall intercession on its behalf be accepted, nor will any compensation be taken from it, nor shall they be helped.[49]

﴿...مِنْ قَبْلِ أَنْ يَأْتِيَ يَوْمٌ لَا بَيْعٌ فِيهِ وَلَا خُلَّةٌ وَلَا شَفَاعَةٌ ﴿٢٥٤﴾﴾

...before the day comes, in which there is no bargaining, neither any friendship nor intercession.[50]

﴿يَوْمَ لَا يُغْنِي مَوْلًى عَنْ مَوْلًى شَيْئًا ﴿٤١﴾﴾

The day on which a friend shall not avail (his) friend the slightest...[51]

﴿فَمَا لَهُ مِنْ هَادٍ ﴿٣٣﴾﴾

...there shall be no helper for you (from Allāh)...[52]

﴿مَا لَكُمْ لَا تَنَاصَرُونَ ﴿٢٥﴾ بَلْ هُمُ الْيَوْمَ مُسْتَسْلِمُونَ ﴿٢٦﴾﴾

---

[49] *Quran*, Sūrah al-Baqarah (2), verse 48.
[50] Ibid., verse 254.
[51] *Quran*, Sūrah al-Dukhān (44), verse 41.
[52] *Quran*, Sūrah al-Mo'min (40), verse 33.

What is the matter with you that you do not help each other? Nay! on this day they are submissive.[53]

﴿وَيَعْبُدُونَ مِنْ دُونِ اللهِ مَا لَا يَضُرُّهُمْ وَلَا يَنْفَعُهُمْ وَيَقُولُونَ هَٰؤُلَاءِ شُفَعَاؤُنَا عِنْدَ اللهِ ۚ قُلْ أَتُنَبِّئُونَ اللهَ بِمَا لَا يَعْلَمُ فِي السَّمَاوَاتِ وَلَا فِي الْأَرْضِ ۚ سُبْحَانَهُ وَتَعَالَىٰ عَمَّا يُشْرِكُونَ ﴿١٨﴾﴾

And they worship beside Allāh what can neither harm them nor profit them, and they say: "These are our intercessors with Allāh" Say: "Do you (presume to) inform Allāh about what He knows not in the heavens and the earth?" Glory be to Him, and supremely exalted is He above what they set up with Him.[54]

﴿مَا لِلظَّالِمِينَ مِنْ حَمِيمٍ وَلَا شَفِيعٍ يُطَاعُ ﴿١٨﴾﴾

The unjust will not have any friend, nor any intercessor who will be obeyed.[55]

﴿فَمَا لَنَا مِنْ شَافِعِينَ ﴿١٠٠﴾ وَلَا صَدِيقٍ حَمِيمٍ ﴿١٠١﴾﴾

So we have no intercessors, nor a true friend.[56]

There are many other verses in the Quran based on this same theme and they all reject intercession on the Day of Resurrection.

On the other hand, there are also verses within the Quran which do not totally reject intercession, rather they confirm it to a certain extent. For example, it says:

---

[53] *Quran,* Sūrah al-Ṣāffāt (37), verses 25-26.

[54] *Quran,* Sūrah Yūnus (10), verse 18.

[55] *Quran,* Sūrah al-Mo'min (40), verse 18.

[56] *Quran,* Sūrah al-Shuarā' (26), verses 100-101.

﴿ٱللَّهُ ٱلَّذِى خَلَقَ ٱلسَّمَٰوَٰتِ وَٱلْأَرْضَ وَمَا بَيْنَهُمَا فِى سِتَّةِ أَيَّامٍ ثُمَّ ٱسْتَوَىٰ عَلَى ٱلْعَرْشِ ۖ مَا لَكُم مِّن دُونِهِۦ مِن وَلِىٍّ وَلَا شَفِيعٍ ۚ أَفَلَا تَتَذَكَّرُونَ ﴿٤﴾﴾

Allāh is He Who created the heavens and the earth and what is between them in six periods and He is firmly established on the throne; you have not besides Him any guardian nor any intercessor; will you not then mind?[57]

Another verse states:

﴿...لَيْسَ لَهُم مِّن دُونِهِۦ وَلِىٌّ وَلَا شَفِيعٌ... ﴿٥١﴾﴾

...there is no guardian for them, nor any intercessor besides Him.[58]

In addition we read:

﴿قُل لِّلَّهِ ٱلشَّفَٰعَةُ جَمِيعًا ﴿٤٤﴾﴾

Say: Allāh's is the intercession altogether.[59]

We are also told:

﴿لَّهُۥ مَا فِى ٱلسَّمَٰوَٰتِ وَمَا فِى ٱلْأَرْضِ ۗ مَن ذَا ٱلَّذِى يَشْفَعُ عِندَهُۥٓ إِلَّا بِإِذْنِهِۦ ۚ يَعْلَمُ مَا بَيْنَ أَيْدِيهِمْ وَمَا خَلْفَهُمْ ﴿٢٥٥﴾﴾

...whatever is in the heavens and whatever is in the earth is His; who is he that can intercede with Him except by His permission? He knows what is before them and what is behind them...[60]

---

[57] *Quran,* Sūrah al-Sajdah (32), verse 4.

[58] *Quran,* Sūrah al-Anʿām (6), verse 51.

[59] *Quran,* Sūrah al-Zumur (39), verse 44.

[60] *Quran,* Sūrah al-Baqarah (2), verse 255.

The Quran also states:

﴿إِنَّ رَبَّكُمُ اللهُ الَّذِى خَلَقَ السَّمَاوَاتِ وَالْأَرْضَ فِى سِتَّةِ أَيَّامٍ ثُمَّ اسْتَوَىٰ عَلَى الْعَرْشِ ۖ يُدَبِّرُ الْأَمْرَ ۖ مَا مِن شَفِيعٍ إِلَّا مِن بَعْدِ إِذْنِهِ ۝٣﴾

Surely your Lord is Allāh, Who created the heavens and the earth in six periods; and He is firmly established on the throne; regulating the affair; there is no intercessor except after His permission.[61]

Another verse states:

﴿وَقَالُوا اتَّخَذَ الرَّحْمَٰنُ وَلَدًا ۗ سُبْحَانَهُ ۚ بَلْ عِبَادٌ مُكْرَمُونَ ۝٢٦ لَا يَسْبِقُونَهُ بِالْقَوْلِ وَهُم بِأَمْرِهِ يَعْمَلُونَ ۝٢٧ يَعْلَمُ مَا بَيْنَ أَيْدِيهِمْ وَمَا خَلْفَهُمْ وَلَا يَشْفَعُونَ إِلَّا لِمَنِ ارْتَضَىٰ وَهُم مِنْ خَشْيَتِهِ مُشْفِقُونَ ۝٢٨﴾

And they say: "The Beneficent God has taken to Himself a son." Glory be to Him! Nay! They are honoured servants; they do not precede Him in speech and (only) according to His commandment do they act. He knows what is before them and what is behind them, and they do not intercede except for whom He approves, and for fear of Him they tremble.[62]

We are also reminded:

﴿وَلَا يَمْلِكُ الَّذِينَ يَدْعُونَ مِن دُونِهِ الشَّفَاعَةَ إِلَّا مَن شَهِدَ بِالْحَقِّ وَهُمْ يَعْلَمُونَ ۝٨٦﴾

[61] *Quran*, Sūrah Yūnus (10), verse 3.
[62] *Quran*, Sūrah al-Anbiyā' (21), verses 26-28.

> And those whom they call upon besides Him have no authority for intercession, except one who bears witness of the truth, and they know (the facts about the Oneness of Allāh).[63]

Yet another passage states:

﴿لَا يَمْلِكُونَ الشَّفَاعَةَ إِلَّا مَنِ اتَّخَذَ عِنْدَ الرَّحْمَٰنِ عَهْدًا ﴿٨٧﴾﴾

> They shall have no authority for intercession, except the one who has made a covenant with the Beneficent God.[64]

Penultimately we read:

﴿وَلَا تَنْفَعُ الشَّفَاعَةُ عِنْدَهُ إِلَّا لِمَنْ أَذِنَ لَهُ ۚ حَتَّىٰ إِذَا فُزِّعَ عَنْ قُلُوبِهِمْ قَالُوا مَاذَا قَالَ رَبُّكُمْ ۖ قَالُوا الْحَقَّ ۖ وَهُوَ الْعَلِيُّ الْكَبِيرُ ﴿٢٣﴾﴾

> Besides, no intercession (for the fulfillment of any demand and for the accomplishment of any deed) is of any avail before Him, except that it be made for him (and by him) whom He permits. Yet, when the dread and awe (the angels whose intercession those polytheists hope for feel before Allāh's commands) is removed from their hearts, (other angels) ask: "What has your Lord commanded?" They answer: "The truth (that which is always and unalterably true)." He is the All-Exalted, the All-Great.[65]

Finally, the following verse states:

---

[63] *Quran*, Sūrah al-Zukhruf (43), verse 86.

[64] *Quran*, Sūrah Maryam (19), verse 87.

[65] *Quran*, Sūrah Sabā' (34), verse 23.

﴿وَكَمْ مِنْ مَلَكٍ فِي السَّمَاوَاتِ لَا تُغْنِي شَفَاعَتُهُمْ شَيْئًا إِلَّا مِنْ بَعْدِ أَنْ يَأْذَنَ اللهُ لِمَنْ يَشَاءُ وَيَرْضَىٰ ۝٢٦﴾

And how many an angel is there in the heavens whose intercession does not avail at all except after Allāh has given permission to whom He pleases and chooses.[66]

Some of these verses (like the first three) say that intercession is reserved only for Allāh ﷻ, while the rest of them declare that others may also intercede with the permission of Allāh ﷻ.

In any case, all of these verses confirm the general matter of intercession. However, how are these verses related to the preceding ones which totally reject intercession? It is exactly the same relationship which exists between the verses of the Quran which state that knowledge of unseen is reserved solely for Allāh ﷻ , and another set of verses which declare that others may also have that knowledge - with the permission of Allāh ﷻ. For example, He says:

﴿قُلْ لَا يَعْلَمُ مَنْ فِي السَّمَاوَاتِ وَالْأَرْضِ الْغَيْبَ إِلَّا اللهُ ۝٦٥﴾

Say: "No one in the heavens and the earth knows the unseen except Allāh."[67]

﴿وَعِنْدَهُ مَفَاتِحُ الْغَيْبِ لَا يَعْلَمُهَا إِلَّا هُوَ ۝٥٩﴾

And with Him are the keys of the unseen, none have knowledge of it except for Him.[68]

﴿عَالِمُ الْغَيْبِ فَلَا يُظْهِرُ عَلَىٰ غَيْبِهِ أَحَدًا ۝٢٦ إِلَّا مَنِ ارْتَضَىٰ مِنْ رَسُولٍ ۝٢٧﴾

---

[66] *Quran*, Sūrah al-Najm (53), verse 26.

[67] *Quran*, Sūrah al-Naml (27), verse 65.

[68] *Quran*, Sūrah al-Anʿām (6), verse 59.

> The Knower of the Unseen! So He does not reveal His secrets to any, except to him whom He chooses as an apostle.[69]

The same is the case with various verses on the subjects of creating, sustaining, giving death, causality, command, authority and similar things. Some verses reserve these issues solely to be in the discretion of Allāh ﷻ, while other verses confirm that others may also be able to perform these things (by His permission).

It is a well known style of the Quran that it first rejects the idea that anyone other than Allāh ﷻ has any virtue or perfection, but thereafter it confirms the same virtue or perfection for others depending on the permission and pleasure of Allāh ﷻ.

Therefore when read together, the verses show that no one has any virtue by their own power and right, and whatever excellence anyone may possess is solely because Allāh ﷻ has granted it to that person. This is something which Allāh ﷻ puts great emphasis on. In many instances, He attaches the proviso of His will even for those things which are firmly decreed by Him. For example:

﴿فَأَمَّا الَّذِينَ شَقُوا فَفِي النَّارِ لَهُمْ فِيهَا زَفِيرٌ وَشَهِيقٌ
﴿١٠٦﴾ خَالِدِينَ فِيهَا مَا دَامَتِ السَّمَاوَاتُ وَالْأَرْضُ إِلَّا مَا
شَاءَ رَبُّكَ ۚ إِنَّ رَبَّكَ فَعَّالٌ لِمَا يُرِيدُ ﴿١٠٧﴾ وَأَمَّا الَّذِينَ
سُعِدُوا فَفِي الْجَنَّةِ خَالِدِينَ فِيهَا مَا دَامَتِ السَّمَاوَاتُ
وَالْأَرْضُ إِلَّا مَا شَاءَ رَبُّكَ ۖ عَطَاءً غَيْرَ مَجْذُوذٍ ﴿١٠٨﴾﴾

> So as to those who are unhappy, they shall be in the fire; for them shall be sighing and groaning in it; abiding therein so long as the heavens and the earth endure, except as your Lord pleases; surely your Lord

[69] *Quran*, Sūrah al-Jinn (72), verses 26-27.

> is the (mighty) doer of what He intends. And as for those who are made happy, they shall be in the garden, abiding in it as long as the heavens and the earth endure, except as your Lord please; a gift which shall never be cut off.[70]

Note that 'abiding forever' is made dependent on the pleasure of Allāh ﷻ, and the same holds true even in the case of the garden - although it is a gift which will never be cut off.

This verse emphasizes the fact that even when Allāh ﷻ firmly decrees a thing, it does not pass out of His control or authority, just as He states: ﴾Surely your Lord is the (mighty) doer of what He intends﴿.[71] Thus, when Allah gives a thing to someone, it does not go out of His total possession; and when He denies something to someone, it is not done to protect Himself against any need or poverty!

In short, the verses which reject intercession - albeit talking about the Day of Resurrection - do so in the context of intercession independent upon the authority of Allāh ﷻ; while the verses which prove it, do so for Allāh ﷻ and then depending on His permission given to others. Thus intercession is possible for other than Allāh ﷻ, but **only** with His permission.

Now we must review what the meaning of intercession is; who may intercede; on behalf of whom; when will this occur; and how is it related to Divine forgiveness?

Quranic Discourse About Intercession

1. What is the Meaning of Intercession?

"Ash-Shafāʿah"(intercession) is derived from *ash-shafʿ* which means "even" as opposed to "odd". With this meaning, we understand

[70] *Quran*, Sūrah Hūd (11), verses 106-108.

[71] Ibid., verse 107.

that the interceder adds his own recommendation to the plea of the petitioner and in this way, the number of pleaders becomes even, and the weak plea of the single petitioner is strengthened by the prestige of an intercessor.

In our social and communal life, we are accustomed to seeking other people's intercession and help in the fulfillment of our needs. We resort to it in order to get an advantage or to deter a disadvantage.

However in this discussion, we are not talking about an advantage or a disadvantage, a benefit or a harm which is caused by natural factors such as hunger and thirst, heat or cold, illness or health because in such cases, we can attain what we are seeking through natural solutions such as eating and drinking, wearing clothes, getting medical treatment and so on.

What we are talking about here is the benefit and harm, punishment and reward resulting from the social laws made by civil authorities. These actually stem from the very relationship of mastership-and-servitude and for that matter, between every ruler and ruled one. As we know, there are some commandments, orders and prohibitions in society, and a person who follows and obeys them is praised and rewarded, and the one who disobeys them is condemned and punished, and that reward or punishment that is given to them may either be material or spiritual.

When a master orders his servant to perform or refrain from a thing, and the servant obeys him, he receives a reward; and if he disobeys him, then he is punished. Whenever a rule is made, the punishment for infringing on the law is also laid down and this is the foundation upon which all authorities are built on.

When a person is seeking to gain material or spiritual benefits but is not suitably qualified for it, or when a person is trying to ward off harm which is coming to him due to his disobedience, but finds that he has no shield to protect himself, then comes the time for intercession.

In other words, when an individual wants to get a reward without fulfilling one's responsiblities, or wishes to save oneself from punishment without performing what is required from them, then one looks for someone to intercede on one's behalf.

However, intercession is effective only if the person for whom one intercedes is otherwise qualified to get the reward and has already established a relationship with the authority.

If an ignorant person wants to be appointed to a prestigious academic post, no intercession can do them any good, nor can interecession avail in the case of a rebellious traitor who shows no remorse for one's misdeeds and does not submit to the lawful authorities. Therefore, one can clearly understand that intercession works as a supplement to the cause, and it is not an independent cause.

The effect of an intercessor's words depends on some factors which may have an influence upon the concerned authority - in other words, intercession must have a solid ground to stand upon. The intercessor endeavours to find a way to the heart of the authority concerned in order that the said authority may give the reward to, or waive the punishment of the person who is the subject of intercession.

An intercessor does not ask the master to nullify his mastership or to release the servant from his servitude; nor does he plead with him to refrain from forgoing the rules and regulations for his servants, or to abrogate his commandments (either generally or especially in that one case) in order to save the wrong-doer from the due consequences. In addition, the person interceding does not ask the one to discard the standard of reward and punishment (either generally or in that particular case).

In summary, intercession does not interfere with either the institution of mastership and servanthood, nor the master's authority to lay down the rules, nor can it effect the system of reward and punishment – for these three factors are beyond the jurisdiction of intercession.

Therefore what an intercessor does is this: He accepts the inviolability of the above mentioned three aspects, and then he looks at one or more of the following factors and builds his intercession on that basis:

a. He appeals to the attributes of the master that will give rise to forgiveness - such as his nobility, magnanimity and generosity;

b. He draws attention to characteristics of the servant which would justify the showing of mercy and pardon - such as the person's wretchedness, poverty, low status and misery;

c. He puts at stake his own prestige and honour in the eyes of the master.

Thus, the summary of intercession is like this: "I cannot and do not say that you should forget your mastership over your servant or abrogate your commandment or nullify the system of reward and punishment. What I ask from you is that you forgive this defaulting servant of yours because you are magnanimous and generous and because no harm will come to you if you forgive his sins, and/or because your servant is a wretched creature of low status and is steeped in misery; and it is befitting to a master like you to ignore the faults of a slave like him and/or because you have bestowed on me a high prestige, and I implore you to forgive and pardon him in honour of my (request for) intercession."

In this way, the intercessor bestows precedence on the factors of forgiveness and pardon over those of legislation and recompense. He removes the case from the latter's jurisdiction putting it under the former's influence; and as a result of this shift, the consequences of legislation (reward and punishment) do not remain applicable.

The effect of intercession is therefore based on shifting the case from the jurisdiction of reward and punishment to that of pardon and forgiveness; it is not a confrontation between one cause (Divine legislation) and the other (intercession).

By now it should be clear that intercession is in itself one of the causes - it is the intermediate cause that connects a distant cause to its desired effect.

Allāh ﷻ is the ultimate Cause and this causality shows itself in two ways:

First - In creation: Every cause begins from Allāh ﷻ and ends up back to Him; He is the first and the final Cause. He is the real Creator and Originator. All other causes are merely channels to carry His boundless mercy and limitless bounty to His creatures.

Second - In legislation: Allāh ﷻ in His mercy, established a contact with His creatures; He laid down the religion, sent down His commandments, and prescribed suitable reward and appropriate punishment for His obedient and disobedient servants. He sent prophets and apostles to bring us good tidings and to warn us about the consequences of transgression. These messengers conveyed to us His message in the best possible way. Thus His proof over us was complete:

﴿وَتَمَّتْ كَلِمَتُ رَبِّكَ صِدْقًا وَعَدْلًا ۚ لَا مُبَدِّلَ لِكَلِمَاتِهِ ﴿١١٥﴾﴾

> And the word of your Lord has been accomplished with truth and justice, there is none to change His words...[72]

Both aspects of causality of Allāh ﷻ may be, and in fact are related to intercession.

1. Intercession in creation: Quite obviously the intermediary causes of creation are the conduits that bring down Divine mercy, life, sustenance and other bounties to the creatures; and as such they are intercessors between the Creator and the created. Some Quranic verses are based on this very theme such as the following:

﴿...لَهُ مَا فِي السَّمَاوَاتِ وَمَا فِي الْأَرْضِ ۗ مَنْ ذَا الَّذِي يَشْفَعُ

[72] *Quran*, Sūrah al-Anʿām (6), verse 115.

عِنْدَهُ إِلَّا بِإِذْنِهِ...﴿٢٥٥﴾

...Whatever is in the heavens and what is in the earth is His; who is he that can intercede with Him but by His permission...[73]

﴿إِنَّ رَبَّكُمُ اللهُ الَّذِى خَلَقَ السَّمَاوَاتِ وَالْأَرْضَ فِى سِتَّةِ أَيَّامٍ ثُمَّ اسْتَوَىٰ عَلَى الْعَرْشِ يُدَبِّرُ الْأَمْرَ مَا مِنْ شَفِيعٍ إِلَّا مِنْ بَعْدِ إِذْنِهِ﴿٣﴾

Surely your Lord is Allāh, who created the heavens and the earth in six periods, and He is firmly established on the throne, regulating the affair; there is no intercessor except after His permission.[74]

Intercession in the sphere of creation is only the intermediation of causes between the Creator and the created thing and effect, in bringing it into being and regulating its affairs.

2. Intercession in legislation: Intercession, as analyzed earlier, is effective in this sphere too. It is in this context that Allāh ﷻ says:

﴿يَوْمَئِذٍ لَا تَنْفَعُ الشَّفَاعَةُ إِلَّا مَنْ أَذِنَ لَهُ الرَّحْمَـٰنُ وَرَضِىَ لَهُ قَوْلًا﴿١٠٩﴾

On that day shall no intercession avail except for one whom the Beneficent God allows and whose word He is pleased with.[75]

We also read the following in the Quran:

﴿وَلَا تَنْفَعُ الشَّفَاعَةُ عِنْدَهُ إِلَّا لِمَنْ أَذِنَ لَهُ﴿٢٤﴾

---

[73] *Quran*, Sūrah al-Baqarah (2), verse 255.

[74] *Quran*, Sūrah Yūnus (10), verse 3.

[75] *Quran*, Sūrah Tāhā (20), verse 109.

> And intercession will not avail anything with Him, except for the one whom He permits.[76]

The Quran also states:

﴿وَكَم مِّن مَّلَكٍ فِي السَّمَاوَاتِ لَا تُغْنِي شَفَاعَتُهُمْ شَيْئًا إِلَّا مِن بَعْدِ أَن يَأْذَنَ اللَّهُ لِمَن يَشَاءُ وَيَرْضَىٰ ﴿٢٦﴾﴾

> And how many an angel is there in the heavens whose intercession does not help for anything except after Allāh has given permission to whom He pleases and chooses.[77]

In addition, we read the following:

﴿...وَلَا يَشْفَعُونَ إِلَّا لِمَنِ ارْتَضَىٰ... ﴿٢٨﴾﴾

> ...And they do not intercede except for one whom He approves...[78]

Lastly, we see the following verse in the Quran:

﴿وَلَا يَمْلِكُ الَّذِينَ يَدْعُونَ مِن دُونِهِ الشَّفَاعَةَ إِلَّا مَن شَهِدَ بِالْحَقِّ وَهُمْ يَعْلَمُونَ ﴿٨٦﴾﴾

> And those whom they call upon besides Him have no authority for intercession, except one who bears witness of the truth and know (Him).[79]

These verses clearly affirm an intercessory role for various servants of Allāh ﷻ - both humans and angels, but only with Divine permission and pleasure.

This means that Allāh ﷻ has given some of these groups of

---

[76] *Quran*, Sūrah Sabā' (34), verse 24.
[77] *Quran*, Sūrah al-Najm (53), verse 26.
[78] *Quran*, Sūrah al-Anbiyā' (21), verse 28.
[79] *Quran*, Sūrah al-Zukhruf (43), verse 86.

individuals – human beings and angels –some power and authority in certain matters, and to Him belongs the entire kingdom and all of the affairs.

Those intercessors may appeal to the mercy, forgiveness and other relevant attributes of Allāh ﷻ to cover and protect a servant who otherwise would have deserved punishment because of that person's sins and transgressions. The intercession would transfer that person's case from the general law of recompense to the special domain of grace and mercy. (It has already been explained that the effect of intercession is based on shifting a case from the former's to the latter's jurisdiction - it is not a confrontation between one law and the other.)

In this regards, Allāh ﷻ clearly says:

﴿فَأُولَٰئِكَ يُبَدِّلُ اللَّهُ سَيِّئَاتِهِمْ حَسَنَاتٍ ۝٧٠﴾

> So these are they for whom Allāh changes the evil deeds to good ones.[80]

Allāh ﷻ has the power to change one type of deed into another in the same way that He may render an act null and void, like He reminds us in the Quran:

﴿وَقَدِمْنَا إِلَىٰ مَا عَمِلُوا مِنْ عَمَلٍ فَجَعَلْنَاهُ هَبَاءً مَنْثُورًا ۝٢٣﴾

> And We will proceed to what they have done of deeds, so We shall render them as scattered floating dust.[81]

We also read the following in the Quran:

﴿...فَأَحْبَطَ أَعْمَالَهُمْ... ۝٩﴾

> ...so He rendered their deeds null...[82]

---

[80] *Quran*, Sūrah al-Furqān (25), verse 70.

[81] Ibid., verse 23.

[82] *Quran*, Sūrah Muḥammad (47), verse 9.

The Quran also states:

﴿إِن تَجْتَنِبُوا كَبَآئِرَ مَا تُنْهَوْنَ عَنْهُ نُكَفِّرْ عَنكُمْ سَيِّئَاتِكُمْ ﴿٣١﴾﴾

If you avoid the great sins which you are forbidden, then We will expiate from you your (small) sins.[83]

The Quran also clearly states:

﴿إِنَّ اللَّهَ لَا يَغْفِرُ أَن يُشْرَكَ بِهِ وَيَغْفِرُ مَا دُونَ ذَٰلِكَ لِمَن يَشَآءُ ﴿٨﴾﴾

Surely Allāh does not forgive that any thing should be associated with Him, and He forgives what is besides that to whomsoever He pleases.[84]

The last verse which we have quoted is certainly about the cases other than true belief and repentance, because with belief and repentance even polytheism is forgiven, just like any other sin. In addition, Allāh ﷻ may nurture a small deed to make it greater than the original:

﴿أُولَٰئِكَ يُؤْتَوْنَ أَجْرَهُم مَّرَّتَيْنِ ﴿٥٤﴾﴾

These shall be granted their reward twice.[85]

﴿مَن جَآءَ بِالْحَسَنَةِ فَلَهُ عَشْرُ أَمْثَالِهَا ﴿١٦٠﴾﴾

Whoever brings a good deed, shall have ten like it.[86]

Likewise, Allāh ﷻ may treat a nonexistent deed as existing:

---

[83] *Quran*, Sūrah al-Nisā' (4), verse 31.

[84] Ibid., verse 8.

[85] *Quran*, Sūrah al-Qaṣaṣ (28), verse 54.

[86] *Quran*, Sūrah al-Anʿām (6), verse 160.

﴿وَالَّذِينَ آمَنُوا وَاتَّبَعَتْهُمْ ذُرِّيَّتُهُمْ بِإِيمَانٍ أَلْحَقْنَا بِهِمْ
ذُرِّيَّتَهُمْ وَمَا أَلَتْنَاهُمْ مِنْ عَمَلِهِمْ مِنْ شَيْءٍ ۚ كُلُّ امْرِئٍ
بِمَا كَسَبَ رَهِينٌ ٢١﴾

> And (as for) those who believe and their offspring follow them in faith, We will unite with them their offspring and We will not diminish to them any of their work; every person is responsible for what they have done.[87]

In other words, Allāh ﷻ does what He pleases, and decrees as He wills. Of course, He does so pursuant to His servants' interest, and in accordance with an intermediary cause - and intercession of the intercessors (e.g., the prophets, the friends of Allāh ﷻ and those who are very close to Him) is one of those causes, and certainly no rashness or injustice is entailed therein.

It should now be clear that intercession in its true sense, belongs to Allāh ﷻ only. All of His attributes are intermediaries between Him and His creatures and are the channels through which His grace, mercy and decrees pass to the creatures. He is the Real and All-Encompassing intercessor:

﴿قُلْ لِلَّهِ الشَّفَاعَةُ جَمِيعًا ٤٤﴾

> Say: 'Allāh's is the intercession altogether.'[88]

﴿مَا لَكُمْ مِنْ دُونِهِ مِنْ وَلِيٍّ وَلَا شَفِيعٍ ٤﴾

> Other than Him, you have no guardian or intercessor.[89]

﴿لَيْسَ لَهُمْ مِنْ دُونِهِ وَلِيٌّ وَلَا شَفِيعٌ ٥١﴾

---

[87] *Quran*, Sūrah al-Ṭūr (52), verse 21.
[88] *Quran*, Sūrah al-Zumar (39), verse 44.
[89] *Quran*, Sūrah al-Sajdah (32), verse 4.

> There is no guardian for them, nor any intercessor besides Him.[90]

Therefore, all intercessors - other than Allāh ﷻ - are granted that right by His permission, and by His authority only.

In short, intercession with Him is a confirmed reality - in cases where it does not go against Divine glory and honour.

2. Objections Against Intercession

Intercession, as explained above, is a confirmed reality - not in every case, but only in the approved ones, and the Quran and the traditions do not prove anything more than this and a little bit of reflection on the meaning of intercession is enough to lead to this conclusion.

As mentioned, intercession is mediation in causality and effectiveness. Obviously causality cannot be limitless and unconditional. No cause can be a cause of every effect, nor can an effect be governed by every cause - otherwise it would render the system of cause and effect null and void.

Those who do not believe in intercession have fallen into this very trap. They thought that we affirm the intercession in its totality without any condition or limit, and thus all of their objections emanates from this very misunderstanding.

First Objection: Allāh ﷻ has threatened to punish the wrongdoer - now supposedly He waives the punishment on the Day of Judgement. The question here is whether this waiver is justice or injustice. If it is justice, then the original promise of punishment would be injustice, quite unworthy of Divine majesty; and if it is injustice, then the intercession of the prophets, for example, would be a plea for injustice, and that is irrational and should not be attributed to the prophets.

First Reply to the First Objection: What will such individuals

---

[90] *Quran*, Sūrah al-Anʿām (6), verse 51.

[who share this belief] say about those orders which are given only to test the loyalty of a servant and are changed at the last moment, like the order given to Prophet Ibrāhīm ﷺ to kill his son, Ismā'īl ﷺ? Surely its waiver, just like the original order, was based on justice. Such orders are given only to test the hidden quality of the servant concerned. Likewise, it may be said that salvation is written for all of the believers. The laws of the *sharī'ah* were ordained with punishments prescribed for transgressors - in order that the disbelievers should perish because of their disbelief. As for the obedient believers, their rank will be enhanced by their good deeds; and as for the disobedient believers, they will be rescued by intercession - that intercession may be effective either totally or partially. In the later case, they will have to suffer some of the punishments in *al-Barzakh*[91] or on the Day of Judgement itself and then they will get deliverance.

Thus the original law with the prescribed punishment for the defaulters is nothing but justice, and the subsequent waiver of that punishment is also nothing but justice.

Second Reply to the First Objection: The waiver of the prescribed punishment as a result of intercession could be compared with the previous order - in being based on justice or injustice - only if that waiver were a contradiction of the previous order.

Reply to the Above: We have explained that it is not so. Intercession is not a contradiction of or confrontation between one cause (Divine legislation) and the other (intercession); it is in fact merely a shifting of a person's case from one jurisdiction (reward and punishment) to another jurisdiction (mercy and forgiveness).

Second Objection: It is an established practice of Allāh ﷻ, that His actions are safe from contradiction and conflict. Whatever He decrees and orders, without any exception, runs on an established

[91] The period after death until the Day of Resurrection. (Tr.)

pattern, and this is the foundation which the system of cause and effect has been built upon. In this regards, Allāh ﷻ says:

﴿قَالَ هَٰذَا صِرَاطٌ عَلَيَّ مُسْتَقِيمٌ ﴿٤١﴾ إِنَّ عِبَادِي لَيْسَ لَكَ عَلَيْهِمْ سُلْطَانٌ إِلَّا مَنِ اتَّبَعَكَ مِنَ الْغَاوِينَ ﴿٤٢﴾ وَإِنَّ جَهَنَّمَ لَمَوْعِدُهُمْ أَجْمَعِينَ ﴿٤٣﴾﴾

> This is a straight path with Me, Surely as regards My servants, you have no authority over them except those who follow you of the deviators. And surely hell is the promised place for them all.[92]

﴿وَأَنَّ هَٰذَا صِرَاطِي مُسْتَقِيمًا فَاتَّبِعُوهُ ۖ وَلَا تَتَّبِعُوا السُّبُلَ فَتَفَرَّقَ بِكُمْ عَنْ سَبِيلِهِ ﴿١٥٣﴾﴾

> And (know) that this is My path, the straight one, therefore, follow it, and follow not (other) ways, for they will scatter you away from His way.[93]

﴿فَلَنْ تَجِدَ لِسُنَّتِ اللَّهِ تَبْدِيلًا ۖ وَلَنْ تَجِدَ لِسُنَّتِ اللَّهِ تَحْوِيلًا ﴿٤٣﴾﴾

> For you shall not find any alteration in the course of Allāh; and you shall not find any change in the course of Allāh.[94]

Therefore intercession if effective, will certainly create conflict and contradiction in the actions of Allāh ﷻ. If intercession caused a waiver of punishment from all of the sinners of all of their sins, then it will defeat the very purpose of the *sharīʿah* and will turn

---

[92] *Quran*, Sūrah al-Ḥijr (15), verses 41-43.
[93] *Quran*, Sūrah al-Anʿām (6), verse 153.
[94] *Quran*, Sūrah Fāṭir (35), verse 43.

the whole system into a joke. Conversely, if only some sinners, or only some sins are forgiven, then a contradiction in Divine actions and change and alteration in the established course of Allāh ﷻ would also transpire. Certainly, all of the sinners are transgressors and every sin is disobedience of the Divine command. Therefore, forgiving only some of them or only some of their sins, because of intercession, will be impossible.

Objection: Intercession is used in this life of ours where people are influenced by their desires or social connections. It cannot work in the affairs of the *sharīʿah*, nor can it influence the divine Judgement in any way.

Reply: No one doubts that the path of Allāh ﷻ is straight and His course is one without any change or conflict, however at the same time, it should not be forgotten that this one and unchanged course is based on all of His relevant attributes, not only one or two of them.

Allāh ﷻ is the One Who bestows on every creature diverse things like life, death, sustenance, bounty and so on, and these are the decrees which are contradictory or unrelated to each other - they do not have the same connection with the issuing authority i.e. God. If this was the case, then the relationship between cause and effect would become null and void.

For example, Allāh ﷻ does not restore a sick man to health by virtue of His death-giving power; rather He does so because He is Merciful, Benevolent, Giver of health and Bestower of bounties. Likewise, He does not destroy an arrogant tyrant by His mercy and beneficence, but rather He does so because He is the Avenger, the Omnipotent and the Subduer. In this regards, the Quran is the best witness to this fact: Whenever it ascribes an event or affair to Allāh ﷻ, it invariably always mentions the appropriate attribute by which that affair or event is decreed and managed.

You may say that every affair and every thing is decreed by Allāh ﷻ because of its underlying benefit and good, and because

He does whatever He does by His all-relevant attributes, and not by only one or some of them. Therefore, we can state that there is always an action and reaction between benefits and good of various courses of a certain affair. With that said, Allāh ﷻ issues His decree as a result of His knowledge that encompasses all of these aspects - His vision is not limited to one or two sides only. Had there been one fixed cause or attribute, there would have been no change or difference between a believer and a non-believer, between a pious person and a sinner; however there are numerous causes and attributes, and their sum-total often has effects which are quite different from the effect of its individual parts.

Therefore, intercession and the consequent waiver of punishment - based on the total of several causes like mercy, pardon, judgement, and giving everyone their due right - does not entail any change in the established course, nor any deviation from the right path.

Third Objection: Intercession, according to common understanding, prevails upon the authority to act against his original will. In other words, the original will is abrogated and changed because of the intercessor. A just judge would never accept an intercession unless one's knowledge has changed, e.g., the original judgement was wrong, and then a person was made to realize that justice demanded a course opposite to one's original plan. An unjust judge would accept the intercession of one's friends knowing full well that the course suggested was wrong; but one values those personal relations more than the demands of justice and equity. Obviously, both of these alternatives are impossible so far as Allāh ﷻ is concerned; His will is related to His knowledge, and His knowledge is eternal and unchangeable.

Reply: Intercession has nothing to do with the change of will or knowledge. What actually changes is the thing willed about or known. Allāh ﷻ knows that a certain person will pass through various stages in one's own life; for a time one's condition will be excellent - and Allāh ﷻ wills about that person a certain will, and He knows that later, that person's condition will change - and He wills about him another will; and every day He is in a (new) state (of glory), just as He has said in the Quran:

﴿يَمْحُو اللَّهُ مَا يَشَاءُ وَيُثْبِتُ ۖ وَعِنْدَهُ أُمُّ الْكِتَابِ﴾٣٩

Allāh effaces what He pleases and establishes (likewise), and with Him is the bases of the Book.[95]

﴿بَلْ يَدَاهُ مَبْسُوطَتَانِ يُنْفِقُ كَيْفَ يَشَاءُ﴾٦٤

Rather, both of His hands are spread out, He expends as He pleases.[96]

The same happens with our knowledge and will. We know that soon night will come and we will not be able to see in the darkness, however a few hours later the sun will rise, scattering the darkness. When night comes, our will is directed to light a lamp, and later when the morning comes, the will is directed to extinguish that lamp. In this case, there was no change at all in our knowledge and will; what changed was the objects of that knowledge and will, and consequently they ceased to be governed by that knowledge and that will. After all, not every knowledge is related to every known object, nor is every will connected to every purpose.

What is impossible for Allāh ﷻ is disagreement between His knowledge with the thing known, and His will with its object - while that thing or object remains unchanged. In other words, it is impossible for Him to be mistaken in His knowledge or for His will to be ineffective. We see an apparition far away and take it to be a person; but upon coming near it, we find that it was a horse - in this case, our "knowledge" did not agree with the object - it was a

---

[95] *Quran*, Sūrah al-Raʿd (13), verse 39.

[96] *Quran*, Sūrah al-Māʾidah (5), verse 64.

mistake.

Likewise, we intend to do a certain work, but then we realize that it would be wrong to do so; here our "will" was cancelled and became ineffective. But in these cases the objects of our knowledge and will had not changed.

Such "disagreement" is certainly impossible for Allāh ﷻ. But as we have seen, intercession and the subsequent waiver of punishment does not come into this category.

Fourth Objection: Had Allāh ﷻ promised intercession or had His prophets brought this message to their nations, the people would have been emboldened to disobey the commandments of Allāh ﷻ and to transgress the limits of the *sharīʿah.* It would have defeated the whole purpose behind the institutions of prophethood and religion. If we are to avoid this inherent difficulty, then we will have to interpret the relevant Quranic verses and traditions in a way that do not collide with this basic concept.

Reply - First: What would those people say about the verses showing that the mercy and forgiveness of Allāh ﷻ are all-encompassing? For example:

﴿إِنَّ اللَّهَ لَا يَغْفِرُ أَنْ يُشْرَكَ بِهِ وَيَغْفِرُ مَا دُونَ ذَٰلِكَ لِمَنْ يَشَاءُ ﴿٤٨﴾﴾

> Surely Allāh does not forgive that any thing should be associated with Him, and He forgives what is besides that to whomsoever He pleases.[97]

This verse as explained earlier, covers those cases other than repentance, as the exception of polytheism shows - because in cases of repentance even polytheism may be forgiven.

Second: The promise or message of intercession could incite people to disregard the rules of the *sharīʿah,* if it was accompanied

---

[97] *Quran,* Sūrah al-Nisāʾ (4), verse 48.

by one of the following factors:

1. If it had pinpointed either the sinner - by name or description - who was to be forgiven through intercession; or the particular sin that was to be wiped off unconditionally, definitely and without any ambiguity.

2. Or, if intercession was effective against all types of punishments and at all times.

Read the following sentences to understand what the above conditions mean:

1. "All people, or a named group of people, will never be held responsible for any sins that they commit; nor will they ever be punished for their transgressions."
2. "A specifically named sin will never be punished for."

Obviously, such declarations would defeat the basic purpose of the *sharīʿah.*

However, Allāh ﷻ has kept both of these things vague. He has never said what sins or which sinners might benefit from intercession, nor has He said whether all or only some of the punishments will be waived; nor has He made it clear whether or not the intercession will be effective in every condition and at all times! As all of these things have been kept vague, no one can be sure about benefitting from intercession.

In view of this uncertainty, the individual cannot feel bold to trespass the limits of Allāh ﷻ. On the other hand the possibility of intercession could save one from losing the hope of Divine mercy, and keep one away from despair, despondency, pessimism and hopelessness.

In this regards, there is a verse of the Quran which states:

﴿إِنْ تَجْتَنِبُوا كَبَآئِرَ مَا تُنْهَوْنَ عَنْهُ نُكَفِّرْ عَنْكُمْ سَيِّئَاتِكُمْ ﴿٣١﴾﴾

> If you avoid the major sins which you are forbidden, then We will expiate from you your (small) sins...[98]

This verse clearly says that Allāh ﷻ will forgive the small sins and waive the punishment, provided that the servant shuns the major sins. If Allāh ﷻ can say, "If you avoid major sins, then I will forgive the small ones", then He can just as easily say, "If you keep your belief pure until you come to Me with unpolluted faith, then I will accept the intercession of the intercessors on your behalf." The important thing is to keep the faith strong as sins weaken faith, harden the heart and lead to polytheism.

Allāh ﷻ has said the following in the Quran:

﴿فَلَا يَأْمَنُ مَكْرَ اللَّهِ إِلَّا الْقَوْمُ الْخَاسِرُونَ ﴿٩٩﴾﴾

> But none feel secure from Allāh's plan except the people who shall perish.[99]

﴿كَلَّا ۖ بَلْ ۜ رَانَ عَلَىٰ قُلُوبِهِمْ مَا كَانُوا يَكْسِبُونَ ﴿٤﴾﴾

> Nay! Rather what they used to do has become like rust upon their hearts.[100]

﴿ثُمَّ كَانَ عَاقِبَةَ الَّذِينَ أَسَاءُوا السُّوأَىٰ أَنْ كَذَّبُوا بِآيَاتِ اللَّهِ ﴿١٠﴾﴾

> Then evil was the end of those who did evil, because they rejected the signs of Allāh...[101]

The hope of Divine mercy (generated by the belief in intercession), in many cases, leads to repentance, piety and good deeds - and often the servant reaches a stage where intercession is not needed

[98] *Quran*, Sūrah al-Nisā' (4), verse 31.
[99] *Quran*, Sūrah al-A'rāf (7), verse 99.
[100] *Quran*, Sūrah al-Mutaffifīn (83), verse 4.
[101] *Quran*, Sūrah al-Rūm (30), verse 10.

after all. It is in fact the most important benefit of this belief.

Likewise, if it was mentioned in the religious sources as to who will benefit from intercession, or which sins are likely to be interceded about, but it was declared that it would nevertheless entail some types of punishment up to a certain period, then the person will not feel bold to commit sins.

The fact is that the Quran has nowhere pinpointed the sin, nor if a sinner is likely to benefit from intercession or not. On the contrary, it speaks only about averting the punishment from some people; and no objection can be leveled against such a vague expression.

Fifth Objection: At most, that reason may prove the possibility, and not the actuality, of intercession - in fact, it does not prove even that much. So far as the Quran is concerned, it does not show that intercession will actually take place, as some verses refute the idea of intercession altogether, such as:

﴿...أَنْ يَأْتِيَ يَوْمٌ لَا بَيْعٌ فِيهِ وَلَا خُلَّةٌ وَلَا شَفَاعَةٌ ٢٥٤﴾

> ...A day will come in which there is no bargaining, neither any friendship nor intercession.[102]

Other verses say that intercession shall be of no avail, such as:

﴿فَمَا تَنْفَعُهُمْ شَفَاعَةُ الشَّافِعِينَ ٤٨﴾

> So the intercession of the intercessors will not avail them.[103]

Still other verses, after refuting the actuality of intercession, add the proviso like:

﴿إِلَّا بِإِذْنِهِ ٢٥٥﴾

---

[102] *Quran*, Sūrah al-Baqarah (2), verse 254.

[103] *Quran*, Sūrah al-Muddaththir (74), verse 48.

...Except by His permission...[104]

﴿إِلَّا مِنْ بَعْدِ إِذْنِهِ ۝٣﴾

...Except after His permission...[105]

﴿إِلَّا لِمَنِ ارْتَضَىٰ ۝٢٨﴾

...Except for one whom He approves.[106]

This style (a negative followed by the exception of Divine permission or approval) is used in the Quran invariably always to emphasize a negative statement; for example, it says:

﴿سَنُقْرِئُكَ فَلَا تَنْسَىٰ ۝٦ إِلَّا مَا شَاءَ اللَّهُ ۝٧﴾

We will make you recite so you shall not forget, except what Allah pleases...[107]

In addition we read:

﴿خَالِدِينَ فِيهَا مَا دَامَتِ السَّمَاوَاتُ وَالْأَرْضُ إِلَّا مَا شَاءَ رَبُّكَ ۝١٠٧﴾

Abiding therein so long as the heavens and the earth endure, except as your Lord pleases.[108]

Obviously, there is no definite declaration in the Quran proving the actuality of intercession. As for the traditions, those giving its details are not reliable; and the reliable ones do not say more than the Quran does.

Reply: As for the verses refuting intercession, we have already explained that what is rejected is the intercession without the

---

[104] *Quran*, Sūrah al-Baqarah (2),verse 255.

[105] *Quran*, Sūrah Yūnus (10), verse 3.

[106] *Quran*, Sūrah al-Anbiyā' (21), verse 28.

[107] *Quran*, Sūrah al-Aʿlā (87), verses 6-7.

[108] *Quran*, Sūrah Hūd (11), verse 107.

permission of Allāh ﷻ.

In chapter 74 of the Quran, verse 48 states: ﴾The intercession of intercessors shall not avail them﴿, however this is not a proof against intercession - on the contrary it proves its actuality. This verse is found in Sūrah al-Muddaththir and speaks about "them" – meaning a particular group of wrongdoers mentioned in verses 41 to 47, and we are told that it is this specific group who will not benefit from the intercession of intercessors - it does not speak about all sinners. Moreover, it uses the phrase, "the intercession of intercessors" and without a doubt, there is a difference between saying, "Intercession shall not avail them", and saying, "Intercession of intercessors shall not avail them." When an infinitive verb or verbal noun is used in the genitive or possessive case, it proves its actual existence, just as Shaykh ʿAbd al-Qāhir has clearly stated in *Dalā'il al-Iʿjāz*.

Therefore, the expression, "intercession of intercessors" proves that some intercession will definitely take place on that day, although a particular group will not be able to benefit from it.

Also, the plural, "intercessors" points to the presence of a group of intercessors. Look for example at the phrases:

﴿كَانَتْ مِنَ الْغَابِرِينَ ۝٨٣﴾

She was of those who remained behind.[109]

﴿وَكَانَ مِنَ الْكَافِرِينَ ۝٣٤﴾

And he was one of the unbelievers.[110]

﴿فَكَانَ مِنَ الْغَاوِينَ ۝١٧٥﴾

So he is of those who went astray.[111]

---

[109] *Quran*, Sūrah al-Aʿrāf (7), verse 83.

[110] *Quran*, Sūrah al-Baqarah (2), verse 34.

[111] *Quran*, Sūrah al-Aʿrāf (7), verse 175.

﴿لَا يَنَالُ عَهْدِى الظَّالِمِينَ ١٢٤﴾

My convenant does not include the unjust ones.[112]

The plural used in all of these phrases would have been irrelevant if they did not mean the existence of more than two persons having the attributes mentioned.

Likewise the verse: ﴾So the intercession of intercessors shall not avail them﴿, rather than refuting intercession, clearly proves the existence of intercessors and therefore, intercession.

As for the verses that contain the exceptions, "except by His permission", "except after His permission", they clearly prove the actuality of intercession, especially as the infinitive verb "permission" is used in genitive case *(His permission)* – and no one having a taste of ʿArabic literature can entertain any doubt about this.

It is childish to say that the two phrases, "except by His permission" and "except for one whom He approves" mean the same thing, i.e., the Divine will. Moreover, the Quran has used various phrases of exception in various places, such as: "except by His permission", "except after His permission", "except for one whom He approves" and "except one who bears witness of the truth and they know (Him)."

Even if we accept that Divine permission and Divine approval mean the same thing – meaning the Divine will, can it be said that the last mentioned phrase, ﴾except one who bears witness of the truth...﴿ also implies the same thing? Such interpretation implies such inexactness and laxity in talk that even an ordinary Arab would not like this attributed to him, let alone an eloquent one. Can we accuse the most eloquent Divine speech — the Quran — of such inarticulateness?

As for the traditions, we shall show later that they too follow

---

[112] *Quran*, Sūrah al-Baqarah (2), verse 124.

the line adopted by the Quran.

Sixth Objection: The verses do not clearly state that on the Day of Judgement, the punishment will be averted from the wrong-doers, after the sin has been proved and the sentence pronounced. The intercession attributed to the prophets means that they were the intermediaries between the Lord and His servants, they received revelation from their Lord and conveyed it to the people and guided them to the right path, leading them to spiritual and ethical perfection. In this sense, they are the intercessors for the believers in this world, as well as in the hereafter.

Reply: No doubt, it is one of the aspects of intercession - but intercession is not limited to this much. The prophets called their people to true faith and repentance, and this is the intercession mentioned by the objector. Now let us look again at the verse:

﴿إِنَّ اللَّهَ لَا يَغْفِرُ أَنْ يُشْرَكَ بِهِ وَيَغْفِرُ مَا دُونَ ذَٰلِكَ لِمَنْ يَشَاءُ ۝٤٨﴾

> Surely Allāh does not forgive that any thing should be associated with Him, and He forgives what is besides that to whomsoever He pleases.[113]

As described earlier, this verse covers the cases other than the true faith and repentance (as true faith and repentance will wipe out the polytheism as well). The exception of polytheism shows that here the talk is about other things - and intercession, in the meaning explained by us, is one of those cases.

Seventh Objection: Reason does not prove that intercession really exists; and the Quranic verses on this subject are ambiguous - in one place they prove it, and at others refute it; sometimes they add some proviso, other times they speak unconditionally. Therefore, the ethics of religion demands that we should believe in

[113] *Quran*, Sūrah al-Nisā' (4), verse 48.

all of them and leave their meaning to Allāh ﷻ.

Reply: The ambiguous verses, when referred to the decisive ones, become decisive themselves. It is an easy process which is not beyond our ability and power. We shall explain this subject when writing about the verse: ﴾...Among it there are some verses decisive, they are the basis of the Book, and others are ambiguous...﴿[114]

3. Who will Benefit from Intercession?

As explained earlier, it was not in the best interest of religious guidance to pinpoint who will benefit from intercession on the Day of Judgement. But vague hints and ambiguous statements can do no harm, and the Quran has used them to give us a general idea. For example, Allāh ﷻ says:

﴿كُلُّ نَفْسٍ بِمَا كَسَبَتْ رَهِينَةٌ ٣٨ إِلَّا أَصْحَابَ الْيَمِينِ
٣٩ فِي جَنَّاتٍ يَتَسَاءَلُونَ ٤٠ عَنِ الْمُجْرِمِينَ ٤١ مَا
سَلَكَكُمْ فِي سَقَرَ ٤٢ قَالُوا لَمْ نَكُ مِنَ الْمُصَلِّينَ
٤٣ وَلَمْ نَكُ نُطْعِمُ الْمِسْكِينَ ٤٤ وَكُنَّا نَخُوضُ مَعَ
الْخَائِضِينَ ٤٥ وَكُنَّا نُكَذِّبُ بِيَوْمِ الدِّينِ ٤٦ حَتَّىٰ أَتَانَا
الْيَقِينُ ٤٧ فَمَا تَنْفَعُهُمْ شَفَاعَةُ الشَّافِعِينَ ٤٨﴾

> Every soul is held in pledge for what it has earned, except the people of the right hand, in gardens; they shall ask each other about the guilty: "What has brought you into hell?" They will say: "We were not of those who prayed, and we used to not feed the poor; and we used to enter (into vain discourse) with those who entered (into vain discourse); and we used to call the Day of Judgement a lie, until death overtook us."

---

[114] *Quran*, Sūrah Āle 'Imrān (3), verse 7.

So the intercession of intercessors will not avail them.[115]

The verses declare that every soul will remain mortgaged on the Day of Judgement for the sins it has earned - held responsible for the wrongs done in this life. The only exception is for the people of the right hand - they will be released from that pledge, and will settle in the gardens. They will see the wrongdoers who will be held captive of their sins, and herded into the fire of hell; the righteous will ask the sinners why they are going into hell and the guilty will reply by enumerating four sins as the cause of their disgrace and punishment. They will confirm that it was because of those sins that they lost the benefit of the intercession of the intercessors.

These verses imply that the people of the right hand will be free from those sins which deprive a person from the benefit of intercession. Allāh ﷻ will release them from the fetters of sins and wrongs; and this release will be as a result of the intercession of the intercessors.

It must be noted that these verses are a part of chapter 74, Al-Muddaththir. This chapter was revealed in Mecca at the beginning of the call to Islam, as the contents of the sūrah prove. At that time, the prayer and charity as known to us were not promulgated. In this context the prayer mentioned in the verse which reads, ﴾We were not among those who prayed﴿, could only mean turning one's face towards Allāh ﷻ with humility and submission. Likewise, the verse which mentions, ﴾and we did not feed the poor﴿, could only refer to general spending on the poor in the way of Allāh ﷻ. The word *al-khawd* (translated here as entering into vain discourse) literally means to wade into water, and to plung or rush into something. Therefore, the verse which states, We used to enter (into vain discourse)...﴿, implies entanglement into the vain things of this life, which distract a person from remembrance of the hereafter, and it may also mean vilification of the verses which remind one

[115] *Quran*, Sūrah al-Muddaththir (74), verses 38-48.

about the Day of Reckoning.

Therefore, those wrongdoers will be guilty of four sins:

1. Not turning their faces towards Allāh ﷻ with humility and submission;
2. Not spending in the way of Allāh ﷻ;
3. Vilification - of Divine revelations; and
4. Calling the Day of Judgement a lie.

These four evils destroy the foundation of religion.

Religion demands following the purified guides, setting one's face towards Allāh ﷻ, turning away from the worldly distractions, and setting one's eyes on the Day of Judgement. If a person succeeds in it, then one will be free from the third and the fourth sins -vilification of Divine revelation and calling the Day of Judgement a lie. When in this way, a person's fundamental belief is secured, then one will feel the urge to turn towards Allāh ﷻ and help fellow human beings. These two factors are represented in these verses by prayer and spending in the way of Allāh ﷻ. Faith and deeds thus combine to build the structure of religion, while other elements such as belief in the Oneness of God and prophethood, will then naturally follow.

The people of the right hand are the ones who will benefit from the intercession; and they are the ones whose religion and faith Allāh ﷻ is pleased with. They may come on the Day of Judgement with perfect deeds - and in that case there will be no need for any intercession; or they may come burdened with some sins and it is they who will benefit from the intercession. Therefore, the intercession will be for those people of the right hand who may have committed some sins.

In this regards, Allāh ﷻ says:

﴿إِن تَجْتَنِبُوا كَبَآئِرَ مَا تُنْهَوْنَ عَنْهُ نُكَفِّرْ عَنكُمْ سَيِّئَاتِكُمْ ﴿٣١﴾﴾

> If you avoid the great sins which you are forbidden,
> We will expiate from you your (small) sins.[116]

Therefore, anybody coming on the Day of Judgement with a sin which was not expiated will be guilty of a great sin, because had it been a small one, then it would have been expiated long before their arrival on the Judgement plain.

Thus, we conclude from this verse that intercession will only be for those "people of the right hand" who will be guilty of great sins. In this regards, Prophet Muḥammad ﷺ has said: "Verily my intercession is for those of my nation who will have committed the major sins. As for the good doers, there shall be no difficulty for them..."

The designation, "the people of the right hand," is opposite to "the people of the left hand." These Quranic terms are based on the fact that on the Day of Judgement, each person will be given their book of deeds either in their right hand or in their left hand, and this is what Allāh ﷻ has said in the Quran:

﴿يَوْمَ نَدْعُو كُلَّ أُنَاسٍ بِإِمَامِهِمْ ۖ فَمَنْ أُوتِيَ كِتَابَهُ بِيَمِينِهِ فَأُولَٰئِكَ يَقْرَءُونَ كِتَابَهُمْ وَلَا يُظْلَمُونَ فَتِيلًا ﴿٧١﴾ وَمَنْ كَانَ فِي هَٰذِهِ أَعْمَىٰ فَهُوَ فِي الْآخِرَةِ أَعْمَىٰ وَأَضَلُّ سَبِيلًا ﴿٧٢﴾﴾

> (Remember) the day when We will call every people with their leader (imam); then whoever is given one's book in their right hand, these shall read their book; and they will not be dealt with a whit unjustly. And whoever is blind in this, will (also) be blind in the hereafter; and more erring from the way.[117]

---

[116] *Quran*, Sūrah al-Nisā (4), verse 31.

[117] *Quran*, Sūrah al-Isrā' (17), verses 71-72.

We shall describe, when commenting about this verse, that getting the book in one's right hand is synonymous with following the rightful leader (imām); likewise receiving the book in one's left hand means following a misguided leader. In this vein, Allāh ﷻ says the following about Pharaoh:

﴿يَقْدُمُ قَوْمَهُ يَوْمَ الْقِيَامَةِ فَأَوْرَدَهُمُ النَّارَ ۝٩٨﴾

> He will lead his people on the Resurrection Day, and bring them down to the fire.[118]

This verse means that it is not only the four qualities which were previously mentioned which are required, but one must also possess the nomenclature of being one of "the people of the right hand" which determines that the individual followed an approved religion, and that Allāh ﷻ was pleased with them.

Allāh ﷻ says the following in another place in the Quran:

﴿وَلَا يَشْفَعُونَ إِلَّا لِمَنِ ارْتَضَىٰ ۝٢٨﴾

> And they do not intercede except for one whom He is pleased with.[119]

We must note that this approval is general and without any conditions or qualifications, and that it is not like the one mentioned in the following verse:

﴿إِلَّا مَنْ أَذِنَ لَهُ الرَّحْمَٰنُ وَرَضِيَ لَهُ قَوْلًا ۝١٠٩﴾

> ...except of one whom the Beneficent God allows and whose word He is pleased with...[120]

In this verse, the condition which is required is approval or pleasure which is related to a servant's word.

In this verse under discussion [of this overall themse of

---

[118] *Quran*, Sūrah Hūd (11), verse 98.

[119] *Quran*, Sūrah al-Anbiyā᾽ (21), verse 28.

[120] *Quran*, Sūrah Tāhā (20), verse 109.

intercession] the pleasure or approval is related to them, not to their deeds; in other words, "whom He approves" means 'whose religion He approves of.' Accordingly this verse too has the same import as the previous ones.

Again in yet another part of the Quran, Allāh ﷻ says:

﴿يَوْمَ نَحْشُرُ الْمُتَّقِينَ إِلَى الرَّحْمَٰنِ وَفْدًا ﴿٨٥﴾ وَنَسُوقُ الْمُجْرِمِينَ إِلَىٰ جَهَنَّمَ وِرْدًا ﴿٨٦﴾ لَا يَمْلِكُونَ الشَّفَاعَةَ إِلَّا مَنِ اتَّخَذَ عِنْدَ الرَّحْمَٰنِ عَهْدًا ﴿٨٧﴾﴾

The day on which We will gather the pious ones to the Beneficent God as the guests of honour, and We will drive the guilty one's to hell like a (thirsty) herd (to the watering place). They shall not own any intercession, except one who has made a covenant with the Beneficent God.[121]

The one who has made a covenant with Allāh ﷻ will be given the control of intercession, however it should not be forgotten that not every guilty servant is an unbeliever. Allāh ﷻ says:

﴿إِنَّهُ مَنْ يَأْتِ رَبَّهُ مُجْرِمًا فَإِنَّ لَهُ جَهَنَّمَ لَا يَمُوتُ فِيهَا وَلَا يَحْيَىٰ ﴿٧٤﴾ وَمَنْ يَأْتِهِ مُؤْمِنًا قَدْ عَمِلَ الصَّالِحَاتِ فَأُولَٰئِكَ لَهُمُ الدَّرَجَاتُ الْعُلَىٰ ﴿٧٥﴾﴾

Whoever comes to one's Lord (being) guilty, for him is surely hell; he shall not die therein nor shall he live; and whoever comes to Him a believer (and) he has done good deeds indeed, these it is who shall have the high ranks.[122]

---

[121] *Quran*, Sūrah Maryam (19), verses 85-87.
[122] *Quran*, Sūrah Tāhā (20), verses 74-75.

According to these verses, anyone who is not a righteous believer is guilty, no matter whether he is an unbeliever, or a wrong doing believer. The latter group, i.e., those who have true belief, but have also committed sins, are the ones that made a covenant with God and in regards to whom Allāh ﷻ says:

﴿أَلَمْ أَعْهَدْ إِلَيْكُمْ يَا بَنِي آدَمَ أَنْ لَا تَعْبُدُوا الشَّيْطَانَ إِنَّهُ لَكُمْ عَدُوٌّ مُبِينٌ ۝٦٠ وَأَنِ اعْبُدُونِي ۚ هَٰذَا صِرَاطٌ مُسْتَقِيمٌ ۝٦١﴾

> Did I not enjoin you (make a covenant with you), O children of Adam that you should not worship the Satan? Surely he is your open enemy, and that you should worship Me; this is the straight path.[123]

The phrase, ﴾...and that you should worship Me...﴿ is a covenant in the meaning of a command or a directive and the sentence, ﴾...this is the straight path﴿ is also a covenant by implication because the straight path leads to felicity and safety. However, some believers will enter hell because of the sins that they had committed, and then they will be rescued by intercession.

It is to this covenant that the following verse alludes:

﴿وَقَالُوا لَنْ تَمَسَّنَا النَّارُ إِلَّا أَيَّامًا مَعْدُودَةً ۚ قُلْ أَتَّخَذْتُمْ عِنْدَ اللَّهِ عَهْدًا ۝٨٠﴾

> And they (the Jews) Say: "Fire shall not touch us but for a few days. Say: "Have you received a promise (covenant) from Allāh?"[124]

Thus, these verses also lead us to the same conclusion which is

---

[123] *Quran*, Sūrah Yāsīn (36), verses 60-61.

[124] *Quran*, Sūrah al-Baqarah (2), verse 80.

that the group which will benefit from intercession on the Day of Judgement are the believers who committed major sins, however they are people whose religion and belief is something which Allāh ﷻ is pleased with and has approved.

4. Who are the Intercessors?

It has been described that intercession takes place in two spheres: creation and legislation.

So far as the intercession in creation is concerned, all intermediary causes are intercessors because they are placed between the Creator and the created.

As for the intercessors in the sphere of legislation and Judgement, they may be divided into two categories: (1) intercessors in this life, and (2) intercessors in the hereafter.

Intercessors in this life refer to all of the things which bring a person closer to Allāh ﷻ and make one eligible for Divine forgiveness, and the following things fall into this category:

a. Repentance:

﴿قُلْ يَا عِبَادِيَ الَّذِينَ أَسْرَفُوا عَلَىٰ أَنْفُسِهِمْ لَا تَقْنَطُوا مِنْ رَحْمَةِ اللَّهِ ۚ إِنَّ اللَّهَ يَغْفِرُ الذُّنُوبَ جَمِيعًا ۚ إِنَّهُ هُوَ الْغَفُورُ الرَّحِيمُ ﴿٥٣﴾﴾

Say: O My servants who have acted extravagantly against their own souls, do not despair of the mercy of Allah; surely Allah forgives the faults altogether; surely He is the Forgiving, the Merciful. And return to your Lord.[125]

This covers all of the sins - even polytheism - if one repents from it and believes in the One God, then even one's previous sin of

[125] *Quran*, Sūrah al-Zumar (39), verse 53.

polytheism will be wiped out and forgiven.

b. True faith:

﴿يَا أَيُّهَا الَّذِينَ آمَنُوا اتَّقُوا اللَّهَ وَآمِنُوا بِرَسُولِهِ يُؤْتِكُمْ كِفْلَيْنِ مِنْ رَحْمَتِهِ وَيَجْعَلْ لَكُمْ نُورًا تَمْشُونَ بِهِ وَيَغْفِرْ لَكُمْ وَاللَّهُ غَفُورٌ رَحِيمٌ ﴿٢٨﴾﴾

O you who believe! Have the awe of Allāh and believe in His Apostle: He will give you two portions of His mercy, and make for you a light with which you will walk, and forgive you, and indeed Allāh is Forgiving, Merciful.[126]

c. Good deeds:

﴿وَعَدَ اللَّهُ الَّذِينَ آمَنُوا وَعَمِلُوا الصَّالِحَاتِ لَهُمْ مَغْفِرَةٌ وَأَجْرٌ عَظِيمٌ ﴿٩﴾﴾

Allāh has promised those who believe and do good deeds (that there is) for them pardon and great recompense.[127]

﴿يَا أَيُّهَا الَّذِينَ آمَنُوا اتَّقُوا اللَّهَ وَابْتَغُوا إِلَيْهِ الْوَسِيلَةَ ﴿٣٥﴾﴾

O you who believe! Have the awe of Allāh and seek an approach (medium) to Him...[128]

Indeed there are many verses on this theme.

d. The Quran:

---

[126] *Quran*, Sūrah al-Ḥadīd (57), verse 28.

[127] *Quran*, Sūrah al-Mā'idah (5), verse 9.

[128] Ibid., verse 35.

﴿يَهْدِى بِهِ اللَّهُ مَنِ اتَّبَعَ رِضْوَانَهُ سُبُلَ السَّلَامِ وَيُخْرِجُهُمْ مِنَ الظُّلُمَاتِ إِلَى النُّورِ بِإِذْنِهِ وَيَهْدِيهِمْ إِلَىٰ صِرَاطٍ مُسْتَقِيمٍ ﴿١٦﴾﴾

...whereby Allāh guides him who follows His pleasure, into the ways of peace, and takes them out of the darknesses towards the light by His will and guides them to the straight path.[129]

e. Anything related to a good deed, such as building or maintaining of the mosques, holy places and upholding or giving due importance to the auspicious days.

f. The prophets and the apostles, as they seek forgiveness for their people:

﴿...وَلَوْ أَنَّهُمْ إِذْ ظَلَمُوا أَنْفُسَهُمْ جَاءُوكَ فَاسْتَغْفَرُوا اللَّهَ وَاسْتَغْفَرَ لَهُمُ الرَّسُولُ لَوَجَدُوا اللَّهَ تَوَّابًا رَحِيمًا ﴿٦٤﴾﴾

...And had they, when they were unjust to themselves, come to you and asked forgiveness of Allāh, and the Apostle had (also) asked forgiveness for them, then they would have found Allāh Oft-returning (to mercy), Merciful.[130]

g. The angels, as they too ask for forgiveness for the believers.

﴿الَّذِينَ يَحْمِلُونَ الْعَرْشَ وَمَنْ حَوْلَهُ يُسَبِّحُونَ بِحَمْدِ رَبِّهِمْ وَيُؤْمِنُونَ بِهِ وَيَسْتَغْفِرُونَ لِلَّذِينَ آمَنُوا... ﴿٧﴾﴾

Those who bear the throne and those around it celebrate the praise of their Lord and believe in Him

---

[129] Ibid., verse 16.

[130] *Quran*, Sūrah al-Nisā' (4), verse 64.

and ask forgiveness for those who believe...[131]

﴿وَالْمَلَائِكَةُ يُسَبِّحُونَ بِحَمْدِ رَبِّهِمْ وَيَسْتَغْفِرُونَ لِمَنْ فِي الْأَرْضِ ۝٥﴾

...and the angels celebrate the praise of their Lord and ask forgiveness for those on the earth...[132]

h. The believers themselves, as they seek pardon for their believing brothers and sisters and for themselves.

﴿وَاعْفُ عَنَّا وَاغْفِرْ لَنَا وَارْحَمْنَا ۚ أَنْتَ مَوْلَانَا ۝٢٨٦﴾

...And pardon us, and forgive us, and have mercy on us, You are our Guardian...[133]

Intercessors in the hereafter: We use the term intercessor, in the meaning explained in the beginning of this discussion and in this regards, the following fall under this category:

a. The prophets and the apostles:

﴿وَقَالُوا اتَّخَذَ الرَّحْمَٰنُ وَلَدًا ۗ سُبْحَانَهُ ۚ بَلْ عِبَادٌ مُكْرَمُونَ ۝٢٦ لَا يَسْبِقُونَهُ بِالْقَوْلِ وَهُمْ بِأَمْرِهِ يَعْمَلُونَ ۝٢٧ يَعْلَمُ مَا بَيْنَ أَيْدِيهِمْ وَمَا خَلْفَهُمْ وَلَا يَشْفَعُونَ إِلَّا لِمَنِ ارْتَضَىٰ ۝٢٨﴾

And they say: 'The Beneficent God has taken to Himself a son.' Glory be to Him. Nay! they are honoured servants - they do not precede Him in speech and (only) according to His commandment do they act. He knows what is before them and what is behind them,

[131] *Quran*, Sūrah al-Mo'min (40), verse 7.
[132] *Quran*, Sūrah al-Shūra (42), verse 5.
[133] *Quran*, Sūrah al-Baqarah (2), verse 286.

> and they do not intercede except for those whom He approves...[134]

Those who were called 'son' of God, are in fact His honoured servants and they do intercede for those except whom He approves. Among them is ʿIsā (Jesus) - son of Maryam and he was a prophet. Therefore it means that the prophets do intercede but only for those approved people.

In this regards, Allāh ﷻ says:

﴿وَلَا يَمْلِكُ الَّذِينَ يَدْعُونَ مِن دُونِهِ الشَّفَاعَةَ إِلَّا مَن شَهِدَ بِالْحَقِّ وَهُمْ يَعْلَمُونَ ﴿٨٦﴾﴾

> And those whom they call upon besides Him have no authority for (meaning they do not own) intercession, but one who bears witness of the truth and they know (Him).[135]

b. The angels

In the two preceding verses, we saw that the angels too may intercede, because they too were called daughters of Allāh ﷻ and in this regards, Allāh ﷻ says:

﴿وَكَم مِّن مَّلَكٍ فِي السَّمَاوَاتِ لَا تُغْنِي شَفَاعَتُهُمْ شَيْئًا إِلَّا مِن بَعْدِ أَن يَأْذَنَ اللَّهُ لِمَن يَشَاءُ وَيَرْضَىٰ ﴿٢٦﴾﴾

> And how many an angel is there in the heavens whose intercession does not avail at all except after Allāh has given permission to whom He pleases and chooses.[136]

﴿يَوْمَئِذٍ لَّا تَنفَعُ الشَّفَاعَةُ إِلَّا مَنْ أَذِنَ لَهُ الرَّحْمَٰنُ وَرَضِيَ

[134] *Quran*, Sūrah al-Anbiyāʾ (21), verses 26-28.

[135] *Quran*, Sūrah al-Zukhruf (43), verse 86.

[136] *Quran*, Sūrah al-Najm (53), verse 26.

لَهُ قَوْلًا ﴿١٠٩﴾ يَعْلَمُ مَا بَيْنَ أَيْدِيهِمْ وَمَا خَلْفَهُمْ ﴿١١٠﴾

On that day shall no intercession avail except for him whom the Beneficent God allows and whose word He is pleased with, He knows what is before them and what is behind them...[137]

c. The witnesses

﴿وَلَا يَمْلِكُ الَّذِينَ يَدْعُونَ مِنْ دُونِهِ الشَّفَاعَةَ إِلَّا مَنْ شَهِدَ بِالْحَقِّ وَهُمْ يَعْلَمُونَ ﴿٨٦﴾﴾

And those whom they call upon besides Him have no authority for (or, do not own) intercession, except one who bears witness of the truth and they know (him).[138]

This verse shows that those who bear witness of the truth own (or have authority for) intercession. The witness (*shahīd*) mentioned in this verse does not mean one who is killed in the battlefield. It refers to the witnessing of deeds, as was described in Sūrah al-Fātiha, and will be further explained under the verse:

﴿وَكَذَٰلِكَ جَعَلْنَاكُمْ أُمَّةً وَسَطًا لِتَكُونُوا شُهَدَاءَ عَلَى النَّاسِ وَيَكُونَ الرَّسُولُ عَلَيْكُمْ شَهِيدًا ﴿١٤٣﴾﴾

And thus we have made you a medium (i.e. just) nation that you may be witnesses over the people and (that) the Apostle may be a witness over you...[139]

d. The believers

They will be joined to the witnesses on the Day of Judgement and it follows that they too may intercede, just like the witnesses may

[137] *Quran*, Sūrah Tāhā (20), verses 109-110.

[138] *Quran*, Sūrah al-Zukhruf (43), verse 86.

[139] *Quran*, Sūrah al-Baqarah (2), verse 143.

be able to and in this regards, Allāh ﷻ says:

﴿وَالَّذِينَ آمَنُوا بِاللَّهِ وَرُسُلِهِ أُولَٰئِكَ هُمُ الصِّدِّيقُونَ ۖ وَالشُّهَدَاءُ عِنْدَ رَبِّهِمْ...﴿١٩﴾﴾

> And (as for) those who believe in Allāh and His apostles, these it is that are the truthful one and the witnesses with their Lord...[140]

5. Intercession: About What?

The intercession in creation is related to every cause in this world in regards to the [rule of] cause and effect.

As for the intercession in matters of legislation and judgement, some of them wipe out every sin and its punishment, starting from polytheism to the smallest of sins as long as repentance is done and true faith is acquired, before the Day of Resurrection. Some wipe out effects of some particular sins, like certain specified good deeds.

As for the issue under discussion which is intercession of the prophets and other believers on the Day of Judgement, we have already explained that those believers who committed major sins, however were among those whom Allah was pleased with, will achieve and benefit from intercession.

6. When will Intercession be Achieved?

Here, we are talking too about the intercession on the Day of Judgement which will waive off the punishment of one's sins. Earlier, we quoted the verses from Sūrah al-Muddaththir which mentioned:

﴿كُلُّ نَفْسٍ بِمَا كَسَبَتْ رَهِينَةٌ ﴿٣٨﴾ إِلَّا أَصْحَابَ الْيَمِينِ

---

[140] *Quran*, Sūrah al-Ḥadīd (57), verse 19.

﴿ ٣٩ فِي جَنَّاتٍ يَتَسَاءَلُونَ ٤٠ عَنِ الْمُجْرِمِينَ ٤١ ﴾

> Every soul is held in pledge for what it has earned, except the people of the right hand, in gardens they shall ask each other about the guilty. [141]

As explained earlier, the verses clearly speak about who will benefit from intercession, and who will not benefit from it. They also imply that intercession will free the wrongdoing believers from the fetters of their sins and protect them from abiding in hell for eternity.

However, there is nothing to show that intercession will benefit a person against the turmoil of the Day of Resurrection. Rather, the verse proves that it will be effective only for rescuing the guilty believers from hell, or preventing them from entering into it in the first instance.

It may be inferred from the verses that this talk (which was quoted above from Sūrah al-Muddaththir) takes place after the people of the garden have settled in the gardens, and the people of the hell are in the hell; and that the intercessors shall then intercede for a group of the guilty ones and rescue them from the fire of hell. The phrase ﴾in gardens﴿ implies this as does the question, ﴾What has brought you into hell?﴿ Both phrases imply a more or less permanent abode. Likewise the comment ﴾so the intercession... avails them not﴿, denotes something occurring in present time – meaning after both groups have settled in their respective abodes.

As for *al-barzakh* (the period between death and the Day of Resurrection) and the presence of Prophet Muḥammad ﷺ and the Imāms of the Ahlulbayt ﷺ during the time of death, and for the questioning in the grave and the help given by them to the believers to overcome those difficulties as will be described under the verse:

---

[141] *Quran*, Sūrah al-Muddaththir (74), verses 38-41.

﴿وَإِنْ مِنْ أَهْلِ الْكِتَابِ إِلَّا لَيُؤْمِنَنَّ بِهِ قَبْلَ مَوْتِهِ﴿١٥٩﴾﴾

And there shall not be any one from among the people of the book but he must certainly believe in him before his death.[142]

that these things have nothing to do with intercession. Rather, it is in regards to the exercising of the authority given to them by Allāh ﷻ over the creation, that Allāh ﷻ says:

﴿وَعَلَى الْأَعْرَافِ رِجَالٌ يَعْرِفُونَ كُلًّا بِسِيمَاهُمْ ۚ وَنَادَوْا أَصْحَابَ الْجَنَّةِ أَنْ سَلَامٌ عَلَيْكُمْ ۚ لَمْ يَدْخُلُوهَا وَهُمْ يَطْمَعُونَ ﴿٤٦﴾ وَإِذَا صُرِفَتْ أَبْصَارُهُمْ تِلْقَاءَ أَصْحَابِ النَّارِ قَالُوا رَبَّنَا لَا تَجْعَلْنَا مَعَ الْقَوْمِ الظَّالِمِينَ ﴿٤٧﴾ وَنَادَىٰ أَصْحَابُ الْأَعْرَافِ رِجَالًا يَعْرِفُونَهُمْ بِسِيمَاهُمْ قَالُوا مَا أَغْنَىٰ عَنْكُمْ جَمْعُكُمْ وَمَا كُنْتُمْ تَسْتَكْبِرُونَ ﴿٤٨﴾ أَهَٰؤُلَاءِ الَّذِينَ أَقْسَمْتُمْ لَا يَنَالُهُمُ اللَّهُ بِرَحْمَةٍ ۚ ادْخُلُوا الْجَنَّةَ لَا خَوْفٌ عَلَيْكُمْ وَلَا أَنْتُمْ تَحْزَنُونَ ﴿٤٩﴾﴾

And between the two (the Fire and the Paradise) is a barrier, and on the elevated places there shall be men (like the Prophets and other exalted spiritual dignitaries) who will recognise every one by their appearance. And they shall call out to the (prospective) inmates of Paradise, 'Peace be on you!' These (prospective inmates of Paradise) will not have (yet) entered therein, though they will be hoping (for this

[142] *Quran*, Sūrah al-Nisā' (4), verse 159. We will not present the commentary of this verse in this book; the readers are requested to refer to *al-Mizān* in print or online for this passage. (Tr.)

> entry). And when their eyes are turned towards the fellows of the Fire, they will say, 'Our Lord! place us not with these wrong-doing people.' The occupants of the elevated places will call out to certain people (from the fellows of the Fire), whom they will recognise by their appearance, 'Behold! neither your multitude nor that (amassing) in which you took pride have been of any avail to you. Are these (owners of Paradise) the ones about whom you swore that Allāh would not extend His mercy to them?' (Allāh has ordered them saying) 'Enter Paradise! No fear shall remain on you, nor shall you ever grieve.'[143]

This passage gives us a glimpse of the authority or rule vested to them by the permission of Allāh ﷻ.

If we look at the following verse from this angle, it also throws light on this aspect:

﴿يَوْمَ نَدْعُو كُلَّ أُنَاسٍ بِإِمَامِهِمْ ۖ فَمَنْ أُوتِيَ كِتَابَهُ بِيَمِينِهِ ﴿٧١﴾﴾

> (Remember) the day when We will call every people with their leader (*imām*); then whoever is given his book in his right hand...[144]

The intermediary position of the leader (*imām*) in calling every people and giving them their books is a type of authority and rule vested in him by Allāh ﷻ.

To make a long story short, intercession will definitely happen at the very last stage on the Day of Judgement; it will bring the Divine forgiveness to the guilty believers, prevent them from entering into hell and take those out who would have entered

[143] *Quran*, Sūrah al-Aʿrāf (7), verses 46-49.

[144] *Quran*, Sūrah al-Isrāʾ (17), verse 71.

into it; it will be an extension of mercy and/or a manifestation of benevolence and magnanimity.

Traditions on this Topic

Al-Ḥusayn b. Khālid narrates from Imām al-Riḍā who narrated through his forefathers from the Commander of the Faithful that he said: "The Messenger of Allāh said: 'Whoever does not believe in my reservoir, and whoever does not believe in my intercession, may Allāh not extend to him my intercession.' Then he continued: 'Verily my intercession is for those of my nation who would have committed major sins; and as for the good-doers, there shall be no difficulty for them.'" Al-Ḥusayn b. Khālid said: "I asked al-Riḍā: 'O son of the Messenger of Allāh! Then what is the meaning of the words of Allāh, Mighty and Great is He: ﴾*...And they do not intercede except for him whom He approves?*﴿' He replied: 'They do not intercede except for him whose religion Allāh is pleased with.'"[145]

The author says: The statement of the Prophet: "Verily my intercession is...", has been narrated by both the Shīʿa and Sunni through numerous chains of narrators, and earlier we showed that this tradition is based on the theme of the Quranic verses.

Sumāʿah b. Mihrān narrates from Abū Ibrāhīm that he said about the words of Allah: ﴾*Perhaps your Lord will raise you to a praised position*﴿: "The people, on the Day of Resurrection, will remain standing for forty years, and the sun will be ordered to reside above their heads and they will be bridled by sweat, and the earth will be told not to accept any of their sweat. In such a state, they will approach [Prophet] Adam to intercede for them and he will direct them to [Prophet] Noah, and [Prophet] Noah will direct them to [Prophet] Abraham, and [Prophet] Abraham will direct them to [Prophet] Moses, and [Prophet] Moses will direct them to

[145] *Al-Amālī* of Shaykh al-Ṣaduq.

[Prophet] Jesus, and [Prophet] Jesus will direct them saying: 'You should seek the help of Muḥammad, the last prophet.' Thereupon, Muḥammad ﷺ will say: 'I will do it;' and will proceed until arriving at the door of the garden, he will knock on it. It will be asked, 'Who is it?' (while Allāh knows better!), and he will say: 'Muḥammad.' Then it will be said: 'Open for him.' When the door will be opened he will turn to his Lord, falling in prostration (*sajdah*). He will not raise his head until he is told: 'Speak up and ask, you will be given; and intercede, your intercession shall be granted.' He will raise his head and turn to his Lord and then will fall (again) into prostration. Then he will be promised as before; then he will raise his head. (Thereupon, he shall intercede) until he will intercede even for him who would have been burnt in the fire. Therefore, on the Day of Resurrection, no one among all of the nations will be more eminent than Muḥammad ﷺ and it is (the meaning of) the words of Allah: ﴾*Perhaps your Lord will raise you to a praised position*﴿.[146]

The author says: This meaning is narrated by both the Shīʿa and Sunni in great number, in explicit detail as well as in brief, through numerous chains of narrators and it proves that the "praised position" means the position of intercession. This tradition does not conflict with the intercession of other prophets, because probably their intercession will be an offshoot of our Prophet's, and it will begin with him.

ʿUbayd b. Zurārah said: "Abū ʿAbdillah ﷺ was asked whether a believer would have the right of intercession. He said: 'Yes.' Then someone said: 'Will a believer then need the intercession of Muḥammad ﷺ on that day?' He said: 'Yes. The believers will also come with wrongs and sins; and there will be no one but that they will need the intercession of Muḥammad on that day.'"

ʿUbayd said: "Someone asked him about the words of the Messenger of Allah: 'I am the Chief of the children of Adam, and I

[146] *Tafsīr* of al-ʿAyyāshī.

say this without boasting.' He said: 'Yes.' (Then) he said: 'He will hold the chain for the door of the garden and open it; then he will fall into prostration and Allāh will tell him 'Raise your head and intercede, your intercession will be granted, and ask, for you shall be given.' Thereupon he will raise his head and intercede – and his intercession will be accepted; and he will ask and it will be given."[147]

Muḥammad b. al-Qāsim narrates through his chains from Bishr b. Shurayh al-Baṣrī that he said: "I asked Muḥammad b. ʿAlī ﷺ: 'Which verse in the Book of Allāh is the one which inspires the most hope?' He said: 'What do your people say (about it)?' I said: 'They say, (it is the verse), ﴾*Say: 'O My servants! Who have acted extravagantly against their own souls, do not despair of the mercy of Allah.'*﴿" He said: 'But we, the people of the house, do not say so.' I said: 'Then what do you say about it?' He said: 'We say (it is the verse), ﴾*And soon will your Lord give you so that you shall be well pleased*﴿. (It means) the intercession; by Allāh the intercession; by Allāh the intercession.'"[148]

The author says: The words of Allāh ﷻ, ﴾*Perhaps your Lord will raise you to a praised position*﴿, refers to the Prophet's ﷺ glorious position of intercession, as the numerous traditions of the Prophet ﷺ himself prove.

Moreover the wording of the verse also supports it as it states: ﴾...will raise you...﴿ shows that it is a position which Prophet Muḥammad ﷺ will attain in the future – meaning on the Day of Judgement. The word "praised" is general and unconditional and implies that he shall be praised by all of humanity - past and present. The word *al-ḥamd* means to praise someone for a good done to you intentionally and so this definition shows that the Prophet ﷺ will do something by his own will and power which will benefit all of them and in return everyone will praise him.

---

[147] Ibid.

[148] *Tafsīr* of Furāt b. Ibrāhīm.

That is why the Imām said in the tradition of ʿUbayd b. Zurārah, "...and there will be no one but that he will need the intercession of Muḥammad on that day."

We shall explain this issue further...[149]

The context of this verse, so far as intercession is concerned, is like the following verses:

﴿إِنَّ رَبَّكُمُ اللَّهُ الَّذِي خَلَقَ السَّمَاوَاتِ وَالْأَرْضَ فِي سِتَّةِ أَيَّامٍ ثُمَّ اسْتَوَىٰ عَلَى الْعَرْشِ ۖ يُدَبِّرُ الْأَمْرَ ۖ مَا مِنْ شَفِيعٍ إِلَّا مِنْ بَعْدِ إِذْنِهِ ۚ ذَٰلِكُمُ اللَّهُ رَبُّكُمْ فَاعْبُدُوهُ ۚ أَفَلَا تَذَكَّرُونَ ﴿٥٤﴾﴾

Surely your Lord is Allāh Who created the heavens and the earth in six periods, and He is firmly established on the Throne (*ʿarsh*) regulating the affair; there is no intercessor except by His permission; this is Allāh, your Lord therefore worship Him; will you not then ponder?[150]

﴿اللَّهُ الَّذِي خَلَقَ السَّمَاوَاتِ وَالْأَرْضَ وَمَا بَيْنَهُمَا فِي سِتَّةِ أَيَّامٍ ثُمَّ اسْتَوَىٰ عَلَى الْعَرْشِ ۖ مَا لَكُمْ مِنْ دُونِهِ مِنْ وَلِيٍّ وَلَا شَفِيعٍ ۚ أَفَلَا تَتَذَكَّرُونَ ﴿٤﴾﴾

Allāh is He Who created the heavens and the earth and what is between them in six periods, and He is firmly established on the Throne (*ʿarsh*); you have not

[149] Please note that further discussions on this topic can be read in the *al-Mizān* available in print or online. In order to keep this book to it minimal length, we do not quote all of the relevant passages in regards to intercession here. (Tr.)

[150] *Quran*, Sūrah al-Aʿrāf (7), verse 54.

besides Him any guardian nor any intercessor; will you not then ponder?[151]

Under the topic of intercession, it was mentioned that it includes creative causation, as well as legislative intercession. Every cause intercedes with Allāh ﷻ for its effect, and becomes a medium for bestowing the grace of existence on it, by adhering to the Divine attributes of grace and mercy. The system of "cause and effect" is found in intercession as well as in prayer and invocation. Allāh ﷻ says:

﴿يَسْأَلُهُ مَن فِي السَّمَاوَاتِ وَالْأَرْضِ ۚ كُلَّ يَوْمٍ هُوَ فِي شَأْنٍ ﴿٢٩﴾﴾

All of those who are in the heavens and the earth do beseech Him; every day He is in a (new) splendor.[152]

﴿وَآتَاكُم مِّن كُلِّ مَا سَأَلْتُمُوهُ ﴿٣٤﴾﴾

And He gave you all that you ask Him for.[153]

﴿يَعْلَمُ مَا بَيْنَ أَيْدِيهِمْ وَمَا خَلْفَهُمْ وَلَا يُحِيطُونَ بِشَيْءٍ مِّنْ عِلْمِهِ إِلَّا بِمَا شَاءَ﴾

﴾He knows what is before them and what is behind them, and they cannot comprehend anything out of His knowledge except what He pleases.﴿

This sentence comes after the topic of intercession, and in its context it is like the below mentioned verses:

[151] *Quran*, Sūrah al-Sajdah (32), verse 4.

[152] *Quran*, Sūrah al-Raḥmān (55), verse 29.

[153] *Quran*, Sūrah Ibrāhīm (14), verse 34.

﴿بَلْ عِبَادٌ مُكْرَمُونَ ۝٢٦ لَا يَسْبِقُونَهُ بِالْقَوْلِ وَهُم بِأَمْرِهِ يَعْمَلُونَ ۝٢٧ يَعْلَمُ مَا بَيْنَ أَيْدِيهِمْ وَمَا خَلْفَهُمْ وَلَا يَشْفَعُونَ إِلَّا لِمَنِ ارْتَضَىٰ وَهُم مِّنْ خَشْيَتِهِ مُشْفِقُونَ ۝٢٨﴾

Nay! They are honoured servants; they do not precede Him in speech and (only) according to His commandment do they act. He knows what is before them and what is behind them, and they do not intercede except for him whom He approves, and for fear of Him they tremble.[154]

Apparently, the third person plural pronouns in the verse under discussion refer to the intercessors who are implied in the preceding sentence. To say that ﴾He knows what is before them and what is behind them is to say that He encompasses them completely. He has given them permission to intercede﴿ - but that does not mean they can do anything without His prior permission; nor can others take undue advantage of that intercession.

The following two verses throw light on the same subject:

﴿وَمَا نَتَنَزَّلُ إِلَّا بِأَمْرِ رَبِّكَ ۖ لَهُ مَا بَيْنَ أَيْدِينَا وَمَا خَلْفَنَا وَمَا بَيْنَ ذَٰلِكَ ۚ وَمَا كَانَ رَبُّكَ نَسِيًّا ۝٦٤﴾

And we do not come down but by the command of your Lord; His is whatever is before us and whatever is behind us and whatever is between these, and your Lord is not forgetful.[155]

﴿عَالِمُ الْغَيْبِ فَلَا يُظْهِرُ عَلَىٰ غَيْبِهِ أَحَدًا ۝٢٦ إِلَّا مَنِ

[154] *Quran*, Sūrah al-Anbiyā (21), verses 26-28.

[155] *Quran*, Sūrah Maryam (19), verse 64.

ارْتَضَىٰ مِنْ رَسُولٍ فَإِنَّهُ يَسْلُكُ مِنْ بَيْنِ يَدَيْهِ وَمِنْ خَلْفِهِ رَصَدًا ﴿٢٧﴾ لِيَعْلَمَ أَنْ قَدْ أَبْلَغُوا رِسَالَاتِ رَبِّهِمْ وَأَحَاطَ بِمَا لَدَيْهِمْ وَأَحْصَىٰ كُلَّ شَيْءٍ عَدَدًا ﴿٢٨﴾﴾

> The Knower of the Unseen! So He does not reveal His secret to any, except to him whom He chooses of an apostle; for surely He makes a guard to march before him and after him, so that He may know that they have indeed delivered the messages of their Lord, and He encompasses what is with them and He takes account of everything.[156]

These two verses show that Allāh ﷻ incorporates the angels and the prophets, such that they cannot do anything without His permission; they cannot descend unless commanded to do so, and they cannot deliver except what He wishes them to deliver. It may be inferred that ﴿what is before them﴾ refers to what is seen by them; and ﴿what is behind them﴾ refers to what is not seen by them and is far away from them. In other words, the two phrases refer to the seen and the unseen. In short, this sentence says that Allāh ﷻ knows very well what is present with them and what is yet to come to them. The talk is then completed by the words, ﴿and they cannot comprehend anything out of His knowledge except what He pleases﴾. He knows them and encompasses what they know, but they cannot comprehend His knowledge except that which He pleases.

We have proved that the intercessor in this verse means both creative causes and legislative interceders. The pronouns used in three places in this verse are those of the third person plural, and the masculine gender, which is normally used for rational beings.

Someone may think that these pronouns can not be used for

---

[156] *Quran*, Sūrah al-Jinn (72), verses 26-28.

creative causes (as these causes are not "people" or rational beings) – however this is not the case. Intercession, interceding, glorifying the Creator and offering thanks to Him are normally the acts of rational beings and for this reason the Quran mostly uses such pronouns even for inert or lifeless things, when it declares them to perform such deeds. Allāh ﷻ says:

﴿وَإِنْ مِنْ شَيْءٍ إِلَّا يُسَبِّحُ بِحَمْدِهِ وَلَٰكِنْ لَا تَفْقَهُونَ تَسْبِيحَهُمْ ﴿٤٤﴾﴾

And there is not a single thing but that it glorifies Him with His praise, but you do not understand their glorification.[157]

﴿ثُمَّ اسْتَوَىٰ إِلَى السَّمَاءِ وَهِيَ دُخَانٌ فَقَالَ لَهَا وَلِلْأَرْضِ ائْتِيَا طَوْعًا أَوْ كَرْهًا قَالَتَا أَتَيْنَا طَائِعِينَ ﴿١١﴾﴾

Then He directed Himself to the heaven and it was vapour, so He said to it and to the earth - come both willing or unwillingly. They both said: We come willingly.[158]

In both verses the pronouns of rational beings have been used for "everything" – even for the heaven and the earth, and there are many similar verses such as these [in the Quran].

The sentence (which comes from Sūrah al-Baqarah (2), verse 255) which reads: ﴾and they cannot comprehend anything out of His knowledge except what He pleases﴿ shows the total authority and perfect management of Allāh ﷻ and as we know, perfect management demands that the subordinate should not know what is going to happen next; otherwise he might try to wriggle out of

[157] *Quran*, Sūrah al-Isrā' (17), verse 44.
[158] *Quran*, Sūrah Fuṣṣilat (41), verse 11.

a forthcoming unpleasant situation and the plan of the manager might be put into disorder.

It is easy to see in the light of the above discussion, the meaning of this sentence: it wants to show us that the management of all of the affairs are in the hands of Allāh ﷻ alone, and it is done by His knowledge and His control of the intermediary causes which He Himself has created. As far as these intermediary causes are concerned (and especially those with life and intellect), their effectiveness and their knowledge is derived from His knowledge, will and pleasure - and ultimately is a reflection of Divine knowledge and power, and nothing can proceed against the will and decree of Allāh ﷻ in any way.

The sentence moreover shows that knowledge (not "the thing known") belongs to Allāh ﷻ alone. No creature has any knowledge except what Allāh ﷻ pleases to bestow upon them. It is the same as when Allāh ﷻ says that power, honour and life belong to Him only. For example:

﴿وَلَوْ يَرَى الَّذِينَ ظَلَمُوا إِذْ يَرَوْنَ الْعَذَابَ أَنَّ الْقُوَّةَ لِلَّهِ جَمِيعًا وَأَنَّ اللَّهَ شَدِيدُ الْعَذَابِ ١٦٥﴾

> And if only those who are unjust could see, when they see the chastisement, that the power is solely Allāh's, and that Allāh is severe in requiting (evil).[159]

﴿أَيَبْتَغُونَ عِنْدَهُمُ الْعِزَّةَ فَإِنَّ الْعِزَّةَ لِلَّهِ جَمِيعًا ١٣٩﴾

> Do they seek honour from them? For surely all honour is (only) with Allāh.[160]

﴿هُوَ الْحَيُّ لَا إِلَٰهَ إِلَّا هُوَ ٦٦﴾

---

[159] *Quran*, Sūrah al-Baqarah (2), verse 165.

[160] *Quran*, Sūrah al-Nisā' (4), verse 139.

He is the Living, there is no god but He.[161]

The following verses may also be brought as evidence that knowledge belongs only to Allāh ﷻ:

﴿إِنَّهُ هُوَ الْعَلِيمُ الْحَكِيمُ ۝٨٣﴾

Surely He is the Knowing, the Wise.[162]

﴿وَاللَّهُ يَعْلَمُ وَأَنْتُمْ لَا تَعْلَمُونَ ۝٢١٦﴾

And Allāh knows while you do not know.[163]

Indeed, there are many other verses in the Qurān with the same meaning.

﴿وَسِعَ كُرْسِيُّهُ السَّمٰوَاتِ وَالأَرْضَ﴾

﴿His Chair extends over the heavens and the earth.﴾

The word "*al-kursī*" means chair and metaphorically it is sometimes used for "kingdom"; thus, "the chair of a king" means the sphere of his authority and region under his rule and sovereignty.

The preceding sentences show that the whole universe belongs to Allāh ﷻ and is encompassed by His knowledge. This sentence also means that His "Chair" extends over the whole universe as well.

It is reasonable to believe that the extension of the "Chair" refers to all-encompassing Divine authority. The "Chair" thus would mean the Divine position by which the heavens and the earth are maintained, possessed, managed and known.

Ultimately, the "Chair" would be a degree of Divine knowledge, and an extension of the "Chair" would mean maintenance and

---

[161] *Quran*, Sūrah al-Moʾmin (40), verse 66.

[162] *Quran*, Sūrah Yūsuf (12), verse 83.

[163] *Quran*, Sūrah al-Baqarah (2), verse 216.

preservation of everything that is in the heavens and the earth, with all of its characteristics; and that is why the sentence is followed by the words, ﴾and the preservation of them both tires Him not.﴿

﴾وَلاَ يَئُودُهُ حِفْظُهُمَا وَهُوَ الْعَلِيُّ الْعَظِيمُ﴿

﴾And the preservation of them both tires Him not, and He is the Most High, the Great.﴿

The word "*al-awd*" means to tire, to weigh down, to depress. Although, the objective pronoun after the verb "tires" is generally taken to refer to "Allāh" (as is seen in the translation), equally correct is that it may be taken to refer to the "Chair," and then it would be translated as "tires **it** not." The declaration at the end of the verse that ﴾the preservation of the heavens and the earth tires Him not﴿ is befitting to its beginning: ﴾slumber does not overtake Him nor sleep.﴿

This verse in short, says that there is no god except Allāh ﷻ, for Him is Life and to Him belongs the attribute of *al-qayyumiyyah* (Standing, Self-Subsisting by Whom all subsist), in its unrestricted sense without any weakness or defect. That is why the verse ends off with the words, ﴾and He is the Most High, the Great.﴿

Therefore: He is the Most High: the hands of creatures cannot reach Him and in no way can they weaken His authority or enfeeble His being. He is the Greatest: the great number of creatures does not overwhelm Him, and the magnitude of the heavens and the earth do not tire Him in any way.

This sentence also shows that eminence and greatness in their true sense are for Allāh ﷻ only. This restriction is real, because eminence and greatness are parts of perfection, and every perfection in its real sense, is found only in Allāh ﷻ. Also, the restriction may have been used to strengthen the claim that the eminence and greatness are reserved for Allāh ﷻ only - the heavens and the earth are insignificant before His majesty and greatness.

Traditions on this Topic

The well-known scholar, al-ʿAyyāshī narrates in his *Tafsīr* from [Imām] al-Ṣādiq ؑ that, "Abū Dharr said: 'O Messenger of Allāh! What is the best of that which has been revealed to you?' He said: 'The Verse of the Chair. The seven heavens and the seven earths in the "Chair" are but like a ring thrown in a vast open space.' Then he said: 'Surely the excellence of the Throne (*al-ʿArsh*) over the Chair (*al-Kursī*) is like that of the open space over a ring.'"

The author says: The known scholar, al-Suyūtī has quoted the first part of this tradition in *al-Durr al-Manthūr* from Ibn Rahwayh (in his *al-Musnad*) who has narrated it from ʿAwf b. Mālik from Abū Dharr; and also he has quoted Aḥmad (b. Ḥanbal), Ibn Dāris and al-Ḥakim (who said that it is a correct tradition) and al-Bayhaqī (in his *Shuʿabu Imān*) who have narrated it from Abū Dharr.

Aḥmad (b. Ḥanbal) and al-Tabarānī have narrated from Abū Amāmah who said: "I asked: 'O Messenger of Allāh! Which (verse) revealed to you is the greatest of all?' He said: '﴾Allāh is He besides Whom there is no god, the Ever-Living, the Self-Subsisting by Whom all subsist﴿ - the Verse of the Chair.'" (*al-Durr al-Manthūr*)

The author says: al-Suyūtī has also narrated the same through al-Khatīb al-Baghdādī (in his *Tārikh*) from Anas from the Prophet ﷺ.

In the same book he quotes al-Darimī who has narrated from Ayfaʿ b. ʿAbdullāh al-Kalāʾī that he said: "A man asked: 'O Messenger of Allāh! Which verse in the Book of Allāh is the greatest?' He said: 'The Verse of the Chair: ﴾Allāh is He besides Whom there is no god, the Ever-Living, the Self-Subsisting by Whom all subsist...﴿'"

The author says: This verse was named the Verse of the Chair in the early period of Islam during the lifetime of the Prophet ﷺ, and was thus described by the Prophet ﷺ himself. The traditions quoted from him, the Imams of the Ahlul Bayt ﷷ and the companions prove that this verse was given a special name, and shows how much importance was attached to it, and it can only be because of the highest nobility of its meaning and the elegance and grace of its style.

Āyatul Kursī establishes the pristine belief about the oneness of God, ﴾Allāh is He besides Whom there is no god﴿, and then goes on to the attribute of "Standing" which is the foundation of all of His names which describe His attributes of action. Then it gives details about those attributes in even small and big things and affairs of the universe, showing that whatever emanates from His authority is part of that authority.

It is because of these fine points that the traditions have called it "the greatest verse of the Quran." It deals in detail with various aspects of monotheism and the Divine authority.

Of course, there are some other verses which deal with this subject as well, for example:

﴿ٱللَّهُ لَآ إِلَٰهَ إِلَّا هُوَ لَهُ ٱلْأَسْمَآءُ ٱلْحُسْنَىٰ ٨﴾

> Allāh is He besides Whom there is no god; His are the very best names.[164]

However it lacks the details which have been given in the Verse of the Chair. It is for this reason that some traditions have said that this verse is the chief of all of the other verses in the Quran.

For the proof of this statement, one can refer to the tradition narrated in *al-Durr al-Manthūr* narrated by Abū Hurayrah from the Prophet ﷺ. Some other traditions say: "Everything has a summit, and the summit of the Quran is the Verse of the Chair" – this has been narrated in the *Tafsīr* of al-ʿAyyāshī from ʿAbdullāh b. Sinān

---

[164] *Quran*, Sūrah Ṭāḥā (20), verse 8.

from [Imām] al-Ṣādiq ﷺ.

Shaykh al-Ṭūsī has narrated in his book, *al-Amālī*, through the chain of narrators from Abū Amāmah al-Bahilī that he heard ʿAlī b. Abī Ṭālib ﷺ say: "I do not think that a man who enters into Islam upon attaining wisdom, or one who was born into Islam (i.e., into a Muslim family) should pass a night's darkness..." At this juncture Abū Amāmah interrupted by asking, "and what is the meaning of a night's darkness?" ʿAlī ﷺ said: "the whole night" - "until he recites this verse: ﴾Allāh is He besides Whom there is no god...﴿ and he recited the complete verse up to the end: ﴾and the preservation of them both tires Him not; and He is the Most High, the Great﴿." Then he said: "If you only knew what it is (or as in another version it says, "what is in it") you would not leave it under any condition. Surely, the Messenger of Allāh ﷺ said, 'I have been given the 'Verse of the Chair' from the treasure (that is) below the Throne; and no prophet before me was given it." Then ʿAlī ﷺ continued: "I have not spent a single night, since I heard it from the Messenger of Allāh, without reciting it."

The author says: This has been narrated in *al-Durr al-Manthūr* quoting ʿUbayd, Ibn Abī Shaybah, al-Dārimī, Muḥammad b. Naṣr, Ibnū Ḍarīs and al-Daylamī, all from [Imām] ʿAlī ﷺ. In addition, there are a multitude of traditions, from both Sunni and Shīʿa sources about the excellence of this verse.

The tradition of the Prophet ﷺ quoted in this tradition ("I have been given the Verse of the Chair from below the Throne") has been narrated in *al-Durr al-Manthūr* on the authority of al-Bukhārī (in his *Tarīkh*) and Ibnū Ḍarīs from the Prophet ﷺ. It may be inferred from it that The Chair is below The Throne and is encompassed by it, but we will speak about this later.

Zurārah said: "I asked Abū ʿAbdillāh ﷺ about the words of Allāh: ﴾His Chair extends over the heavens and the earth﴿ - whether the heavens and the earth encompass the Chair or the Chair extends over the heavens and the earth? He said: 'Verily, everything is in the Chair.'" (*al-Kāfī*)

The author says: The same point has been emphasized in many traditions in response to similar questions, however this question looks strange - because no one has ever recited the verse in a way that could justify such confusion. Apparently, the questions were based not on the recital of the Quran, but on the common understanding that the Chair was a particular body kept over the heavens or over the seventh heaven (i.e. above the material world), and from there the affairs of the material world were managed.

That being the picture of the Chair in their minds, it was reasonable to suppose that the heavens and the earth encompassed the Chair because it was placed over the heavens the way a wooden or iron chair is placed over a floor, and with this background it would seem more appropriate to say that the heavens and the earth encompassed the Chair and that gave rise to the question as to why Allāh ﷻ instead said: "His Chair extends over the heavens and the earth"?

A question of this same type was asked about the Throne and the reply was given that the extension (or encompassing) was not the way that a material thing encompasses another material thing.

Hafs b. al-Ghiyāth said: "I asked Abū ʿAbdillāh ؑ about what the words of Allāh mean: ﴾His Chair extends over the heavens and the earth﴿? He replied: '[It means] His knowledge.'"[165]

There is another tradition in the same book from the same Imām about this verse which says: "The heavens and the earth and whatever is between them is in the Chair - and the Throne is that knowledge which no one can measure."

The author says: These two traditions show that the Chair is one of the levels of the knowledge of Allāh ﷻ, and many other traditions also support this interpretation.

As will be explained later, there exists a level of knowledge

---

[165] *Maʿānī al-Akhbār.*

which is not limited or measured - in other words there is a world on a higher plane than ours whose constituents are not bound by material dimensions. They exist and at the same time are known to Allāh ﷻ, and that knowledge also is unlimited. God Willing, we shall describe it in detail when commenting on the verse of the Quran:

﴿وَمَا يَعْزُبُ عَن رَّبِّكَ مِن مِّثْقَالِ ذَرَّةٍ فِي ٱلْأَرْضِ وَلَا فِي ٱلسَّمَآءِ وَلَآ أَصْغَرَ مِن ذَٰلِكَ وَلَآ أَكْبَرَ إِلَّا فِي كِتَابٍ مُّبِينٍ ﴿٦١﴾﴾

> And there does not lie concealed from your Lord the weight of an atom in the earth or in the heaven, nor anything less than that nor greater, but it is in a clear book.[166]

This boundless knowledge has been referred to in the tradition of the Imām ؑ in these words, "And the Throne is that knowledge which no one can measure."

The significance of the tradition is not to show the great number of the things known, because number is not unlimited and anything which is created is finite. What the tradition wants to say is that the limitations and restrictions of this material world are not found in that world. Existence on that level, is perfect and the conditions, dimensions and distinctions of this material world are not found there. It is as Allāh ﷻ says:

﴿وَإِن مِّن شَيْءٍ إِلَّا عِندَنَا خَزَآئِنُهُۥ وَمَا نُنَزِّلُهُۥٓ إِلَّا بِقَدَرٍ مَّعْلُومٍ ﴿٢١﴾﴾

> And there is not a thing but with Us are the treasures of it, and We do not send it down but in

[166] *Quran*, Sūrah Hūd (10), verse 61.

a known measure.[167]

When those existing things are known by unlimited knowledge, that is when they exist without any limitations attached to them, then that knowledge is called the Throne; and when they exist in the world of limitations and are known with those limitations, then that knowledge is called the Chair.

At this stage we may probably say that the words: ﴾He knows what is before them and what is behind them﴿ alludes to this plane of knowledge. What is before them (i.e. the future) and what is behind them (i.e. the past) is not what is with them (i.e. the present). It refers to a plane where past, present, and future lose their limitations of time and are all equally present.

Hannān said: "I asked Abū ʿAbdillāh ﷺ about the Throne and the Chair and he replied: 'Verily, the Throne has many diverse attributes. Allāh in the Quran uses various adjectives to describe its different aspects. He says:

﴿وَهُوَ رَبُّ الْعَرْشِ الْعَظِيمِ ١٢٩﴾

And He is the Lord of the great Throne.[168]

It means - Lord of the great kingdom or authority, and He says:

﴿الرَّحْمَٰنُ عَلَى الْعَرْشِ اسْتَوَىٰ ٥﴾

The Beneficent (God) on the firm Throne.[169]

It means that He is firm in His kingdom and it is the knowledge of the "how" of things.

The Throne, although together with it is also distinct from the Chair, because they are two of the greatest doors of the unseen and they both are unseen - they are together in the unseen, because

---

[167] *Quran*, Sūrah al-Ḥijr (15), verse 21.

[168] *Quran*, Sūrah al-Tawbah (9), verse 129.

[169] *Quran*, Sūrah Tāhā (20), verse 5.

the Chair is the manifest door of the unseen, from which appears creation and from which all of the things come; and the Throne is the concealed door of the unseen in which is found the knowledge of the states, conditions and existence; of measure and limit; of will and intention; as well as the knowledge of words, actions and omissions; and the knowledge of the beginning and the return. Thus, these two are two gates of knowledge joined together, because the dominion of the Throne is other than the dominion of the Chair, and the Throne's knowledge is more hidden than the knowledge of the Chair.

That is why Allāh ﷻ said, ﴾the Lord of the great Throne﴿ that is, its attribute is greater than that of the Chair, but both are joined in it.

It has been mentioned in a tradition from Hannān that: "I said: 'May I be your ransom, then why did it become associated with the Chair in excellence?' He (the Imām ؑ) said: 'It was associated with it because the knowledge of the state and condition is found in it; and in it are found the manifest doors of *al-bada* (the decree hidden from others); as well as its reality, and the dimensions of its joining and separating. Therefore, they are two neighbours, one of which contains the other in itself. As well, by similitude are termed those who know, so they may offer proof for the truth of their claims. He chooses especially whom He pleases for His mercy, and He is the Mighty, the Powerful.'"[170]

The author says: The words of the tradition, "The Chair is the manifest door of the unseen," may be understood in the light of the short explanation given earlier. The level of the knowledge of measured things is nearer to our material world, than infinite knowledge which has no limits. A further explanation will be given under the exegesis of the follow verse:

[170] *Al-Tawḥīd.*

﴿إِنَّ رَبَّكُمُ اللهُ الَّذِى خَلَقَ السَّمَاوَاتِ وَالْأَرْضَ فِي سِتَّةِ أَيَّامٍ ثُمَّ اسْتَوَىٰ عَلَى الْعَرْشِ﴾

Surely your Lord is Allāh Who created the heavens and the earth in six periods of time, and He is firm on the Throne.[171]

"And by similitude are turned those who know" is an indication that the words: Throne, Chair and other similar expressions are similitudes which have been given to the people for their understanding, and only those who have knowledge understand this.

Imām al-Ṣādiq said among other things, in a tradition: "Everything which Allāh has created is in the receptacle of the Chair except His Throne, because that is far too great for the Chair to encompass."[172]

The author says: Its meaning may be understood from the earlier discourse and it is in conformity with other traditions. Contrary to it, there is a tradition which says that the Throne is that knowledge which Allāh gave to His prophets and apostles; and the Chair is that knowledge which no one was made aware of, and this has been narrated by [Shaykh] al-Ṣadūq through [the companion] Mufaḍḍal from Imām al-Ṣādiq. But in view of all of the other traditions, it can only be surmised that the narrator was confused and changed the names of the Throne and the Chair from their proper places. If this is not accepted then the tradition will have to be discarded, like the one that is attributed to Zaynab al-ʿAttārah.

Al-ʿAyyāshī narrates in his *Tafsīr* from Imām ʿAlī that the latter said: "Verily the heavens and the earth and whatever is between them is created in the hollow of the Chair; and it has four

[171] *Quran*, Sūrah al-Aʿrāf (7), verse 54.

[172] *Al-Iḥtijāj.*

angels who bear it by the order of Allāh."

The author says: Shaykh al-Ṣadūq has narrated this tradition from Imām ʿAlī through Asbāgh b. Nubātah and it is the only tradition narrated from the Ahlul Bayt which says that there are angels who bear the Chair, however other traditions mention such bearers only for the Throne; and it is in conformity with the Book of Allāh which says:

﴿الَّذِينَ يَحْمِلُونَ الْعَرْشَ وَمَنْ حَوْلَهُ يُسَبِّحُونَ بِحَمْدِ رَبِّهِمْ ﴿٧﴾﴾

> Those who bear the Throne and those around it celebrate the praise of their Lord...[173]

﴿وَيَحْمِلُ عَرْشَ رَبِّكَ فَوْقَهُمْ يَوْمَئِذٍ ثَمَانِيَةٌ ﴿١٧﴾﴾

> And the Throne of your Lord will be borne on that day by eight [angels].[174]

It may be said that the Chair is somewhat joined with the Throne, like a manifest side of a thing is joined with its hidden side, and in this way the bearers of one may be called the bearers of the other.

Al-ʿAyyāshī narrates in his *Tafsīr* from Muʿāwiyah b. ʿAmmār that he asked Imām al-Ṣādiq about (the verse), ﴾Who is it that can intercede with Him except by His permission?﴿, and he replied: "We are those intercessors."

The author says: It has also been narrated by al-Barqī in *al-Maḥāsin*, that you know that the intercession in this verse is common to creative and legislative interceding and therefore includes the intercession of the Prophet and the Imāms. This tradition therefore, gives an example of the intercessors.

---

[173] *Quran*, Sūrah al-Mo'min (40), verse 7.
[174] *Quran*, Sūrah al-Ḥāqqah (69), verse 17.

﴿لاَ إِكْرَاهَ فِي الدِّينِ قَدْ تَبَيَّنَ الرُّشْدُ مِنَ الغَيِّ﴾

﴾There is no compulsion in the religion; truly the right way has become clearly distinct from error.﴿

The word "*al-ikrāh*" means to compel someone to a work without one's willingness; the word "*al-rushd*" is to get to the reality of an affair and to reach the right path; and the word "*al-ghayy*" is it's opposite. These two words are more general than "*al-hudā*" (to find the path which leads to a destination) and "*al-ḍalāl*" (not to find such a path) respectively.

Obviously, when the word "*al-rushd*" is used for reaching the right path, it is done in the way of applying a general word for a particular example: a walker reaches reality when one travels on the right path. Thus the words "*al-rushd*" and "*al-hudā*" are for two different meanings, but one is used for the other because of special associations. Allāh ﷻ says:

﴿فَإِنْ آنَسْتُمْ مِنْهُمْ رُشْدًا﴿٦﴾﴾

Then if you find in them maturity of intellect...[175]

﴿وَلَقَدْ آتَيْنَا إِبْرَاهِيمَ رُشْدَهُ مِنْ قَبْلُ﴿٥١﴾﴾

And certainly We gave to Ibrāhīm his rectitude (*rushdahu*) from before.[176]

The same applies to "*al-ghayy*" and "*al-ḍalāl*".

That is why we mentioned before that "*al-ḍalāl*" is to deviate from the right path but with knowledge and remembrance of the goal and destination; while "*al-ghayy*" is to deviate from the right path without even remembering the goal or destination - without knowing what one wants or where one wants to go.

The portion of the verse which reads: ﴾There is no compulsion

[175] *Quran*, Sūrah al-Nisā' (4), verse 6.

[176] *Quran*, Sūrah al-Anbiyā' (21), verse 51.

in the religion﴿ negates and disapproves compulsion or coercion in religion.

Religion is a set of truths which are believed in, and some of them are then acted upon. In short, religion is belief and faith, it is a matter of conscience, and such a thing cannot be created by coercion and compulsion. One may force someone to do a certain physical action against one's will, but one cannot be forced to believe against one's will. Belief follows reason and understanding, and nothing but reason and understanding can create it.

This part may be treated as a bit of information or a piece of legislation as well. If it is information of a creative decree, then it will give rise to a legislative order that compulsion should not be used in matters of belief and faith.

If it is an order in the form of information, then the meaning is clear.

Apparently, this alternative is more correct, because the next sentence:

﴿قَدْ تَبَيَّنَ الرُّشْدُ مِنَ الغَيِّ﴾

﴾Truly the right way has become clearly distinct from error﴿

gives the reason for this legislation, and this prohibition of compulsion in religion is based on a factor of creation: the fact that compulsion can influence physical actions, but not matters that are connected with the heart and the conscience.

The next portion of the verse reads:

﴿قَدْ تَبَيَّنَ الرُّشْدُ مِنَ الغَيِّ﴾

﴾Truly the right way has become clearly distinct from error﴿.

As mentioned above, it gives the reason for the prohibition of compulsion.

A wise person resorts to compulsion only when the truth of the order cannot be explained, either because the person who is being coerced, has no capacity to understand it, or for some other reasons. However, there is no need for compulsion in an important matter whose advantages and disadvantages are clearly defined, and the reward and punishment of accepting or rejecting are all well explained. A person, in such a clear matter, should be free to choose one's course of action oneself - whether one takes it or rejects it, whether one wants the rewards of obedience or is prepared to take upon the punishment.

The realities of religion have been explained, and its path is well laid out; the Divine revelation and prophetic explanations have illuminated this highway to the utmost degree. It has been made clear that the religion of Islam is the truth and that the only right thing is to accept it and follow it, and if one deviates from this road, then one will fall into perdition. Why should anyone, then after all of these clarifications, have to compel others to follow the religion?

This is one of the verses which shows that Islam is not based on the sword and killing, and that it does not allow Muslims to compel or coerce other people to accept Islam. It is contrary to the view held by many Muslims and non-Muslims alike that Islam is the religion of the sword, in fact they bring as their evidence, the legislation of *jihād* which is one of the pillars of Islam.

We have already clarified, while writing the commentary on the verses of fighting, that fighting ordained by Islam is not for the purpose of material advancement, nor is it for spreading the religion by force. It was ordained only for reviving the truth and defending the most precious treasure of nature which is the faith of monotheism.

When monotheism is accepted by the people - even if they remain Jews or Christians - Islam does not fight with them. Therefore, the objection arises from clouded thinking.

The verse: ﴾There is no compulsion in the religion﴿, is not abrogated by the verse of the sword, although some writers think so. The order is followed by its reason: ﴾Truly the right way has become clearly distinct from error﴿. Such an order cannot be cancelled unless and until its reason is also abrogated. So long as the reason is valid, the rule must remain valid. There is no need to emphasize that the verse of the sword cannot negate the clear distinction of the right way from error. For example, the verses:

﴿وَاقْتُلُوهُمْ حَيْثُ وَجَدْتُمُوهُمْ ﴿٨٩﴾﴾

And kill them wherever you find them...[177]

and:

﴿وَقَاتِلُوا فِي سَبِيلِ اللَّهِ ﴿١٩٠﴾﴾

And fight in the way of Allāh...[178]

have no effect whatsoever on the clear distinction of the truth from falsehood; and therefore they cannot abrogate an order based on that distinction.

In other words, this order is based on the fact that the right way is made clearly distinct from error; and this distinction is as valid after the revelation of the verses of fighting as it was before that. Since the cause has not changed, the effect, that is the said order, cannot be changed or cancelled either.

﴿فَمَنْ يَكْفُرْ بِالطَّاغُوتِ وَيُؤْمِنْ بِاللَّهِ فَقَدِ اسْتَمْسَكَ بِالْعُرْوَةِ الْوُثْقَى لاَ انْفِصَامَ لَهَا﴾

﴾Therefore, whoever disbelieves in the rebels (false

[177] *Quran*, Sūrah al-Nisā' (4), verse 89.

[178] *Quran*, Sūrah al-Baqarah (2), verse 190.

> deities) and believes in Allāh, he indeed has laid hold on the strongest handle, for which there is no break off❯.

The word "*al-tāghūt*" means rebellion and transgression. This paradigm conveys an intensification on the meaning of the root, just like *al-malakūt* (great kingdom) and *al-jabarīt* (great power), *al-tāghūt* is used for the agents and causes of rebellion and transgression like false deities and idols, satans, jinn and wrong leaders among the human beings; and in short, everyone who is followed without the permission of Allāh ﷻ. This word is common for masculine and feminine genders, as well as for singular, dual and plural numbers.

In this sentence, disbelief in the rebels has been mentioned before the belief in Allāh ﷻ. This sequence keeps in view the next sentence ❮he indeed has laid hold on the strongest handle❯.

When a person wants to hold on to a thing, then one must first discard all of the other things. In other words, one has to first leave all of the unwanted things, then comes the stage of holding fast to the desired thing. Therefore, the verse first mentions the rejection (of the rebels), and then the belief (in Allāh ﷻ) follows.

The word "*al-istimsāk*" means to hold fast; and the word "*al-'urwāh*" notes that part of a thing which is made to hold it by, like the handle of a bucket or a pot. Also this word is used for evergreen plants and trees. Its root meaning is attachment; and it is said that*'arahu* and *i'tarahu* both mean 'something which was attached to him.'

The sentence, ❮he indeed has laid hold on the strongest handle❯, is based on an allegory and conveys the idea that belief in Allāh ﷻ has the same relation with eternal bliss - that a pot's handle has with that pot and its contents. You cannot be sure of your hold unless you keep the handle in your grip; likewise, one cannot be hopeful about eternal and real bliss unless one believes in Allāh ﷻ

and rejects all of the false deities.

The word "*al-infisām*" is to be cut off, to be broken. The phrase, ﴾for which there is no break off﴿ describes the condition or state of the handle, and emphasizes the phrase, the strongest handle.

﴿وَاللَّهُ سَمِيعٌ عَلِيمٌ﴾

﴾And Allāh is All-Hearing, All-Knowing.﴿

The next sentence, ﴾and Allāh is All-Hearing, All-Knowing﴿, points to the fact that belief and disbelief are matters connected with the heart and the tongue, and Allāh is aware of them all.

﴿اللَّهُ وَلِيُّ الَّذِينَ آمَنُوا يُخْرِجُهُم مِّنَ الظُّلُمَاتِ إِلَى النُّورِ وَالَّذِينَ كَفَرُوا أَوْلِيَاؤُهُمُ الطَّاغُوتُ يُخْرِجُونَهُم مِّنَ النُّورِ إِلَى الظُّلُمَاتِ أُولَٰئِكَ أَصْحَابُ النَّارِ هُمْ فِيهَا خَالِدُونَ ﴿٢٥٧﴾﴾

﴾Allāh is the Master of the faithful: He brings them out of the darknesses into the light; and as for the faithless, their patrons are the rebels, who drive them out of the light into the darknesses. They shall be the inmates of the Fire, and they shall remain in it [forever]﴿.

Some explanation had been given, in the previous verse, about ﴾bringing out of the darkness into the light﴿. It was described there that this bringing out and other such phrases express real things, and that they are not used in any allegorical sense.

There are two other interpretations given by other commentators of the Quran, which we will quote here before commenting upon them.

First Interpretation: This bringing out of the darkness into the light and other such phrases are allegorical expressions. They are used for a person's actions and physical stillness and movements, and for the good or evil results of those actions. Accordingly, "light" is used for correct belief which removes the darkness of ignorance, the confusion of doubt and the perplexity of the heart; also it is a metaphor for good deeds because its connection with the right path is clear and its effect on bliss are self-evident - and "light" has all of these attributes and qualities.

On the other hand, "darkness" is metaphorically used for wrong belief, confusion and doubt as well as for evil deeds. According to this interpretation, the bringing out from darkness into the light (attributed to Allāh ﷻ), and taking out of the light into the darkness (attributed to the rebels and false deities) refers only to true and wrong beliefs, and good and evil deeds respectively - there is nothing other than those beliefs and deeds. Allāh ﷻ or the false deities do not do any action (like bringing out) in this respect, nor is there any effect of such action (like light and darkness).

Second Interpretation: Surely Allāh ﷻ does the actions like bringing the people out of the darkness into the light, giving life, bestowing abundance and mercy and similar things. Further to this, surely there are effects of such actions, like light and darkness, the soul and mercy, and the coming down of the angels. But our intellect cannot comprehend these and our senses cannot perceive them. Even then, we believe as we have been told by Allāh ﷻ - and Allāh ﷻ speaks the truth - that these things do exist and they are the actions of Allāh ﷻ, although we do not understand them.

This interpretation like the first one, treats words like: light, darkness, taking out, etc... as metaphors. The only difference between the two is that the first one says that the light and the darkness are our correct and wrong deeds and beliefs; and this one says that the light and the darkness are things other than our beliefs and deeds, but we have no way of knowing, comprehending and understanding them; however both of these interpretations are far from the truth - one has failed to reach the target, and the other has overshot it.

The fact is that these things, which Allāh ﷻ has said He creates and does when we obey Him or disobey Him, are real things - there is no allegory in such expressions, and these Divine actions are related to our beliefs and deeds, and are inseparable from them and this is something which we have already explained.

Of course, it is admitted that the sentences, ﴾He brings them out of the darknesses into the light﴿, and ﴾(they) take them out of the light into the darknesses﴿, are metaphors and mean "He guides them" and "others misguide them" respectively.

In other words, there are two separate matters to decide:

1) Whether the light, darkness and other such expressions refer to some real things in this life or are they merely metaphors?

2) If they refer to some real things, then is the use for example, of the word light for guidance real or metaphorical?

According to what we have already explained, such expressions refer to real things in this life; and using the light as an example for guidance is metaphorical.

In any case, the two sentences mentioned above, are metaphors to denote guidance and misguidance.

If we were to interpret them in their literal sense, then it would mean that the believer and the disbeliever both have light and darkness together. ﴾Allāh brings the believers out of the darknesses into the light﴿, if literally interpreted, would mean that the believer was first in the darkness! Conversely, the second sentence would mean that the disbeliever was first in the light!

How can this meaning be correct about the overwhelming majority of believers and disbelievers who are born in believing or disbelieving families and that they remain in light or in darkness (as the case may be) from their birth? Such literal interpretation would mean that a child remained in light and darkness at one and the same time; and when on attaining maturity, a person accepts the true faith by one's own choice, then that person is removed out of the darkness into the light; and if a person disbelieves, then one is taken out of the light into the darkness. The absurdity of such an interpretation is quite obvious.

Of course, it may be said that a human being in one's creation, has the light of natural faith, but that it is a general light which needs details and particularization. In this way, one has the natural light, but at the same time, is in darkness so far as detailed knowledge and good deeds are concerned. Looking from these different angles, it is possible for the light and the darkness to be present in one place at the same time.

When a believer acquires correct faith, then one goes out from that darkness into the light of knowledge and good deeds. Whereas a disbeliever, by one's disbelief goes out from the natural light into the darkness of disbelief and evil deeds.

Allāh ﷻ, in both sentences has used the "light" (in the singular) and the "darkness" (in the plural) and this is to indicate that the truth is only one - there is no difference in it; and that falsehood is multifaceted, diverse and variable and there is no unity in it. Allāh ﷻ says in another place:

﴿وَأَنَّ هَـٰذَا صِرَاطِى مُسْتَقِيمًا فَاتَّبِعُوهُ ۖ وَلَا تَتَّبِعُوا السُّبُلَ فَتَفَرَّقَ بِكُمْ عَن سَبِيلِهِ ۝﴾

And (know) that this is My path, the straight one, therefore follow it; and follow not (any other) ways, for they will scatter you away from His path.[179]

---

[179] *Quran*, Sūrah al-Anʿām (6), verse 53.

Traditions on this Topic

Abū Dāwūd, al-Nisāʾi, Ibn al-Mundhīr, Ibn Abī Hātim, al-Naḥḥās (in his book, *Al-Nāsikh wa al-Mansūkh*), Ibn Mandih (in his work *Al-Gharāʾib*), Ibn Ḥibbān, Ibn Marduwayh, al-Bayhaqī (in his work *Al-Sunan*), al-Ḍiyāʾ (in his book *Al-Mukhtarah*) have narrated from Ibn ʿAbbās that he said: "(It was customary for) a woman of the Anṣār that if her child died in infancy, she would make a vow that if her next child lived, she would turn him into a Jew. Thus, when the tribe of Nadīr was banished (from Medina), there were many children of the Anṣār among them. They said that they would not leave their sons (to migrate). Then Allāh ﷻ sent down the verse: ﴾There is no compulsion in the religion.﴿"[180]

The author says: The same thing has been narrated, by other chains, from Saʿīd b. Jubayr and al-Shaʿbī.

ʿAbd b. Ḥamīd, Ibn Jarīr and Ibn al-Mundhīr have narrated from Mujāhid that he said: "(The tribe of) Nadīr had suckled some people from the tribe of Aws. When the Prophet ordered their banishment, their foster sons from the Aws said: 'We will go with them and enter into their religion.' But their families prevented them and compelled them to (accept) Islam. Then came down the verse about them: ﴾There is no compulsion in the religion﴿."[181]

The author says: This has also been narrated from other sources and it is not in conflict with the preceding tradition (about the vow of the women of Anṣār), as both may be correct.

Ibn Isḥāq and Ibn Jarīr have narrated from Ibn ʿAbbās that he said about the words of Allāh ﷻ: ﴾There is no compulsion in the religion﴿ that it was revealed about a man from the Anṣār (from the clan of Banū Salīm b. ʿAwf), named al-Ḥusayn who had two Christian sons, and he himself was a Muslim. He said to the

[180] *Al-Durr al-Manthūr.*

[181] Ibid.

Prophet ﷺ: "Should I not compel them because they have refused, and (remain) on Christianity." Thereupon, Allāh ﷻ sent down this (verse) about them.[182]

Imām al-Ṣādiq ؑ said: "The light is the progeny of Muḥammad and the darknesses are their enemies."[183]

The author says: This tradition gives examples of the light and the darknesses, and explains its inner meaning and interpretation.

---

[182] Ibid.

[183] *Al-Kāfī.*

Section 4

Is Āyatul Kursī One Verse or Three Verses?

At this point, a question may come up: Is Āyatul Kursī limited to only one verse (chapter 2, verse 255) and thus concludes with ﴾And He is the All-Exalted, the All-Supreme﴿; or does it also include the two verses which follow (chapter 2, verses 256 and 257), ending with ﴾In it they will abide for eternity﴿?

The answer is that the widely accepted belief is that Āyatul Kursī is not more than one verse (chapter 2, verse 255) and therefore it concludes with ﴾And He is the All-Exalted, the All-Supreme﴿.

What are some of the reasons for making this claim? We enumerate the below proofs:

First: The first proof is that the phrase itself, **Āyatul** Kursī, shows that it is only one verse (as the word ***āyat*** - أيـة is singular), and if it included verses 256 and 257 as well, then the term which would have been used is **Verses** of the Throne (**Āyāt** al-Kursī) as this would denote multiple verses – not just one.

Second: The only verse which makes use of the word 'the Throne' is verse 255 in which we read ﴾His **seat** (*kursī*) embraces the heavens and the earth﴿ and it is because of this that the verse is known as Āyatul Kursī.

Third: In numerous traditions in which the merits of Āyatul Kursī has been mentioned, it states that this passage concludes with ❰And He is the All-Exalted, the All-Supreme❱. For example, in a tradition narrated in *Layālī al-Akhbār*, the Prophet ﷺ has been quoted as saying:

مَنْ قَرَءَ أَرْبَعَ آيَاتٍ مِنَ الْبَقَرَةِ وَ آيَةَ الْكُرْسِيِّ وَ أَيَتَيْنِ بَعْدَهَا وَ ثَلاَثَةَ آيَاتٍ مِنْ آخِرِهَا لَمْ يَرَ فِي نَفْسِهِ وَ مَالِهِ شَيْئاً يَكْرَهُهُ وَ لاَ يُقَرِّبُهُ شَيْطَانَ وَ لاَ يَنْسىٰ الْقُرآنَ.

A person who recites four verses from [the beginning of Sūrah] al-Baqarah, and Āyatul Kursī and the two verses which follow it [i.e. 256 and 257] and the three verses at the end of the chapter [of Sūrah al-Baqarah], will never experience anything which one will dislike in terms of one's life or wealth, Satan will never approach him and he will never forget the Quran.[184]

In this tradition we see that 'the two verses which follow it (i.e. 256 and 257)' have been clearly mentioned to be recited after Āyatul Kursī and this shows that these two verses are not part of Āyatul Kursī.

In addition, there is a tradition narrated from ʿAbdullāh b. Masʿūd in which he quotes the Noble Messenger ﷺ as saying:

مَنْ قَرَءَ عَشْرَ آيَاتٍ مِنْ سُورَةُ الْبَقَرَةِ فِي لَيْلَةٍ فِي بَيْتٍ لَمْ يَدْخُلِ ذٰالِكَ الْبَيْتَ شَيْطَانَ حَتّٰى يَصْبَحَ أَرْبَعُ آيَاتٍ مِنْ أَوَّلِهَا وَ آيَةِ الْكُرْسِيِّ وَ أَيَتَينِ بَعْدَهَا وَ خَوَاتِيمِهَا.

[184] This tradition is also found in *al-Kāfī*, vol. 2, p. 621 in the section of the Merits of the Quran. (Tr.)

> A person who recites ten verses from Sūrah al-Baqarah in his house every night will not have Satan enter the house until the day break, and (these ten verses are) the first four verses of it [Sūrah al-Baqarah], Āyatul Kursī [verse 255] and the two verses which follow it [verses 256 and 257] and the last three verses which close off this chapter.

All of these traditions clearly show us that Āyatul Kursī is only one verse (chapter 2, verse 255) and concludes with ❮And He is the All-Exalted, the All-Supreme❯.

Fourth: The unanimous verdict of the commentators of the Quran from among the Shīʿa and Sunnī, when recounting the merits and specialties of Āyatul Kursī have only mentioned one verse (chapter 2, verse 255) and they do not speak about the two verses which follow as being a part of Āyatul Kursī.

Fifth: The clear opinions from a majority of the scholars in regards to this issue clearly back up this point, such as the writings in *Majmaʿ al-Baḥrain* which read:

آيَةُ الْكُرسِيِّ مَعْرُوفَةٌ وَ هِيَ إِلىٰ قَوْلِهِ: وَ هُوَ الْعَلِيُّ الْعَظِيمُ

> It is well known that Āyatul Kursī is until His words, ❮And He is the All-Exalted, the All-Supreme❯.

As for those who state that it extends up to ❮And they shall remain in it [forever]❯, they try to prove their argument through the use of two points:

1. Their statement that it is well-known among the Muslims that Āyatul Kursī extends from verse 255 through to 257 of chapter 2 of the Quran.
2. In a good number of traditions, it has been mentioned that Āyatul Kursī should be recited until you reach the part ❮And they shall remain in it [forever]❯ – meaning the end

of verse 257.

However, none of these arguments are strong enough, as the evidences for the first opinion are much stronger and thus more widely accepted.

Section 5

Lessons to Learn from Āyatul Kursī

There are numerous subtle points which we can derive from Āyatul Kursī[185] - some of which we will mention here.

Verse 255 of Sūrah al-Baqarah reads:

﴿ٱللَّهُ لَآ إِلَٰهَ إِلَّا هُوَ ٱلۡحَيُّ ٱلۡقَيُّومُۚ لَا تَأۡخُذُهُۥ سِنَةٞ وَلَا
نَوۡمٞۚ لَّهُۥ مَا فِي ٱلسَّمَٰوَٰتِ وَمَا فِي ٱلۡأَرۡضِۗ مَن ذَا ٱلَّذِي
يَشۡفَعُ عِندَهُۥٓ إِلَّا بِإِذۡنِهِۦۚ يَعۡلَمُ مَا بَيۡنَ أَيۡدِيهِمۡ وَمَا
خَلۡفَهُمۡۖ وَلَا يُحِيطُونَ بِشَيۡءٖ مِّنۡ عِلۡمِهِۦٓ إِلَّا بِمَا شَآءَۚ
وَسِعَ كُرۡسِيُّهُ ٱلسَّمَٰوَٰتِ وَٱلۡأَرۡضَۖ وَلَا يَـُٔودُهُۥ حِفۡظُهُمَاۚ
وَهُوَ ٱلۡعَلِيُّ ٱلۡعَظِيمُ ٢٥٥﴾

Allāh - there is no god except Him – He is the Living One, the All-Sustainer. Neither drowsiness befalls Him nor sleep. To Him belongs whatever is in the

[185] Extracted from *Tafsīr-e Nūr* of Shaykh Mohsin Qara'ati, translated by Saleem Bhimji.

heavens and whatever is on the earth. Who is it that may intercede with Him except by His permission? He knows that which is before them and that which is behind them, and they do not comprehend anything of His knowledge except what He wishes. His throne embraces the heavens and the earth, and He is not wearied by their preservation, and He is the All-Exalted, the All-Supreme.

1. In the entire world of existence, there is not a single entity which is worthy of being worshipped and adored in the truest sense of the word, other than Allāh ﷻ. (اللَّـهُ لَا إِلَٰـهَ إِلَّا هُـوَ)
2. The true and perpetual life of all creations stems from Him and Him alone. (الْحَيُّ)
3. Everything in existence is continuously attached to Allāh ﷻ and thus, all are in need of Him for their overall guidance and care. (الْقَيُّـومُ)
4. Whatever is in existence comes 'from' Allāh ﷻ – from His power of creation. (لَـهُ مَـا فِي السَّـمَاوَاتِ وَمَـا فِي الْأَرْضِ)
5. Not only is all which exists in the entire sphere of creation from Allāh ﷻ, but rather, even their efficiency also stems from Him. (مَـنْ ذَا الَّـذِي يَشْـفَعُ)
6. Those who may intercede and intervene for the human being in the court of Allāh ﷻ are not individuals or things which we desire – rather, it is based on His permission. (مَـنْ ذَا الَّـذِي يَشْـفَعُ عِنْـدَهُ إِلَّا بِإِذْنِـهِ)
7. There is none who is more compassionate and caring than Allāh ﷻ and therefore, any affinity, mercy and compassion which is shown by anyone who is permitted to intercede - all originate from Him and Him alone. (إِلَّا بِإِذْنِـهِ)
8. Allāh ﷻ is aware of everything and in every state – nothing is

hidden from His knowledge, and therefore if an individual sins, then they need to display some humility and embarrassment in His presence. (يَعْلَمُ مَا بَيْنَ أَيْدِيهِمْ وَمَا خَلْفَهُمْ)

9. Allāh ﷻ has a comprehensive knowledge over everything and no one can have access to even the slightest of the knowledge which Allāh ﷻ has without His permission. (وَلَا يُحِيطُونَ بِشَيْءٍ مِنْ عِلْمِهِ إِلَّا بِمَا شَاءَ)
10. The governance, power, and authority of Allāh ﷻ is not at all limited. (وَسِعَ كُرْسِيُّهُ السَّمَاوَاتِ وَالْأَرْضَ)
11. It is not difficult for Allāh ﷻ to safeguard all of that which He has created. (وَلَا يَئُودُهُ حِفْظُهُمَا)
12. That entity which is able to protect all of that which has been created is easily able to protect His creations from any of the dangers which may threaten them; therefore, for this level of protection, we have been encouraged to continuously recite Āyatul Kursī. (وَلَا يَئُودُهُ حِفْظُهُمَا)

Verse 256 of Sūrah al-Baqarah reads:

﴿لَآ إِكۡرَاهَ فِي ٱلدِّينِۖ قَد تَّبَيَّنَ ٱلرُّشۡدُ مِنَ ٱلۡغَيِّۚ فَمَن يَكۡفُرۡ بِٱلطَّٰغُوتِ وَيُؤۡمِنۢ بِٱللَّهِ فَقَدِ ٱسۡتَمۡسَكَ بِٱلۡعُرۡوَةِ ٱلۡوُثۡقَىٰ لَا ٱنفِصَامَ لَهَاۗ وَٱللَّهُ سَمِيعٌ عَلِيمٌ ٢٥٦﴾

There is no compulsion in religion – the right way is indeed clearly distinct from error. So whoever disbelieves in the devil and believes in Allāh, he indeed lays hold on the firmest handle which shall never break. And Allāh is Hearing, Knowing.

1. Any religion which is based on clear proofs and logical arguments is never in need of forcing or compelling others to believe and accept it. (لَا إِكْرَاهَ فِي الدِّينِ)

2. The only place where force and compulsion have any effect is on the actions and movements of an individual and never on their minds, thoughts or beliefs. (لَا إِكْرَاهَ فِي الدِّينِ)

3. The difference between the path of truth and falsehood has been so clearly defined that the argument of Allāh ﷻ over humanity is solidified. The way that the path of truth is made clear to humanity is through the powers of the intellect, revelation (from Allāh ﷻ to His prophets), and through the performance of miracles from the deputed men of Allāh ﷻ. In the current era, all of this goes back to the religion of Islam, and it can be stated that Islam IS progress, growth and development. (قَدْ تَبَيَّنَ الرُّشْدُ مِنَ الْغَيِّ)

4. Religion is the only true source of development of humanity and mankind. (قَدْ تَبَيَّنَ الرُّشْدُ مِنَ الْغَيِّ)

5. The religion of Islam is not congruent with arrogance. (فَمَنْ يَكْفُرْ بِالطَّاغُوتِ)

6. Until that time that the oppressors and despots are not removed, there is no way for the true teachings of monotheism (*al-tawḥīd*) to shine through. One must first disavow all forms of despotism and disbelief and only then can true faith in Allāh ﷻ be brought into the heart. (فَمَنْ يَكْفُرْ بِالطَّاغُوتِ وَيُؤْمِنْ بِاللَّهِ)

7. The continuous and perpetual disavowal and distancing from the despotic forces and maintaining faith in Allāh ﷻ are things which much always be there. This point is made clear to us by the usage of present tense verbs in this verse for these two realities. (يَكْفُرْ وَيُؤْمِنْ)

8. It is not only sufficient for the 'rope of Allāh ﷻ' to be something firm and unbreakable, rather what is more important is that our grip of that rope is also strong and powerful. (فَقَدِ اسْتَمْسَكَ بِالْعُرْوَةِ الْوُثْقَىٰ)

9. Reliance upon the oppressors and wrong doers, and really anything other than Allāh ﷻ is something which is bound to vanish and leave, and thus, the only thing which will remain forever is the unwavering faith and commitment to Allāh ﷻ. (لَا انْفِصَامَ لَهَا)

10. True belief in Allāh ﷻ and maintaining strong ties to the close friends of Allāh ﷻ (*awliyā'*) is something which will last forever, however the relationship between oppressors and despots and their followers will be disavowed on the Day of Judgement. (لَا انْفِصَامَ لَهَا)

11. Unwavering commitment and belief in Allāh ﷻ, and disavowal of the despots and oppressors is something which must take on a real form and manifestation in the life of an individual and must not be a hypocritical stand because Allāh ﷻ hears and sees everything. (وَاللَّهُ سَمِيعٌ عَلِيمٌ)

Verse 257 of Sūrah al-Baqarah reads:

﴿ٱللَّهُ وَلِيُّ ٱلَّذِينَ ءَامَنُواْ يُخْرِجُهُم مِّنَ ٱلظُّلُمَٰتِ إِلَى ٱلنُّورِۖ وَٱلَّذِينَ كَفَرُوٓاْ أَوْلِيَآؤُهُمُ ٱلطَّٰغُوتُ يُخْرِجُونَهُم مِّنَ ٱلنُّورِ إِلَى ٱلظُّلُمَٰتِۗ أُوْلَٰٓئِكَ أَصْحَٰبُ ٱلنَّارِۖ هُمْ فِيهَا خَٰلِدُونَ ٢٥٧﴾

> Allāh is the Master of those who believe -- He brings them out of the darknesses into the light. And those who disbelieve, their friends are the devils who take them out of light into darkness. They are the companions of the Fire; therein they shall abide forever.

1. The true believers all have one and only one true guardian and protector which is Allāh ﷻ; while the disbelievers – those who reject the truth – have multiple guardians, friends and

protectors which are referred to as despots, dictators, tyrants, etc... and indeed it is easier to accept one protector rather than multiple ones. It is for this reason that Allāh ﷻ says in regards to the believers that: ﴾Allāh is the [only] guardian of those who believe﴿; while for the disbelievers He state: ﴾for them (the disbelievers) there are [multiple] devils...﴿

2. The previous verse mentioned: ﴾Indeed the truth has been made clear from the path of falsehood﴿, while the current verse explains to us, via an example, the meaning of 'the clear path' and 'the path of falsehood' and we are told that the authority (*wilāyah*) of Allāh ﷻ – His guardianship is represented in our own [spiritual] progress and growth while the authority (*wilāyah*) of the despots is a path of deviation. (اللَّهُ وَلِيُّ الَّذِينَ آمَنُوا يُخْرِجُهُمْ مِنَ الظُّلُمَاتِ إِلَى النُّورِ ۖ وَالَّذِينَ كَفَرُوا أَوْلِيَاؤُهُمُ الطَّاغُوتُ يُخْرِجُونَهُمْ مِنَ النُّورِ إِلَى الظُّلُمَاتِ)

3. The path of the truth is only one, however there are multiple paths of deviation. When speaking about the path of the truth, the Quran uses the term light (*nūr*) which is singular, however when taking about the paths of deviance and misguidedness, the word employed is darknesses (*ḍhulumāt*) which is plural. (مِنَ النُّورِ إِلَى الظُّلُمَاتِ)

4. The path of the truth is one of Divine Light (*nūr*), and as it is known, light is something which moves, grows, gives hope and brings comfort, ease and tranquility. (النُّورِ)

5. A true believer must never feel that they are at a dead end in life. (اللَّهُ وَلِيُّ الَّذِينَ آمَنُوا يُخْرِجُهُمْ مِنَ الظُّلُمَاتِ إِلَى النُّورِ)

6. The despots and other such wicked individuals maneuver their way through the space of disbelief and polytheism. (وَالَّذِينَ كَفَرُوا أَوْلِيَاؤُهُمُ الطَّاغُوتُ)

7. A person who does not place themselves under the mastership and authority of Allāh ﷻ, whether they like it or not, will find

that the despots will take them under their wing and they will become a part of their legion. (اللَّهُ وَلِيُّ الَّذِينَ آمَنُوا يُخْرِجُهُمْ مِنَ الظُّلُمَاتِ إِلَى النُّورِ ۖ وَالَّذِينَ كَفَرُوا أَوْلِيَاؤُهُمُ الطَّاغُوتُ يُخْرِجُونَهُمْ مِنَ النُّورِ إِلَى الظُّلُمَاتِ)

8. Any mastership or authority other than that of Allāh ﷻ is the mastership of the despot. (اللَّهُ وَلِيُّ الَّذِينَ آمَنُوا يُخْرِجُهُمْ مِنَ الظُّلُمَاتِ إِلَى النُّورِ وَالَّذِينَ كَفَرُوا أَوْلِيَاؤُهُمُ الطَّاغُوتُ يُخْرِجُونَهُمْ مِنَ النُّورِ إِلَى الظُّلُمَاتِ)
9. By paying attention to the eventual outcome of oppressors, an individual will automatically be drawn to accepting the Truth. (أُولَٰئِكَ أَصْحَابُ النَّارِ)

Section 6

Benefits of Āyatul Kursī

We have numerous traditions narrated from the Noble Prophet ﷺ and his family, the Ahlul Bayt ‍, in regards to the mystical worth and spiritual greatness of Āyatul Kursī[186] - some of which we will mention here.

1. Fifty Words

There is a tradition from Imām ʿAlī ‍ in which he has said:

> سَمِعْتُ رَسُولَ اللّٰهِ ﷺ يَقُولُ: يَا عَلِيُّ ... سَيِّدُ الْكَلَامِ أَلْقُرَآنُ وَ سَيِّدُ الْقُرَآنِ أَلْبَقَرَةُ وَ سَيِّدُ الْبَقَرَةِ آيَةُ الْكُرْسِيِّ. يَا عَلِيُّ أَنَّ فِيهَا لَخَمْسِينَ كَلِمَةً فِي كُلِّ كَلِمَةٍ خَمْسُونَ بَرَكَةً
>
> I heard the Messenger of Allāh ﷺ say: ‘O’ ʿAlī ... the chief of all speech is the Quran; and the chief of the Quran is [Sūrah] al-Baqarah; and the chief of [Sūrah] al-Baqarah is Āyatul Kursī. O’ ʿAlī! Indeed contained

---

[186] Please note that to save space, we will include the full text of Āyatul Kursī and all other chapters of the Quran in Appendix One of this book rather than mentioning in this portion of the book. (Tr.)

within it [Āyatul Kursī] are fifty words and within each word is fifty blessings.'[187]

2. Benefits of Reciting it Every Morning

Whoever recites Āyatul Kursī in the morning will find that Allāh, the Most High, will appoint one angel to protect that person from all types of tribulations until the evening; and if a person recites Āyatul Kursī twice in the morning, then two angels will be appointed to protect that person until the evening from all forms of tribulations; and if a person recites Āyatul Kursī three times in the morning, then three angels will be appointed to protect that person until the evening from all forms of tribulations; and if a person recites Āyatul Kursī four times in the morning, then four angels will be appointed to protect that person until the evening from all forms of tribulations; and if one recites it five times, then all of the angels are addressed by Allāh ﷻ, who says to them to leave the person alone and that He Himself will be the person's protector and guardian; and if a person recites Āyatul Kursī at night, then it will be a means of one's protection until the morning.

3. Reward of Reciting it in Optional Prayers

It has been narrated that Imām Jaʿfar al-Ṣādiq ﵇ has said:

مَنْ قَرَأَ قُلْ هُوَ اللّٰهُ أَحَدٌ وَ إِنَّا أَنْزَلْنَاهُ فِي لَيْلَةِ الْقَدْرِ وَ آيَةَ الْكُرْسِيِّ فِي كُلِّ رَكْعَةٍ مِنْ تَطَوُّعِهِ فَقَدْ فَتَحَ اللّٰهُ لَهُ بِأَفْضَلِ أَعْمَالِ الْآدَمِيِّينَ إِلاَّ مَنْ أَشْبَهَهُ فَزَادَ عَلَيْهِ

A person who recites ﴾Say: He Allāh is One﴿ [Sūrah al-Ikhlāṣ] and ﴾Indeed We have revealed it on the night of al-Qadr﴿ [Sūrah al-Qadr] and Āyatul Kursī in every *rakʿat* of one's recommended prayers will find

---

[187] *Majmaʿ al-Bayān*, vol. 2, p. 360.

that Allāh will grant him the success of performing the best of actions of all of humanity - with the exception of that person who performs the (same) actions as him or does greater (deeds).[188]

4. Exalted Words of the Noble Quran

Imām Jaʿfar al-Ṣādiq ﷺ has said:

إِنَّ لِكُلِّ شَيْءٍ ذِرْوَةٌ وَ ذِرْوَةُ الْقُرْآنِ آيَةُ الْكُرْسِيِّ

Indeed for everything (in existence) there is something greater (than the thing itself) and Āyatul Kursī is that which is greater and loftier than the [entire] Quran.[189]

5. Reciting it in a Specific Manner

The Messenger of Allāh ﷺ has said:

مَـنْ قَـرَأَ أَرْبَـعَ آيَـاتٍ مِـنْ أَوَّلِ الْبَقَـرَةِ وَ آيَـةَ الْكُـرْسِيِّ وَ أَيَتَـينِ بَعْدَهَـا وَ ثَـلاَثَ آيَـاتٍ مِـنْ أَخِرِهَـا لَـمْ يَـرَ فِي نَفْسِـهِ وَ مَالِـهِ شَـيْئاً يُكْرِهُـهُ وَ لاَ يُقَرِّبُـهُ شَـيْطَانٌ وَ لاَ يَنْـسىٰ الْقُـرآنَ.

A person who recites the first four verses of [Sūrah] al-Baqarah, and [also] Āyatul Kursī and the two verses which follow it [verses 256 and 257], and the three verses at the end of this chapter [Sūrah al-Baqarah] - will never see anything bad or that which will cause one grief in their self, nor their wealth, and (in addition to this) the devil will not go close to that person, and they will never forget the Quran.[190]

NOTE: The verses referred to in this tradition are as follows:

---

188 *Thawāb al-Aʿmāl wa ʿIqāb al-Aʿmāl*, p. 80.

189 *Majmaʿ al-Bayān*, vol. 2, p. 360.

190 *Thawāb al-Aʿmāl wa ʿIqāb al-Aʿmāl*, p. 234.

﴿الٓمٓ ﴿١﴾ ذَٰلِكَ ٱلْكِتَٰبُ لَا رَيْبَ فِيهِ هُدًى لِّلْمُتَّقِينَ ﴿٢﴾ ٱلَّذِينَ يُؤْمِنُونَ بِٱلْغَيْبِ وَيُقِيمُونَ ٱلصَّلَوٰةَ وَمِمَّا رَزَقْنَٰهُمْ يُنفِقُونَ ﴿٣﴾ وَٱلَّذِينَ يُؤْمِنُونَ بِمَآ أُنزِلَ إِلَيْكَ وَمَآ أُنزِلَ مِن قَبْلِكَ وَبِٱلْءَاخِرَةِ هُمْ يُوقِنُونَ ﴿٤﴾﴾

Alif, Lām, Mīm. That is the Book, there is no doubt in it, a guidance to the God conscious, who believe in the Unseen, and maintain the prayer, and spend out of what We have provided them with; and who believe in what has been sent down to you and what was sent down before you, and are certain of the Hereafter.

﴿لِّلَّهِ مَا فِى ٱلسَّمَٰوَٰتِ وَمَا فِى ٱلْأَرْضِ وَإِن تُبْدُوا۟ مَا فِىٓ أَنفُسِكُمْ أَوْ تُخْفُوهُ يُحَاسِبْكُم بِهِ ٱللَّهُ فَيَغْفِرُ لِمَن يَشَآءُ وَيُعَذِّبُ مَن يَشَآءُ وَٱللَّهُ عَلَىٰ كُلِّ شَىْءٍ قَدِيرٌ ﴿٢٨٤﴾ ءَامَنَ ٱلرَّسُولُ بِمَآ أُنزِلَ إِلَيْهِ مِن رَّبِّهِۦ وَٱلْمُؤْمِنُونَ كُلٌّ ءَامَنَ بِٱللَّهِ وَمَلَٰٓئِكَتِهِۦ وَكُتُبِهِۦ وَرُسُلِهِۦ لَا نُفَرِّقُ بَيْنَ أَحَدٍ مِّن رُّسُلِهِۦ وَقَالُوا۟ سَمِعْنَا وَأَطَعْنَا غُفْرَانَكَ رَبَّنَا وَإِلَيْكَ ٱلْمَصِيرُ ﴿٢٨٥﴾ لَا يُكَلِّفُ ٱللَّهُ نَفْسًا إِلَّا وُسْعَهَا لَهَا مَا كَسَبَتْ وَعَلَيْهَا مَا ٱكْتَسَبَتْ رَبَّنَا لَا تُؤَاخِذْنَآ إِن نَّسِينَآ أَوْ أَخْطَأْنَا رَبَّنَا وَلَا تَحْمِلْ عَلَيْنَآ إِصْرًا كَمَا حَمَلْتَهُۥ عَلَى ٱلَّذِينَ مِن قَبْلِنَا رَبَّنَا وَلَا تُحَمِّلْنَا مَا لَا طَاقَةَ لَنَا بِهِۦ وَٱعْفُ عَنَّا وَٱغْفِرْ لَنَا وَٱرْحَمْنَآ أَنتَ مَوْلَىٰنَا فَٱنصُرْنَا عَلَى ٱلْقَوْمِ ٱلْكَٰفِرِينَ ﴿٢٨٦﴾﴾

To Allāh belongs whatever is in the heavens and whatever is in the earth; and whether you disclose what is in your hearts or hide it, Allāh will bring you to account for it. Then He will forgive whomever He wishes and punish whomever He wishes, and Allāh has power over all things. The Apostle has faith in what has been sent down to him from his Lord, and all of the faithful. Each [of them] has faith in Allāh, His angels, His scriptures and His apostles. [They declare,] 'We make no distinction between any of His apostles.' And they say, 'We hear and we obey. Our Lord, forgive us, and toward You is the return.' Allāh does not burden any soul beyond its capacity. Whatever [good] it earns is to its benefit, and whatever [evil] it incurs is to its harm. 'Our Lord! Take us not to task if we forget or make mistakes! Our Lord! Place not upon us a burden as You placed on those who were before us! Our Lord! Lay not upon us what we have no strength to bear! Excuse us and forgive us, and be merciful to us! You are our Master, so help us against the faithless people!'

6. Reward for Reciting it Before Going to Sleep

Imām ʿAlī al-Riḍā ﷺ has said:

مَنْ قَرَأَ آيَةَ الْكُرْسِيِّ عِنْدَ مَنَامِهِ لَمْ يَخَفِ الْفَالِجَ إِنْ شَاءَ اللّٰهُ
وَ مَنْ قَرَأَهَا بَعْدَ كُلِّ صَلاَةٍ لَمْ يَضُرَّهُ ذُوْ حُمَّةٍ

A person who recites Āyatul Kursī before going to sleep will never, by the will of Allāh, be struck with a disease that will render him handicapped (meaning that he will never have a stroke), and whoever recites it (Āyatul Kursī) after every obligatory *ṣalāt* will not be harmed by any creatures which sting or bite.[191]

7. Tradition from Salmān al-Fārsī [al-Muḥammadī)

It has been mentioned in a tradition from Salmān al-Fārsī [al-Muḥammadī] that the Messenger of Allāh ﷺ has said that whoever writes Āyatul Kursī with a mixture of saffron (and water) on the palm of his right hand and then licks it with his tongue, and repeats this action seven times will never forget a single thing, and the angels will plead with Allāh ﷻ for his forgiveness.

8. Reciting it Over Water

It has been mentioned that if a person recites Āyatul Kursī three times over water, pours this water over oneself and then performs a two *rakʿat ṣalāt* and in each *rakʿat*, recites Sūrah al-Ḥamd and Āyatul Kursī once, then whatever desires one has will be fulfilled by Allāh - God Willing; and if a person performs the above mentioned actions and then goes into the presence of a person in authority, one will be respected (in such a gathering). In addition, whoever writes Āyatul Kursī and then ties the writing to one's forearm, then wherever one goes, one will be respected and honoured; and if a man recites Āyatul Kursī and then blows a breath over a sweet pomegranate and gives it to his pregnant wife who has not yet entered into the fourth month of her pregnancy, then the child will be a boy - God Willing.

9. Removal of 1,000 Tribulations

It has been narrated from Imām Muḥammad al-Bāqir ؏ that:

مَـنْ قَـرَأَ آيَـةَ الْكُـرْسِي دَفَـعَ اللَّـهُ عَنْـهُ أَلْـفَ مَكْـرُوهٍ مِـنْ مَـكَارِهِ الدُّنْيَـا أَيْـسَرُهُ الْفَقْـرُ، وَ أَلْـفَ مَكْـرُوهٍ مِـنْ مَـكَارِهِ الْآخِـرَةِ أَيْـسَرُهُ عَـذَابُ الْقَـبْرِ.

---

[191] *Thawāb al-Aʿmāl wa ʿIqāb al-Aʿmāl*, p. 235.

> Whoever recites Āyatul Kursī once, 1,000 tribulations from this world will be removed from him and 1,000 tribulations from the next world will be removed from him – the minimal of these in this world is poverty and the most nominal of these in the next world being the punishment in the grave.

10. Advice from Imām al-Ṣādiq

It has been narrated that a man once came to complain to Imām al-Ṣādiq that he was suffering from fever to which the Imām replied:

اكْتُبْ آيَةَ الْكُرْسِي فِي إِنَاءٍ ثُمَّ دُفَّهُ بِجُرْعَةٍ مِنْ مَآءٍ فَاشْرَبْهُ.

> Write Āyatul Kursī in a dish and wash that dish with water; then drink that water and as a result of this, you will be cured from the fever.

11. Eradication of One's Enemies

It has been stated that to be victorious over one's enemies, Āyatul Kursī should be recited forty times, and when you reach the spot between the two '*meems*' – meaning when you reach 'يَعْلَمُ * مَا بَيْنَ أَيْدِيهِمْ' [as indicated by the *], bring to mind the name of your enemy. The above mentioned point can also be used in order to fulfill any other important matter on the condition that you bring to memory that request between the two '*ayns*' – meaning when you reach 'يَشْفَعُ * عِنْدَهُ' [as indicated by the *].

In addition, if Āyatul Kursī is recited seven times over salt and that salt is then put into food and given to someone whom you have affection for, then that person (who eats the food) will develop a stronger love and affection for the person (who performed this action).

12. Reciting it after Wuḍhū

It has been narrated from Imām al-Bāqir ﷺ that:

مَنْ قَرَءَ عَلىٰ آثَرِ وُضُوئِهِ آيَةَ الْكُرْسِيِّ أَعْطَاهُ اللّٰهُ تَعَالىٰ ثَوَابَ أَرْبَعِينَ عَاماً وَرَفَعَ لَهُ أَرْبَعِينَ دَرَجَةً وَ زَوَّجَهُ اللّٰهُ أَرْبَعِينَ حَوراً

A person who recites Āyatul Kursī after performing *wuḍhū* will be granted the following by Allāh, the Most High: the reward of forty years of worship; they will be raised up forty levels in rank; and (in paradise) that individual will be wed with forty of the heavenly damsels.[192]

13. Salvation from the Punishment of Allāh ﷻ

Whoever passes by a graveyard and recites Sūrah al-Ikhlāṣ eleven times will be given a reward equivalent to the number of people buried in that graveyard. In addition, we have been advised to recite Sūrah al-Ḥamd, Āyatul Kursī, Sūrah al-Ikhlāṣ, Sūrah al-Falaq and Sūrah al-Nās three times each; Sūrah al-Qadr seven times and Sūrah al-Mulk once (when visiting a graveyard) as these recitations free the deceased ones from any forms of punishment that [they may be experiencing].[193] [NOTE: The text of these chapters is presented at the end of this book.]

14. Supplication of the Throne

ʿAbdullāh b. Masʿūd has stated that:

One morning the Messenger of Islam ﷺ was sitting in the *masjid* when [the angel] Jibrāʾīl, the trustworthy, descended in the most beautiful of ways [not that people are able to see the angels, however individuals

---

[192] *Biḥār al-Anwār*, vol. 80, p. 317.

[193] Ibid., vol. 102, p. 299.

such as the prophets and their successors are able to see them] and said to him, 'Peace be upon you O' Messenger of Allāh! Allāh conveys His regards to you and has sent a gift for you.' The Prophet replied: 'And upon you be peace O' my brother, Jibrā'īl! What is this gift?'

At this point, Jibrā'īl took out a scroll which had green writing on it. The Prophet and those present with him stood up as a sign of reverence to this gift, and the Prophet ﷺ placed it over his head (as a sign of respect) and then said: 'O trustworthy Spirit! What is this gift and what Divine reward does it have?'

The angel replied: 'O Messenger of Allāh! Other than Allāh, no one else knows the Divine reward associated with it, however know that whoever reads this supplication and is sick, will be cured; whoever is in a state of sadness and sorrow will be made happy; and whoever has a spiritual sickness in one's heart, will by the grace of Allāh, attain treatment through this; whoever has an important task which needs to be done will find that it will be accomplished; and that person will be safeguarded from all tribulations and tragedies; and if a person recites it even one time with the intention of being forgiven for one's sins, then Allāh will grant that individual the reward of four prophets and four close angels; and if a person writes this supplication on the burial shroud (*kafān*), then one's body will never decay; and on the Day of Raising (from the graves) one will be raised up with a beautiful, appealing and illuminating countenance... The scroll had the below written on it.'

بِسْمِ اللهِ الرَّحْمٰنِ الرَّحِيمِ

In the Name of Allāh, the Most Gracious, the Most Merciful

لَا إِلٰهَ إِلَّا اللهُ الْـحَلِيمُ الْكَرِيمُ

There is no god except for Allāh, the Forbearing, the Generous.

لَا إِلٰهَ إِلَّا اللهُ الْعَلِيُّ الْعَظِيمُ

There is no god except for Allāh, the Exalted, the Magnificient.

لَا إِلٰهَ إِلَّا اللهُ الْمَلِكُ الْـحَقُّ الْمُبِينُ

There is no god except for Allāh, the King, the Truth, the Manifest.

لَا إِلٰهَ إِلَّا اللهُ الْـحَقُّ الْعَدْلُ الْيَقِينُ

There is no god except for Allāh, the Truth, the Just, the Evident.

لَا إِلٰهَ إِلَّا اللهُ رَبُّنَا وَ رَبُّ آبَآئِنَا الْأَوَّلِينَ

There is no god except for Allāh, our Lord and the Lord of our fore-fathers.

لَا إِلٰهَ إِلَّا أَنْتَ سُبْحَانَكَ إِنِّي كُنْتُ مِنَ الظَّالِمِينَ

There is no god except for You, all Praise belongs to You, surely I am of those who was oppressive [to my own self].

لَا إِلٰهَ إِلَّا اللهُ وَحْدَهُ لاَ شَرِيكَ لَهُ

There is no god except for Allāh, the One who has no partners;

لَهُ الْمُلْكُ وَ لَهُ الْـحَمْدُ

to Him belongs the Dominion and [all of] the Praise.

يُـحْيِي وَ يُمِيتُ وَ يُمِيتُ وَ يُـحْيِي

He gives life and He causes to die; and He causes to die and He gives life;

وَ هُوَ حَيٌّ لَا يَمُوتُ بِيَدِهِ الْـخَيْرُ

and He is the Ever-Living who shall never die and in His hands [power] is all goodness;

وَ هُوَ عَلٰى كُلِّ شَيْءٍ قَدِيرٌ

and He has power over all things.

لَا إِلٰهَ إِلَّا اللهُ مُحَمَّدٌ رَسُولُ اللهُ صَلَّى اللهُ عَلَيْهِ وَ آلِهِ

There is no god except for Allāh, Muḥammad, prayers of Allāh be upon him and his family, is the Messenger of Allāh.

وَ الْـحَمْدُ لِلّٰهِ رَبِّ الْعَالَمِينَ

And all praise belongs to Allāh, the Lord of the Worlds.

لَا إِلٰهَ إِلَّا اللهُ إِقْرَاراً بِرُبُوبِيَّتِهِ

There is no god except for Allāh, [and I testify] to the recognition of His Lordship.

وَ سُبْحَانَ اللهِ خُضُوعاً لِعَظَمَتِهِ

And glory be to Allāh alone, all praise [as I humbly] submit to His greatness.

وَ نَشْهَدُ أَنَّ مُحَمَّداً عَبْدُهُ وَ رَسُولُهُ

And we bear witness that indeed Muḥammad is His servant and His messenger.

أَللّٰهُمَّ يَا نُورَ السَّمٰوَاتِ وَ الْأَرْضِ

O Allāh! O Light of the heavens and the earth.

وَ يَا غِيَاثَ السَّمٰوَاتِ وَ الْأَرْضِ

And O Helper of the heavens and the earth.

وَ يَا فَاطِرَ السَّمٰوَاتِ وَ الْأَرْضِ

And O Splitter of the heavens and the earth.

يَا ذَا الْـجَلَالِ وَ الْإِكْرَامِ

O Possessor of Majesty and Nobility.

يَا حَيُّ يَا قَيُّومُ

O Ever-Living, O Self-Subsisting.

أَللّٰهُمَّ صَلِّ عَلٰى مُحَمَّدٍ وَآلِ مُحَمَّدٍ

O Allāh! Send [Your] prayers upon Muḥammad and the family of Muḥammad,

وَ ارْحَمْ مُحَمَّداً وَ آلَ مُحَمَّدٍ

and shower down [Your] mercy upon Muḥammad and the family of the Muḥammad,

وَ بَارِكْ عَلٰى مُحَمَّدٍ وَ آلِ مُحَمَّدٍ

and send [Your] blessings upon Muḥammad and the family of Muḥammad,

كَأَفْضَلِ مَا صَلَّيْتَ وَ بَارَكْتَ وَ تَرَحَّمْتَ وَ تَحَنَّنْتَ عَلٰى إِبْرَاهِيمَ وَ آلِ إِبْرَاهِيمَ

just as You have sent down Your prayers and Your blessings and Your mercy and Your salutations upon Ibrāhīm and the family of Ibrāhīm,

إِنَّكَ حَمِيدٌ مَجِيدٌ

indeed You are Praised, Glorious.

أَللّٰهُمَّ إِنَّكَ تَعْلَمُ سِرِّى وَ عَلَانِيَتِي وَ مَا فِي نَفْسِى

O Allāh! Indeed You know my hidden [words, deeds, and thoughts] and what I openly perform and what is in my soul.

فَاقْبَلْ مَعْذِرَتِي وَ تَعْلَمُ حَاجَتِي فَأَعْطِنِي سُؤْلِي

So then accept my excuses, and [since] You know my needs, grant me that which I ask for;

وَ اغْفِرْ لِي ذُنُوبِي إِنَّهُ لَا يَغْفِرُ الذُّنُوبَ إِلَّا أَنْتَ

and forgive me my sins as indeed none have the power to forgive the sins except for You,

يَا أَرْحَمَ الرَّاحِمِينَ

O the Most Merciful of those who show mercy!

أَللّٰهُمَّ إِنِّي أَسْأَلُكَ بِحَقِّ وَجْهِكَ الْكَرِيمِ عَلَيْكَ يَا رَبِّ

O Allāh, indeed I ask You by the right of Your noble countenance, which You have imposed upon Yourself, O my [dear] Lord!

وَ أَسْأَلُكَ بِـحَقِ عِزَّتِكَ عَلَيْكَ يَا رَبِّ

And I ask You by the right of Your Glory, which You have imposed upon Yourself, O my [dear] Lord!

وَ أَسْأَلُكَ بِـحَقِّ عَظَمَةِ جَلَالِكَ عَلَيْكَ يَا رَبِّ

And I ask You by the right of the greatness of Your Splendor, which You have imposed upon Yourself, O my [dear] Lord!

وَ أَسْأَلُكَ بِـحَقِّ مَلَائِكَتِكَ الْمُقَرَّبِينَ وَ أَنْبِيَائِكَ الْمُرْسَلِينَ عَلَيْكَ يَا رَبِّ

And I ask You by the right of Your close angels and Your deputed prophets, which You have imposed upon Yourself, O my [dear] Lord!

وَ أَسْأَلُكَ بِـحَقِّ جَبْرَءِيلَ عَلَيْكَ يَا رَبِّ

And I ask You by the right of [the angel] Jibrāʾīl, which You have imposed upon Yourself, O my [dear] Lord!

وَ أَسْأَلُكَ بِـحَقِّ مِيكَائِيلَ عَلَيْكَ يَا رَبِّ

And I ask You by the right of [the angel] Mīkāʾīl, which You have imposed upon Yourself, O my [dear] Lord!

وَ أَسْأَلُكَ بِـحَقِّ إِسْرَافِيلَ عَلَيْكَ يَا رَبِّ

And I ask You by the right of [the angel] Isrāfīl, which You have imposed upon Yourself, O my [dear] Lord!

وَ أَسْأَلُكَ بِـحَقِّ عَزْرَآئِيلَ عَلَيْكَ يَا رَبِّ

And I ask You by the right of [the angel] ʿAzrāʾīl, which You have imposed upon Yourself, O my [dear] Lord!

وَ أَسْأَلُكَ بِحَقِّ حَمَلَةِ عَرْشِكَ وَ الْكَرُوبِيِّينَ عَلَيْكَ يَا رَبِّ

And I ask You by the right of the carriers of Your throne and the archangels, which You have imposed upon Yourself, O my [dear] Lord!

وَ أَسْأَلُكَ بِحَقِّ آدَمَ وَ مُحَمَّدٍ وَ مَنْ بَيْنَهُمَا مِنَ الْأَنْبِيَآءِ وَ الْمُرْسَلِينَ عَلَيْكَ يَا رَبِّ

And I ask You by the right of Ādam and Muḥammad and those from amongst the prophets and messengers who came between them, which You have imposed upon Yourself, O my [dear] Lord!

وَ أَسْأَلُكَ بِحَقِّ مُحَمَّدٍ ﷺ الْمُصْطَفَى خَاتَمِ النَّبِيِّينَ عَلَيْكَ يَا رَبِّ

And I ask You by the right of Muḥammad al-Muṣṭafā, the Seal of the prophets, which You have imposed upon Yourself, O my [dear] Lord!

وَ أَسْأَلُكَ بِحَقِّ عَلِيِّ بْنِ أَبِي طَالِبٍ أَمِيرِ الْمُؤْمِنِينَ وَ إِمَامِ الْمُتَّقِينَ عَلَيْكَ يَا رَبِّ

And I ask You by the right of ʿAlī the son of Abī Ṭālib, the Commander of the Faithful, and the Leader of the Pious, which You have imposed upon Yourself, O my [dear] Lord!

وَ أَسْأَلُكَ بِحَقِّ فَاطِمَةَ الزَّهْرَاءِ سَيِّدَةِ نِسَآءِ الْعَالَمِينَ عَلَيْكَ يَا رَبِّ

And I ask You by the right of Fāṭima al-Zahrā', the Leader of the Women of the Worlds, which You have imposed upon Yourself, O my [dear] Lord!

وَ أَسْأَلُكَ بِـحَقِّ الْـحَسَنِ الْمُجْتَبىٰ عَلَيْكَ يَا رَبِّ

And I ask You by the right of al-Ḥasan, the Chosen, which You have imposed upon Yourself, O my [dear] Lord!

وَ أَسْأَلُكَ بِـحَقِّ الْـحُسَيْنِ الْإِمَامِ الشَّهِيدِ الْمَظْلُومِ الْمَقْتُولِ بِكَرْبَلَاءَ عَلَيْكَ يَا رَبِّ

And I ask You by the right of al-Ḥusayn, the Leader, the Martyr, the Oppressed, the one who was killed in Kerbalāʾ, which You have imposed upon Yourself, O my [dear] Lord!

وَ أَسْأَلُكَ بِـحَقِّ عَلِيِّ بْنِ الْـحُسَيْنِ زَيْنِ الْعَابِدِينَ عَلَيْكَ يَا رَبِّ

And I ask You by the right of ʿAlī the son of al-Ḥusayn, the Ornament of the Worshippers, which You have imposed upon Yourself, O my [dear] Lord!

وَ أَسْأَلُكَ بِـحَقِّ مُحَمَّدِ بْنِ عَلِيٍّ الْبَاقِرِ لِعِلْمِ النَّبِيِّينَ عَلَيْكَ يَا رَبِّ

And I ask You by the right of Muḥammad the son of ʿAlī, the Splitter of Knowledge of the Prophets, which You have imposed upon Yourself, O my [dear] Lord!

وَ أَسْأَلُكَ بِـحَقِّ جَعْفَرِ بْنِ مُحَمَّدٍ الصَّادِقِ الْبَارِّ عَلَيْكَ يَا رَبِّ

And I ask You by the right of Jaʿfar the son of Muḥammad, the Truthful, the Righteous, which You have imposed upon Yourself, O my [dear] Lord!

وَ أَسْأَلُكَ بِـحَقِّ مُوسَى بْنِ جَعْفَرٍ الْكَاظِمِ فِي اللهِ عَلَيْكَ يَا رَبِّ

And I ask You by the right of Mūsā the son of Jaʿfar, the one who Swallows his Anger in the way of Allāh, which You have imposed upon Yourself, O my [dear] Lord!

وَ أَسْأَلُكَ بِحَقِّ عَلِيِّ بْنِ مُوسَى الرِّضَا عَلَيْكَ يَا رَبِّ

And I ask You by the right of ʿAlī the son of Mūsā, the Pleased One [with Allāh], which You have imposed upon Yourself, O my [dear] Lord!

وَ أَسْأَلُكَ بِحَقِّ مُحَمَّدِ بْنِ عَلِيٍّ التَّقِيِّ عَلَيْكَ يَا رَبِّ

And I ask You by the right of Muḥammad the son of ʿAlī, the Pious, which You have imposed upon Yourself, O my [dear] Lord!

وَ أَسْأَلُكَ بِحَقِّ عَلِيِّ بْنِ مُحَمَّدٍ النَّقِيِّ عَلَيْكَ يَا رَبِّ

And I ask You by the right of ʿAlī the son of Muḥammad, the Refined, which You have imposed upon Yourself, O my [dear] Lord!

وَ أَسْأَلُكَ بِحَقِّ الْحَسَنِ بْنِ عَلِيٍّ الزَّكِيِّ الرَّضِيِّ عَلَيْكَ يَا رَبِّ

And I ask You by the right of al-Ḥasan the son of ʿAlī, the Spiritually Cleansed, the Pleased, which You have imposed upon Yourself, O my [dear] Lord!

وَ أَسْأَلُكَ بِحَقِّ مُحَمَّدِ بْنِ الْحَسَنِ الْقَآيِمِ بِأَمْرِكَ وَ الْحُجَّةِ عَلٰى عِبَادِكَ عَلَيْكَ يَا رَبِّ

And I ask You by the right of Muḥammad the son of al-Ḥasan, the one who will Rise to Implement Your Command and the Proof over Your servants, which You have imposed upon Yourself, O my [dear] Lord!

وَ أَسْأَلُكَ بِحَقِّ صُحُفِ إِبْرَاهِيمَ عَلَيْكَ يَا رَبِ

And I ask You by the right of the Scripture *(Ṣuḥuf)* of Ibrāhīm, which You have imposed upon Yourself, O my [dear] Lord!

وَ أَسْأَلُكَ بِـحَقِّ زَبُورِ دَاوُدَ عَلَيْكَ يَا رَبِّ

And I ask You by the right of the Psalms *(Zabūr)* of Dāwūd, which You have imposed upon Yourself, O my [dear] Lord!

وَ أَسْأَلُكَ بِـحَقِّ تَوْرَاةِ مُوسَى عَلَيكَ يَا رَبِّ

And I ask You by the right of the Torah *(Tawrāh)* of Mūsā, which You have imposed upon Yourself, O my [dear] Lord!

وَ أَسْأَلُكَ بِـحَقِّ إِنْجِيلِ عِيسىٰ عَلَيْكَ يَا رَبِّ

And I ask You by the right of the Evangel *(Injīl)* of ʿIsā, which You have imposed upon Yourself, O my [dear] Lord!

وَ أَسْأَلُكَ بِـحَقِّ اسْمِكَ الْمَكْتُوبِ فِي فُرْقَانِ مُحَمَّدٍ صَلَّى اللهُ عَلَيْهِ وَ آلِهِ عَلَيْكَ يَا رَبِّ

And I ask You by the right of Your written name which is contained in the Distinguisher *(Furqān)* of Muḥammad, prayers of Allāh be upon him and his family, which You have imposed upon Yourself, O my [dear] Lord!

وَ أَسْأَلُكَ بِـحَقِّ اسْمِكَ بِسْمِ اللهِ الرَّحْمٰنِ الرَّحِيمِ عَلَيْكَ يَا رَبِّ

And I ask You by the right of Your name, In the Name of Allāh, the Most Gracious, the Most Merciful, which You have imposed upon Yourself, O my [dear] Lord!

وَ أَسْأَلُكَ بِـحَقِّ سُورَةِ الْـحَمْدِ عَلَيْكَ يَا رَبِّ

And I ask You by the right of *Sūrah al-Ḥamd*, which You have imposed upon Yourself, O my [dear] Lord!

وَ أَسْأَلُكَ بِـحَقِّ سُورَةِ الْبَقَرَةِ عَلَيْكَ يَا رَبِّ

And I ask You by the right of *Sūrah al-Baqarah*, which You have imposed upon Yourself, O my [dear] Lord!

وَ أَسْأَلُكَ بِـحَقِّ سُورَةِ آلِ عِمْرَانَ عَلَيْكَ يَا رَبِّ

And I ask You by the right of *Sūrah Āle ʿImrān*, which You have imposed upon Yourself, O my [dear] Lord!

وَ أَسْأَلُكَ بِـحَقِّ سُورَةِ النِّسَآءِ عَلَيْكَ يَا رَبِّ

And I ask You by the right of *Sūrah al-Nisāʾ*, which You have imposed upon Yourself, O my [dear] Lord!

وَ أَسْأَلُكَ بِـحَقِّ سُورَةِ الْـمَـائِدَةِ عَلَيْكَ يَا رَبِّ

And I ask You by the right of *Sūrah al-Māʾidah*, which You have imposed upon Yourself, O my [dear] Lord!

وَ أَسْأَلُكَ بِـحَقِّ سُورَةِ الأَنْعَامِ عَلَيْكَ يَا رَبِّ

And I ask You by the right of *Sūrah al-Anʿām*, which You have imposed upon Yourself, O my [dear] Lord!

وَ أَسْأَلُكَ بِـحَقِّ سُورَةِ الأَعْرَافِ عَلَيْكَ يَا رَبِّ

And I ask You by the right of *Sūrah al-Aʿrāf*, which You have imposed upon Yourself, O my [dear] Lord!

وَ أَسْأَلُكَ بِـحَقِّ سُورَةِ الأَنْفَالِ عَلَيْكَ يَا رَبِّ

And I ask You by the right of *Sūrah al-Anfāl*, which You have imposed upon Yourself, O my [dear] Lord!

وَ أَسْأَلُكَ بِـحَقِّ سُورَةِ التَّوْبَةِ عَلَيْكَ يَا رَبِّ

And I ask You by the right of *Sūrah al-Tawbah*, which You have imposed upon Yourself, O my [dear] Lord!

وَ أَسْأَلُكَ بِـحَقِّ سُورَةِ يُونُسِ عَلَيْكَ يَا رَبِّ

And I ask You by the right of *Sūrah Yunūs*, which You have imposed upon Yourself, O my [dear] Lord!

وَ أَسْأَلُكَ بِـحَقِّ سُورَةِ هُودِ عَلَيْكَ يَا رَبِّ

And I ask You by the right of *Sūrah Hūd*, which You have imposed upon Yourself, O my [dear] Lord!

وَ أَسْأَلُكَ بِـحَقِّ سُورَةِ يُوسُفِ عَلَيْكَ يَا رَبِّ

And I ask You by the right of *Sūrah Yūsuf*, which You have imposed upon Yourself, O my [dear] Lord!

وَ أَسْأَلُكَ بِـحَقِّ سُورَةِ الرَّعْدِ عَلَيْكَ يَا رَبِّ

And I ask You by the right of *Sūrah al-Raʿd*, which You have imposed upon Yourself, O my [dear] Lord!

وَ أَسْأَلُكَ بِـحَقِّ سُورَةِ إِبْرَاهِيمِ عَلَيْكَ يَا رَبِّ

And I ask You by the right of *Sūrah Ibrāhīm*, which You have imposed upon Yourself, O my [dear] Lord!

وَ أَسْأَلُكَ بِـحَقِّ سُورَةِ الْـحِجْرِ عَلَيْكَ يَا رَبِّ

And I ask You by the right of *Sūrah al-Ḥijr*, which You have imposed upon Yourself, O my [dear] Lord!

وَ أَسْأَلُكَ بِـحَقِّ سُورَةِ النَّحْلِ عَلَيْكَ يَا رَبِّ

And I ask You by the right of *Sūrah al-Naḥl*, which You have imposed upon Yourself, O my [dear] Lord!

وَ أَسْأَلُكَ بِـحَقِّ سُورَةِ الإِسْرَاءِ عَلَيْكَ يَا رَبِّ

And I ask You by the right of *Sūrah al-Isrā'*, which You have imposed upon Yourself, O my [dear] Lord!

وَ أَسْأَلُكَ بِـحَقِّ سُورَةِ الْكَهْفِ عَلَيْكَ يَا رَبِّ

And I ask You by the right of *Sūrah al-Kahf*, which You have imposed upon Yourself, O my [dear] Lord!

وَ أَسْأَلُكَ بِـحَقِّ سُورَةِ مَرْيَمِ عَلَيْكَ يَا رَبِّ

And I ask You by the right of *Sūrah Maryam*, which You have imposed upon Yourself, O my [dear] Lord!

وَ أَسْأَلُكَ بِـحَقِّ سُورَةِ طٰهٰ عَلَيْكَ يَا رَبِّ

And I ask You by the right of *Sūrah Ṭāhā*, which You have imposed upon Yourself, O my [dear] Lord!

وَ أَسْأَلُكَ بِـحَقِّ سُورَةِ الأَنْبِيَآءِ عَلَيْكَ يَا رَبِّ

And I ask You by the right of *Sūrah al-Anbiyā'*, which You have imposed upon Yourself, O my [dear] Lord!

وَ أَسْأَلُكَ بِـحَقِّ سُورَةِ الْـحَجِّ عَلَيْكَ يَا رَبِّ

And I ask You by the right of *Sūrah al-Ḥajj*, which You have imposed upon Yourself, O my [dear] Lord!

وَ أَسْأَلُكَ بِحَقِّ سُورَةِ الْمُؤْمِنُونَ عَلَيْكَ يَا رَبِّ

And I ask You by the right of *Sūrah al-Mu'minūn*, which You have imposed upon Yourself, O my [dear] Lord!

وَ أَسْأَلُكَ بِحَقِّ سُورَةِ النُّوْرِ عَلَيْكَ يَا رَبِّ

And I ask You by the right of *Sūrah al-Nūr*, which You have imposed upon Yourself, O my [dear] Lord!

وَ أَسْأَلُكَ بِحَقِّ سُورَةِ الْفُرْقَانِ عَلَيْكَ يَا رَبِّ

And I ask You by the right of *Sūrah al-Furqān*, which You have imposed upon Yourself, O my [dear] Lord!

وَ أَسْأَلُكَ بِحَقِّ سُورَةِ الشُّعَرَآءِ عَلَيْكَ يَا رَبِّ

And I ask You by the right of *Sūrah al-Shuʿarā*, which You have imposed upon Yourself, O my [dear] Lord!

وَ أَسْأَلُكَ بِحَقِّ سُورَةِ النَّمْلِ عَلَيْكَ يَا رَبِّ

And I ask You by the right of *Sūrah al-Naml*, which You have imposed upon Yourself, O my [dear] Lord!

وَ أَسْأَلُكَ بِحَقِّ سُورَةِ الْقَصَصِ عَلَيْكَ يَا رَبِّ

And I ask You by the right of *Sūrah al-Qaṣaṣ*, which You have imposed upon Yourself, O my [dear] Lord!

وَ أَسْأَلُكَ بِحَقِّ سُورَةِ الْعَنْكَبُوتِ عَلَيْكَ يَا رَبِّ

And I ask You by the right of *Sūrah al-ʿAnkabūt*, which You have imposed upon Yourself, O my [dear] Lord!

وَ أَسْأَلُكَ بِـحَقِّ سُورَةِ الرُّومِ عَلَيْكَ يَا رَبِّ

And I ask You by the right of *Sūrah al-Rūm*, which You have imposed upon Yourself, O my [dear] Lord!

وَ أَسْأَلُكَ بِـحَقِّ سُورَةِ لُقْمَانِ عَلَيْكَ يَا رَبِّ

And I ask You by the right of *Sūrah Luqmān*, which You have imposed upon Yourself, O my [dear] Lord!

وَ أَسْأَلُكَ بِـحَقِّ سُورَةِ السَّجْدَةِ عَلَيْكَ يَا رَبِّ

And I ask You by the right of *Sūrah al-Sajdah*, which You have imposed upon Yourself, O my [dear] Lord!

وَ أَسْأَلُكَ بِـحَقِّ سُورَةِ الأَحْزَابِ عَلَيْكَ يَا رَبِّ

And I ask You by the right of *Sūrah al-Aḥzāb*, which You have imposed upon Yourself, O my [dear] Lord!

وَ أَسْأَلُكَ بِـحَقِّ سُورَةِ سَبَإٍ عَلَيْكَ يَا رَبِّ

And I ask You by the right of *Sūrah Sabā'*, which You have imposed upon Yourself, O my [dear] Lord!

وَ أَسْأَلُكَ بِـحَقِّ سُورَةِ فَاطِرِ عَلَيْكَ يَا رَبِّ

And I ask You by the right of *Sūrah Fāṭir*, which You have imposed upon Yourself, O my [dear] Lord!

وَ أَسْأَلُكَ بِـحَقِّ سُورَةِ يٰسٓ عَلَيْكَ يَا رَبِّ

And I ask You by the right of *Sūrah Yāsīn*, which You have imposed upon Yourself, O my [dear] Lord!

وَ أَسْأَلُكَ بِـحَقِّ سُورَةِ الصَّافَّاتِ عَلَيْكَ يَا رَبِّ

And I ask You by the right of *Sūrah al-Ṣāffāt*, which You have imposed upon Yourself, O my [dear] Lord!

وَ أَسْأَلُكَ بِـحَقِّ سُورَةِ ص عَلَيْكَ يَا رَبِّ

And I ask You by the right of *Sūrah Ṣad*, which You have imposed upon Yourself, O my [dear] Lord!

وَ أَسْأَلُكَ بِـحَقِّ سُورَةِ الزُّمَرِ عَلَيْكَ يَا رَبِّ

And I ask You by the right of *Sūrah al-Zumar*, which You have imposed upon Yourself, O my [dear] Lord!

وَ أَسْأَلُكَ بِـحَقِّ سُورَةِ الغَافِرِ عَلَيْكَ يَا رَبِّ

And I ask You by the right of *Sūrah al-Ghāfir*, which You have imposed upon Yourself, O my [dear] Lord!

وَ أَسْأَلُكَ بِـحَقِّ سُورَةِ فُصِّلَتِ عَلَيْكَ يَا رَبِّ

And I ask You by the right of *Sūrah Fuṣṣilat*, which You have imposed upon Yourself, O my [dear] Lord!

وَ أَسْأَلُكَ بِـحَقِّ سُورَةِ الشُّورىٰ عَلَيْكَ يَا رَبِّ

And I ask You by the right of *Sūrah al-Shūrā*, which You have imposed upon Yourself, O my [dear] Lord!

وَ أَسْأَلُكَ بِـحَقِّ سُورَةِ الزُّخْرُفِ عَلَيْكَ يَا رَبِّ

And I ask You by the right of *Sūrah al-Zukhruf*, which You have imposed upon Yourself, O my [dear] Lord!

وَ أَسْأَلُكَ بِحَقِّ سُورَةِ الدُّخَانِ عَلَيْكَ يَا رَبِّ

And I ask You by the right of *Sūrah al-Dukhān*, which You have imposed upon Yourself, O my [dear] Lord!

وَ أَسْأَلُكَ بِحَقِّ سُورَةِ الْجَاثِيَةِ عَلَيْكَ يَا رَبِّ

And I ask You by the right of *Sūrah al-Jāthiyah*, which You have imposed upon Yourself, O my [dear] Lord!

وَ أَسْأَلُكَ بِحَقِّ سُورَةِ الأَحْقَافِ عَلَيْكَ يَا رَبِّ

And I ask You by the right of *Sūrah al-Aḥqāf*, which You have imposed upon Yourself, O my [dear] Lord!

وَ أَسْأَلُكَ بِحَقِّ سُورَةِ مُحَمَّدٌ عَلَيْكَ يَا رَبِّ

And I ask You by the right of *Sūrah Muḥammad*, which You have imposed upon Yourself, O my [dear] Lord!

وَ أَسْأَلُكَ بِحَقِّ سُورَةِ الْفَتْحِ عَلَيْكَ يَا رَبِّ

And I ask You by the right of *Sūrah al-Fatḥ*, which You have imposed upon Yourself, O my [dear] Lord!

وَ أَسْأَلُكَ بِحَقِّ سُورَةِ الْحُجُرَاتِ عَلَيْكَ يَا رَبِّ

And I ask You by the right of *Sūrah al-Ḥujurāt*, which You have imposed upon Yourself, O my [dear] Lord!

وَ أَسْأَلُكَ بِحَقِّ سُورَةِ قٓ عَلَيْكَ يَا رَبِّ

And I ask You by the right of *Sūrah Qāf*, which You have imposed upon Yourself, O my [dear] Lord!

وَ أَسْأَلُكَ بِـحَقِّ سُورَةِ الذَّارِيَاتِ عَلَيْكَ يَا رَبِّ

And I ask You by the right of *Sūrah al-Dhāriyāt*, which You have imposed upon Yourself, O my [dear] Lord!

وَ أَسْأَلُكَ بِـحَقِّ سُورَةِ الطُّورِ عَلَيْكَ يَا رَبِّ

And I ask You by the right of *Sūrah al-Ṭūr*, which You have imposed upon Yourself, O my [dear] Lord!

وَ أَسْأَلُكَ بِـحَقِّ سُورَةِ النَّجْمِ عَلَيْكَ يَا رَبِّ

And I ask You by the right of *Sūrah al-Najm*, which You have imposed upon Yourself, O my [dear] Lord!

وَ أَسْأَلُكَ بِـحَقِّ سُورَةِ الْقَمَرِ عَلَيْكَ يَا رَبِّ

And I ask You by the right of *Sūrah al-Qamar*, which You have imposed upon Yourself, O my [dear] Lord!

وَ أَسْأَلُكَ بِـحَقِّ سُورَةِ الرَّحْمٰنِ عَلَيْكَ يَا رَبِّ

And I ask You by the right of *Sūrah al-Raḥmān*, which You have imposed upon Yourself, O my [dear] Lord!

وَ أَسْأَلُكَ بِـحَقِّ سُورَةِ الْوَاقِعَةِ عَلَيْكَ يَا رَبِّ

And I ask You by the right of *Sūrah al-Wāqiyah*, which You have imposed upon Yourself, O my [dear] Lord!

وَ أَسْأَلُكَ بِـحَقِّ سُورَةِ الْـحَدِيدِ عَلَيْكَ يَا رَبِّ

And I ask You by the right of *Sūrah al-Ḥadīd*, which You have imposed upon Yourself, O my [dear] Lord!

وَ أَسْأَلُكَ بِـحَقِّ سُورَةِ الْمُجَادِلَةِ عَلَيْكَ يَا رَبِّ

And I ask You by the right of *Sūrah al-Mujādilah*, which You have imposed upon Yourself, O my [dear] Lord!

وَ أَسْأَلُكَ بِـحَقِّ سُورَةِ الْـحَشْرِ عَلَيْكَ يَا رَبِّ

And I ask You by the right of *Sūrah al-Ḥashr*, which You have imposed upon Yourself, O my [dear] Lord!

وَ أَسْأَلُكَ بِـحَقِّ سُورَةِ الْمُمْتَحِنَةِ عَلَيْكَ يَا رَبِّ

And I ask You by the right of *Sūrah al-Mumtaḥinah*, which You have imposed upon Yourself, O my [dear] Lord!

وَ أَسْأَلُكَ بِـحَقِّ سُورَةِ الصَّفِّ عَلَيْكَ يَا رَبِّ

And I ask You by the right of *Sūrah al-Ṣaff*, which You have imposed upon Yourself, O my [dear] Lord!

وَ أَسْأَلُكَ بِـحَقِّ سُورَةِ الْـجُمُعَةِ عَلَيْكَ يَا رَبِّ

And I ask You by the right of *Sūrah al-Jumuʿah*, which You have imposed upon Yourself, O my [dear] Lord!

وَ أَسْأَلُكَ بِـحَقِّ سُورَةِ الْمُنَافِقُونَ عَلَيْكَ يَا رَبِّ

And I ask You by the right of *Sūrah al-Munāfiqūn*, which You have imposed upon Yourself, O my [dear] Lord!

وَ أَسْأَلُكَ بِـحَقِّ سُورَةِ التَّغَابُنِ عَلَيْكَ يَا رَبِّ

And I ask You by the right of *Sūrah al-Taghābun*, which You have imposed upon Yourself, O my [dear] Lord!

وَ أَسْأَلُكَ بِحَقِّ سُورَةِ الطَّلَاقِ عَلَيْكَ يَا رَبِّ

And I ask You by the right of *Sūrah al-Ṭalāq*, which You have imposed upon Yourself, O my [dear] Lord!

وَ أَسْأَلُكَ بِحَقِّ سُورَةِ التَّحْرِيمِ عَلَيْكَ يَا رَبِّ

And I ask You by the right of *Sūrah al-Taḥrīm*, which You have imposed upon Yourself, O my [dear] Lord!

وَ أَسْأَلُكَ بِحَقِّ سُورَةِ الْمُلْكِ عَلَيْكَ يَا رَبِّ

And I ask You by the right of *Sūrah al-Mulk*, which You have imposed upon Yourself, O my [dear] Lord!

وَ أَسْأَلُكَ بِحَقِّ سُورَةِ الْقَلَمِ عَلَيْكَ يَا رَبِّ

And I ask You by the right of *Sūrah al-Qalam*, which You have imposed upon Yourself, O my [dear] Lord!

وَ أَسْأَلُكَ بِحَقِّ سُورَةِ الْحَاقَّةِ عَلَيْكَ يَا رَبِّ

And I ask You by the right of *Sūrah al-Ḥāqqah*, which You have imposed upon Yourself, O my [dear] Lord!

وَ أَسْأَلُكَ بِحَقِّ سُورَةِ الْمَعَارِجِ عَلَيْكَ يَا رَبِّ

And I ask You by the right of *Sūrah al-Maʿārij*, which You have imposed upon Yourself, O my [dear] Lord!

وَ أَسْأَلُكَ بِحَقِّ سُورَةِ نُوحٍ عَلَيْكَ يَا رَبِّ

And I ask You by the right of *Sūrah Nūḥ*, which You have imposed upon Yourself, O my [dear] Lord!

وَ أَسْأَلُكَ بِـحَقِّ سُورَةِ الْـجِنِّ عَلَيْكَ يا رَبِّ

And I ask You by the right of *Sūrah al-Jinn*, which You have imposed upon Yourself, O my [dear] Lord!

وَ أَسْأَلُكَ بِـحَقِّ سُورَةِ الْـمُزَّمِّلِ عَلَيْكَ يا رَبِّ

And I ask You by the right of *Sūrah al-Muzzammil*, which You have imposed upon Yourself, O my [dear] Lord!

وَ أَسْأَلُكَ بِـحَقِّ سُورَةِ الْـمُدَّثِّرِ عَلَيْكَ يا رَبِّ

And I ask You by the right of *Sūrah al-Muddaththir*, which You have imposed upon Yourself, O my [dear] Lord!

وَ أَسْأَلُكَ بِـحَقِّ سُورَةِ الْقِيَامَةِ عَلَيْكَ يا رَبِّ

And I ask You by the right of *Sūrah al-Qiyāmah*, which You have imposed upon Yourself, O my [dear] Lord!

وَ أَسْأَلُكَ بِـحَقِّ سُورَةِ الإِنْسَانِ عَلَيْكَ يا رَبِّ

And I ask You by the right of *Sūrah al-Insān*, which You have imposed upon Yourself, O my [dear] Lord!

وَ أَسْأَلُكَ بِـحَقِّ سُورَةِ الْـمُرْسَلاَتِ عَلَيْكَ يا رَبِّ

And I ask You by the right of *Sūrah al-Mursalāt*, which You have imposed upon Yourself, O my [dear] Lord!

وَ أَسْأَلُكَ بِـحَقِّ سُورَةِ النَّبَاءِ عَلَيْكَ يا رَبِّ

And I ask You by the right of *Sūrah al-Nabā'*, which You have imposed upon Yourself, O my [dear] Lord!

وَ أَسْأَلُكَ بِـحَقِّ سُورَةِ النَّازِعَاتِ عَلَيْكَ يَا رَبِّ

And I ask You by the right of *Sūrah al-Nāzi'āt*, which You have imposed upon Yourself, O my [dear] Lord!

وَ أَسْأَلُكَ بِـحَقِّ سُورَةِ عَبَسَ عَلَيْكَ يَا رَبِّ

And I ask You by the right of *Sūrah al-'Abasa*, which You have imposed upon Yourself, O my [dear] Lord!

وَ أَسْأَلُكَ بِـحَقِّ سُورَةِ التَّكْوِيرِ عَلَيْكَ يَا رَبِّ

And I ask You by the right of *Sūrah al-Takwīr*, which You have imposed upon Yourself, O my [dear] Lord!

وَ أَسْأَلُكَ بِـحَقِّ سُورَةِ الإِنْفِطَارِ عَلَيْكَ يَا رَبِّ

And I ask You by the right of *Sūrah al-Infiṭār*, which You have imposed upon Yourself, O my [dear] Lord!

وَ أَسْأَلُكَ بِـحَقِّ سُورَةِ الْـمُطَفِّفِينَ عَلَيْكَ يَا رَبِّ

And I ask You by the right of *Sūrah al-Muṭaffifīn*, which You have imposed upon Yourself, O my [dear] Lord!

وَ أَسْأَلُكَ بِـحَقِّ سُورَةِ الإِنْشِقَاقِ عَلَيْكَ يَا رَبِّ

And I ask You by the right of *Sūrah al-Inshiqāq*, which You have imposed upon Yourself, O my [dear] Lord!

وَ أَسْأَلُكَ بِـحَقِّ سُورَةِ البُرُوجِ عَلَيْكَ يَا رَبِّ

And I ask You by the right of *Sūrah al-Burūj*, which You have imposed upon Yourself, O my [dear] Lord!

وَ أَسْأَلُكَ بِـحَقِّ سُورَةِ الطَّارِقِ عَلَيْكَ يَا رَبِّ

And I ask You by the right of *Sūrah al-Ṭāriq*, which You have imposed upon Yourself, O my [dear] Lord!

وَ أَسْأَلُكَ بِـحَقِّ سُورَةِ الأَعْلَىٰ عَلَيْكَ يَا رَبِّ

And I ask You by the right of *Sūrah al-Aʿlā*, which You have imposed upon Yourself, O my [dear] Lord!

وَ أَسْأَلُكَ بِـحَقِّ سُورَةِ الْغَاشِيَةِ عَلَيْكَ يَا رَبِّ

And I ask You by the right of *Sūrah al-Ghāshiyah*, which You have imposed upon Yourself, O my [dear] Lord!

وَ أَسْأَلُكَ بِـحَقِّ سُورَةِ الْفَجْرِ عَلَيْكَ يَا رَبِّ

And I ask You by the right of *Sūrah al-Fajr*, which You have imposed upon Yourself, O my [dear] Lord!

وَ أَسْأَلُكَ بِـحَقِّ سُورَةِ الْبَلَدِ عَلَيْكَ يَا رَبِّ

And I ask You by the right of *Sūrah al-Balad*, which You have imposed upon Yourself, O my [dear] Lord!

وَ أَسْأَلُكَ بِـحَقِّ سُورَةِ الشَّمْسِ عَلَيْكَ يَا رَبِّ

And I ask You by the right of *Sūrah al-Shams*, which You have imposed upon Yourself, O my [dear] Lord!

وَ أَسْأَلُكَ بِـحَقِّ سُورَةِ اللَّيْلِ عَلَيْكَ يَا رَبِّ

And I ask You by the right of *Sūrah al-Layl*, which You have imposed upon Yourself, O my [dear] Lord!

وَ أَسْأَلُكَ بِحَقِّ سُورَةِ الضُّحىٰ عَلَيْكَ يَا رَبِّ

And I ask You by the right of *Sūrah al-Ḍuḥā*, which You have imposed upon Yourself, O my [dear] Lord!

وَ أَسْأَلُكَ بِحَقِّ سُورَةِ الشَّرْحِ عَلَيْكَ يَا رَبِّ

And I ask You by the right of *Sūrah al-Sharḥ*, which You have imposed upon Yourself, O my [dear] Lord!

وَ أَسْأَلُكَ بِحَقِّ سُورَةِ التِّينِ عَلَيْكَ يَا رَبِّ

And I ask You by the right of *Sūrah al-Tīn*, which You have imposed upon Yourself, O my [dear] Lord!

وَ أَسْأَلُكَ بِحَقِّ سُورَةِ الْعَلَقِ عَلَيْكَ يَا رَبِّ

And I ask You by the right of *Sūrah al-ʿAlaq*, which You have imposed upon Yourself, O my [dear] Lord!

وَ أَسْأَلُكَ بِحَقِّ سُورَةِ الْقَدرِ عَلَيْكَ يَا رَبِّ

And I ask You by the right of *Sūrah al-Qadr*, which You have imposed upon Yourself, O my [dear] Lord!

وَ أَسْأَلُكَ بِحَقِّ سُورَةِ الْبَيِّنَةِ عَلَيْكَ يَا رَبِّ

And I ask You by the right of *Sūrah al-Bayyinah*, which You have imposed upon Yourself, O my [dear] Lord!

وَ أَسْأَلُكَ بِحَقِّ سُورَةِ الزَّلْزَلَةِ عَلَيْكَ يَا رَبِّ

And I ask You by the right of *Sūrah al-Zalzalah*, which You have imposed upon Yourself, O my [dear] Lord!

وَ أَسْأَلُكَ بِـحَقِّ سُورَةِ الْعَادِيَاتِ عَلَيْكَ يَا رَبِّ

And I ask You by the right of *Sūrah al-ʿĀdiyāt*, which You have imposed upon Yourself, O my [dear] Lord!

وَ أَسْأَلُكَ بِحَقِّ سُورَةِ الْقَارِعَةِ عَلَيْكَ يَا رَبِّ

And I ask You by the right of *Sūrah al-Qārīʿah*, which You have imposed upon Yourself, O my [dear] Lord!

وَ أَسْأَلُكَ بِـحَقِّ سُورَةِ التَّكَاثُرِ عَلَيْكَ يَا رَبِّ

And I ask You by the right of *Sūrah al-Takāthur*, which You have imposed upon Yourself, O my [dear] Lord!

وَ أَسْأَلُكَ بِـحَقِّ سُورَةِ الْعَصْرِ عَلَيْكَ يَا رَبِّ

And I ask You by the right of *Sūrah al-ʿAṣr*, which You have imposed upon Yourself, O my [dear] Lord!

وَ أَسْأَلُكَ بِـحَقِّ سُورَةِ الْـهُمَزَةِ عَلَيْكَ يَا رَبِّ

And I ask You by the right of *Sūrah al-Humazah*, which You have imposed upon Yourself, O my [dear] Lord!

وَ أَسْأَلُكَ بِـحَقِّ سُورَةِ الْفِيلِ عَلَيْكَ يَا رَبِّ

And I ask You by the right of *Sūrah al-Fīl*, which You have imposed upon Yourself, O my [dear] Lord!

وَ أَسْأَلُكَ بِـحَقِّ سُورَةِ الْقُرَيْشِ عَلَيْكَ يَا رَبِّ

And I ask You by the right of *Sūrah al-Quraysh*, which You have imposed upon Yourself, O my [dear] Lord!

وَ أَسْأَلُكَ بِـحَقِّ سُورَةِ الْـمَاعُونِ عَلَيْكَ يَا رَبِّ

And I ask You by the right of *Sūrah al-Maʿūn*, which You have imposed upon Yourself, O my [dear] Lord!

وَ أَسْأَلُكَ بِـحَقِّ سُورَةِ الْكَوْثَرِ عَلَيْكَ يَا رَبِّ

And I ask You by the right of *Sūrah al-Kawthar*, which You have imposed upon Yourself, O my [dear] Lord!

وَ أَسْأَلُكَ بِـحَقِّ سُورَةِ الْكَافِرُونَ عَلَيْكَ يَا رَبِّ

And I ask You by the right of *Sūrah al-Kāfirūn*, which You have imposed upon Yourself, O my [dear] Lord!

وَ أَسْأَلُكَ بِـحَقِّ سُورَةِ النَّصْرِ عَلَيْكَ يَا رَبِّ

And I ask You by the right of *Sūrah al-Naṣr*, which You have imposed upon Yourself, O my [dear] Lord!

وَ أَسْأَلُكَ بِـحَقِّ سُورَةِ الْـمَسَدِ عَلَيْكَ يَا رَبِّ

And I ask You by the right of *Sūrah al-Masad*, which You have imposed upon Yourself, O my [dear] Lord!

وَ أَسْأَلُكَ بِـحَقِّ سُورَةِ الْإِخْلَاصِ عَلَيْكَ يَا رَبِّ

And I ask You by the right of *Sūrah al-Ikhlāṣ*, which You have imposed upon Yourself, O my [dear] Lord!

وَ أَسْأَلُكَ بِـحَقِّ سُورَةِ الْفَلَقِ عَلَيْكَ يَا رَبِّ

And I ask You by the right of *Sūrah al-Falaq*, which You have imposed upon Yourself, O my [dear] Lord!

وَ أَسْأَلُكَ بِـحَقِّ سُورَةِ النَّاسِ عَلَيْكَ يَا رَبِّ

And I ask You by the right of *Sūrah al-Nās*, which You have imposed upon Yourself, O my [dear] Lord!

وَ أَسْأَلُكَ بِـحَقِّ كُلِّ سُورَةٍ أَنْزَلْتَهَا عَلَىٰ نَبِيٍّ مِنْ أَنْبِيَائِكَ عَلَيْكَ يَا رَبِّ

And I ask You by the right of every chapter (*sūrah*) which You have revealed upon Your Prophet from amongst all of Your prophets, which You have imposed upon Yourself, O my [dear] Lord!

وَ أَسْأَلُكَ بِـحَقِّ مِائَةِ أَلْفِ نَبِيٍّ وَ أَرْبَعَةٍ وَ عِشْرِينَ أَلْفَ نَبِيٍّ عَلَيْكَ يَا رَبِّ

And I ask You by the right of the 124,000 prophets [which You have sent to humanity], which You have imposed upon Yourself, O my [dear] Lord!

وَ أَسْأَلُكَ بِـحَقِّ الْأَدْعِيَةِ الَّتِي دَعَاكَ بِهَا أَنْبِيَاؤُكَ وَ رُسُلُكَ وَ أَهْلُ طَاعَتِكَ عَلَيْكَ يَا رَبِّ

And I ask You by the right of the supplications which Your prophets, Your messengers and the people who obey You, called upon You through, which You have imposed upon Yourself, O my [dear] Lord!

وَ أَسْأَلُكَ بِـحَقِّ اسْمِكَ الْمَكْتُوبِ عَلَىٰ اللَّوْحِ الْمَحْفُوظِ عَلَيْكَ يَا رَبِّ

And I ask You by the right of Your written name contained on the Guarded Tablet (*al-Lawḥ al-Maḥfūz*), which You have imposed upon Yourself, O my [dear] Lord!

وَ أَسْأَلُكَ بِـحَقِّ اسْمِكَ الْمَكْتُوبِ عَلىٰ سَاقِ عَرْشِكَ عَلَيْكَ يَا رَبِّ

And I ask You by the right of Your written name which is on the leg of Your Throne, which You have imposed upon Yourself, O my [dear] Lord!

وَ أَسْأَلُكَ بِـحَقِّ اسْمِكَ الْمَكْتُوبِ عَلىٰ الصِّرَاطِ عَلَيْكَ يَا رَبِّ

And I ask You by the right of Your written name which is on the Path (*al-Ṣirāṭ*), which You have imposed upon Yourself, O my [dear] Lord!

وَ أَسْأَلُكَ بِـحَقِّ اسْمِكَ الْمَكْتُوبِ عَلىٰ أَجْنِحَةِ جَبْرَئِيلَ وَ مِيكَائِيلَ عَلَيْكَ يَا رَبِّ

And I ask You by the right of Your written name which is on the wings of [the angels] Jibra'īl and Mīkā'īl, which You have imposed upon Yourself, O my [dear] Lord!

وَ أَسْأَلُكَ بِـحَقِّ اسْمِكَ الْمَكْتُوبِ عَلىٰ أَجْنِحَةِ إِسْرَافِيلَ عَلَيْكَ يَا رَبِّ

And I ask You by the right of Your written name which is on the wings of [the angel] Isrāfīl, which You have imposed upon Yourself, O my [dear] Lord!

وَ أَسْأَلُكَ بِـحَقِّ اسْمِكَ الْمَكْتُوبِ عَلىٰ كَفِّ عَزْرَآئِيلَ عَلَيْكَ يَا رَبِّ

And I ask You by the right of Your written name which is on the palm of [the angel] ʿAzrā'īl, which You have imposed upon Yourself, O my [dear] Lord!

وَ أَسْأَلُكَ بِـحَقِّ اسْمِكَ الْمَكْتُوبِ عَلىٰ بَابِ الْـجِنَانِ عَلَيْكَ يَا رَبِّ

And I ask You by the right of Your written name which is on the door on the Gardens [of Paradise] , which You have imposed upon Yourself, O my [dear] Lord!

وَ أَسْأَلُكَ بِحَقِّ اسْمِكَ الَّذِى دَعَاكَ بِهِ مُنْكَرٌ وَ نَكِيرٌ عَلَيْكَ يَا رَبِّ

And I ask You by the right of Your name by which [the two angels] Munkar and Nakīr call upon You with, which You have imposed upon Yourself, O my [dear] Lord!

وَ أَسْأَلُكَ بِحَقِّ اسْمِكَ الَّذِى دَعَاكَ بِهِ حَمَلَةُ عَرْشِكَ عَلَيْكَ يَا رَبِّ

And I ask You by the right of Your name by which the bearers of Your Throne call upon You with, which You have imposed upon Yourself, O my [dear] Lord!

وَ أَسْأَلُكَ بِحَقِّ اسْمِكَ الَّذِى دَعَاكَ بِهِ مَلَائِكَتُكَ الْمُقَرَّبُونَ وَ الْكَرُوبِيُّونَ عَلَيْكَ يَا رَبِّ

And I ask You by the right of Your name by which the closest of Your angels and the Archangels call upon You with, which You have imposed upon Yourself, O my [dear] Lord!

وَ أَسْأَلُكَ بِحَقِّ غَايَةِ رَحْمَتِكَ عَلَىٰ عِبَادِكَ عَلَيْكَ يَا رَبِّ

And I ask You by the right of the pinnacle of Your Mercy which encompasses Your servants, which You have imposed upon Yourself, O my [dear] Lord!

وَ أَسْأَلُكَ بِحَقِّ تَمَامِ كَلِمَاتِكَ عَلَيْكَ يَا رَبِّ

And I ask You by the right of all of Your words, which You have imposed upon Yourself, O my [dear] Lord!

وَ أَسْأَلُكَ بِحَقِّ عِلْمِكَ أَسْرَارَ عِبَادِكَ عَلَيْكَ يَا رَبِّ

And I ask You by the right of Your hidden knowledge of the [actions of] Your servants, which You have imposed upon Yourself, O my [dear] Lord!

وَ أَسْأَلُكَ بِـحَقِّ اسْمِكَ الْأَعْظَمِ عَلَيْكَ يَا رَبِّ

And I ask You by the right of Your Greatest Name, which You have imposed upon Yourself, O my [dear] Lord!

وَ أَسْأَلُكَ بِـحَقِّ الإِسْمِ الَّذِى لَقَّيْتَهُ آدَمَ عَلَيْهِ السَّلَامُ وَ قَبِلْتَ تَوْبَتَهُ وَ عَفَوْتَ عَنْهُ عَلَيْكَ يَا رَبِّ

And I ask You by the right of the name which You conveyed to Ādam, peace be upon him, and through which You accepted his repentance and through which You forgave him, which You have imposed upon Yourself, O my [dear] Lord!

وَ أَسْأَلُكَ بِـحَقِّ الْكَلِمَاتِ الَّتِى تَلَقَّاهَا مِنْكَ فَتُبْتَ عَلَيْهِ عَلَيْكَ يَا رَبِّ

And I ask You by the right of the words which he (Ādam) conveyed to You through which You turned towards him (in mercy), which You have imposed upon Yourself, O my [dear] Lord!

وَ أَسْأَلُكَ بِـحَقِّ اسْمِكَ الَّذِى دَعَاكَ بِهِ هَابِيلُ فَقَبِلْتَ قُرْبَانَهُ عَلَيْكَ يَا رَبِّ

And I ask You by the right of Your name through which Hābīl called upon You and You accepted his sacrifice, which You have imposed upon Yourself, O my [dear] Lord!

وَ أَسْأَلُكَ بِـحَقِّ الإِسْمِ الَّذِى دَعَاكَ بِهِ شَيْثٌ عَلَيْهِ السَّلَامُ فَاجْتَبَيْتَهُ عَلَيْكَ يَا رَبِّ

And I ask You by the right by the name through which Shayth, peace be upon him, called upon You, by which You chose him, which You have imposed upon Yourself, O my [dear] Lord!

وَ أَسْأَلُكَ بِحَقِّ الإِسْمِ الَّذِى دَعَاكَ بِهِ إِدْرِيسُ عَلَيْهِ السَّلَامُ فَرَفَعْتَهُ
مَكاناً عَلِيًّا عَلَيْكَ يَا رَبِّ

And I ask You by the right of the name through which Idrīs, peace be upon him, called upon You, by which You raised him up to a lofty position, which You have imposed upon Yourself, O my [dear] Lord!

وَ أَسْأَلُكَ بِحَقِّ الإِسْمِ الَّذِى دَعَاكَ بِهِ نُوحُ عَلَيْهِ السَّلَامُ فَنَجَّيْتَهُ وَ مَنْ
مَعَهُ فِى السَّفِينَةِ عَلَيْكَ يَا رَبِّ

And I ask You by the right of the name through which Nūḥ, peace be upon him, called upon You, by which You saved him and those who were with him on the ark, which You have imposed upon Yourself, O my [dear] Lord!

وَ أَسْأَلُكَ بِحَقِّ الإِسْمِ الَّذِى دَعَاكَ بِهِ إِبْرَاهِيمُ عَلَيْهِ السَّلَامُ وَ جَعَلْتَ
النَّارَ عَلَيْهِ بَرْداً وَ سَلاماً عَلَيْكَ يَا رَبِّ

And I ask You by the right of the name through which Ibrāhīm, peace be upon him, called upon You, and You made the fire cool and peaceful for him, which You have imposed upon Yourself, O my [dear] Lord!

وَ أَسْأَلُكَ بِحَقِّ الإِسْمِ الَّذِى دَعَاكَ بِهِ إِسْمَاعِيلُ عَلَيْهِ السَّلَامُ فَفَدَيْتَهُ
بِذِبْحٍ عَظِيمٍ عَلَيْكَ يَا رَبِّ

And I ask You by the right of the name through which Ismāʿīl, peace be upon him, called upon You, by which You ransomed him with a great ransom, which You have imposed upon Yourself, O my [dear] Lord!

وَ أَسْأَلُكَ بِـحَقِّ الإِسْمِ الَّذِى دَعَاكَ بِهِ إِسْحَاقُ عَلَيْهِ السَّلَامُ عَلَيْكَ يَا رَبِّ

And I ask You by the right of the name through which Isḥāq, peace be upon him, called upon You, which You have imposed upon Yourself, O my [dear] Lord!

وَ أَسْأَلُكَ بِـحَقِّ الإِسْمِ الَّذِى دَعَاكَ بِهِ هُودٌ عَلَيْهِ السَّلَامُ فَاسْتَجَبْتَ لَهُ وَ أَهْلَكْتَ عَادًا عَلَيْكَ يَا رَبِّ

And I ask You by the right of the name through which Hūd, peace be upon him, called upon You, through which You answered his call and You destroyed [the people of] ʿAd, which You have imposed upon Yourself, O my [dear] Lord!

وَ أَسْأَلُكَ بِـحَقِّ الإِسْمِ الَّذِى دَعَاكَ بِهِ صَالِحٌ عَلَيْهِ السَّلَامُ فَاسْتَجَبْتَ لَهُ وَ أَهْلَكْتَ ثَمُودَ عَلَيْكَ يَا رَبِّ

And I ask You by the right of the name through which Ṣāliḥ, peace be upon him, called upon You, through which You destroyed [the people of] Thamūd, which You have imposed upon Yourself, O my [dear] Lord!

وَ أَسْأَلُكَ بِـحَقِّ الإِسْمِ الَّذِى دَعَاكَ بِهِ يَعْقُوبُ عَلَيْهِ السَّلَامُ فَرَدَدْتَ عَلَيْهِ بَصَرَهُ وَ وَلَدَهُ وَ كَشَفْتَ عَنْهُ ضُرَّهُ عَلَيْكَ يَا رَبِّ

And I ask You by the right of the name through which Yaʿqūb, peace be upon him, called upon You, through which You returned his eyesight and [brought back] his son [Yūsuf] to him and through which You removed his grief, which You have imposed upon Yourself, O my [dear] Lord!

وَ أَسْأَلُكَ بِـحَقِّ الإِسْمِ الَّذِى دَعَاكَ بِهِ يُوسُفُ عَلَيْهِ السَّلَامُ فَأَنْجَيْتَهُ مِنْ غَيَابَةِ الْجُبِّ وَ مِنَ السِّجْنِ عَلَيْكَ يَا رَبِّ

And I ask You by the right of the name through which Yūsuf, peace be upon him, called upon You, by which You saved him from the depths of the well and from the prison, which You have imposed upon Yourself, O my [dear] Lord!

وَ أَسْأَلُكَ بِـحَقِّ الإِسْمِ الَّذِى دَعَاكَ بِهِ دَاوُدُ عَلَيْهِ السَّلَامُ فَجَعَلْتَهُ خَلِيفَةً فِى الْأَرْضِ عَلَيْكَ يَا رَبِّ

And I ask You by the right of the name through which Dāwūd, peace be upon him, called upon You, through which You made him the representative upon the Earth, which You have imposed upon Yourself, O my [dear] Lord!

وَ أَسْأَلُكَ بِـحَقِّ الإِسْمِ الَّذِى دَعَاكَ بِهِ سُلَيْمَانُ عَلَيْهِ السَّلَامُ فَوَهَبْتَ لَهُ مُلْكاً لَا يَنْبَغِى لِأَحَدٍ مِنْ بَعْدِهِ إِنَّكَ أَنْتَ الْوَهَّابُ عَلَيْكَ يَا رَبِّ

And I ask You by the right of the name through which Sulaymān, peace be upon him, called upon You, through which You granted him a kingdom which none after him would ever be worthy of attaining, as indeed You are the Ultimate Bestower, which You have imposed upon Yourself, O my [dear] Lord!

وَ أَسْأَلُكَ بِـحَقِّ الإِسْمِ الَّذِى دَعَاكَ بِهِ أَيُّوبُ عَلَيْهِ السَّلَامُ فَكَشَفْتَ عَنْهُ ضُرَّهُ وَ أَبْرَأْتَهُ مِنْ سُقْمِهِ عَلَيْكَ يَا رَبِّ

And I ask You by the right of the name through which Ayyūb, peace be upon him, called upon You, through which You relieved him of his difficulties, and You absolved him of his illness, which You have imposed upon Yourself, O my [dear] Lord!

وَ أَسْأَلُكَ بِحَقِّ الإِسْمِ الَّذِى دَعَاكَ بِهِ مُوسَى عَلَيْهِ السَّلَامُ وَ أَتَى إِلَى فِرْعَوْنَ فَأَلْبَسْتَهُ هَيْبَتَكَ عَلَيْكَ يَا رَبِّ

And I ask You by the right of the name through which Mūsā, peace be upon him, called upon You, and came towards Fir'awn (the Pharaoh) and by which You clothed him in Your splendor, which You have imposed upon Yourself, O my [dear] Lord!

وَ أَسْأَلُكَ بِحَقِّ الإِسْمِ الَّذِى دَعَاكَ بِهِ مُوسَى عَلَيْهِ السَّلَامُ عَلَى جَبَلِ الطُّورِ فَكَلَّمْتَهُ تَكْلِيماً عَلَيْكَ يَا رَبِّ

And I ask You by the right of the name through which Mūsā, peace be upon him, called upon You, on the mountain of al-Tūr by which You spoke to him a unique form of speaking, which You have imposed upon Yourself, O my [dear] Lord!

وَ أَسْأَلُكَ بِحَقِّ الإِسْمِ الَّذِى دَعَتْكَ بِهِ آسِيَةُ بِنْتُ مُزَاحِمٍ فَبَنَيْتَ لَهَا عِنْدَكَ بَيْتاً فِي الْجَنَّةِ عَلَيْكَ يَا رَبِّ

And I ask You by the right by the name through which Asiyah the daughter of Muzāḥīm, called upon You, through which You built for her in Your proximity, a house in Paradise, which You have imposed upon Yourself, O my [dear] Lord!

وَ أَسْأَلُكَ بِحَقِّ الإِسْمِ الَّذِى دَعَاكَ بِهِ بَنُو إِسْرَائِيلَ فَجَعَلْتَ لَهُمْ طَرِيقاً فِي الْبَحْرِ يَبَساً عَلَيْكَ يَا رَبِّ

And I ask You by the right of the name through which the Tribes of Isrā'īl (*Banī Isrā'īl*) called upon You, through which You made a way for them through the sea, which You have imposed upon Yourself, O my [dear] Lord!

وَ أَسْأَلُكَ بِحَقِّ الإِسْمِ الَّذِى دَعَاكَ بِهِ دَانِيَالُ فَنَجَّيْتَهُ مِنْ عَدُوِّهِ عَلَيْكَ يَا رَبِّ

And I ask You by the right of the name through which Dānyāl called upon You, through which You saved him from his enemies, which You have imposed upon Yourself, O my [dear] Lord!

وَ أَسْأَلُكَ بِحَقِّ الإِسْمِ الَّذِى دَعَاكَ بِهِ الْخَضِرُ عَلَيْهِ السَّلَامُ عَلَيْكَ يَا رَبِّ

And I ask You by the right of the name through which al-Khiḍr, peace be upon him, called upon You, which You have imposed upon Yourself, O my [dear] Lord!

وَ أَسْأَلُكَ بِحَقِّ الإِسْمِ الَّذِى دَعَاكَ بِهِ عِيسَى عَلَيْهِ السَّلَامُ فَأَبْرَأَ الْأَكْمَهَ وَ الْأَبْرَصَ وَ أَحْيَا الْمَوْتَى بِإِذْنِكَ عَلَيْكَ يَا رَبِّ

And I ask You by the right of the name through which ʿIsā, peace be upon him, called upon You, through which he cured the blind and the leper and gives life to the dead by Your permission, which You have imposed upon Yourself, O my [dear] Lord!

وَ أَسْأَلُكَ بِحَقِّ الإِسْمِ الَّذِى دَعَاكَ بِهِ مُحَمَّدٌ صَلَّى اللهُ عَلَيْهِ وَ آلِهِ فَاسْتَجَبْتَ لَهُ وَ كَفَيْتَهُ هَوْلَ عَدُوِّهِ عَلَيْكَ يَا رَبِّ

And I ask You by the right of the name through which Muḥammad, prayers of Allāh be upon him and his family, called upon You, through which You answered him and You sufficed him from the intrigues of his enemies, which You have imposed upon Yourself, O my [dear] Lord!

وَ أَسْأَلُكَ بِـحَقِّ الإِسْمِ الَّذِى دَعَاكَ بِهِ أَنْبِيَآؤُكَ وَ رُسُلُكَ فَأَجَبْتَ لَهُمْ
دُعَاءَهُمْ وَ آتَيْتَهُمْ سُؤْلَهُمْ عَلَيْكَ يَا رَبِّ

And I ask You by the right of the name through which all of Your prophets and Your messengers called upon You with, through which You answered their calls and You granted them that which they asked from You, which You have imposed upon Yourself, O my [dear] Lord!

وَ أَسْأَلُكَ بِـحَقِّ الإِسْمِ الَّذِى دَعَاكَ بِهِ الْأَنْبِيَآءُ وَ الْأَوْلِيَآءُ وَ الْأَصْفِيَآءُ وَ
الزُّهَّادُ وَ الْعُبَّادُ وَ الْأَبْدَالُ عَلَيْكَ يَا رَبِّ

And I ask You by the right of the name through which all of the prophets (*al-anbiyāʾ*) and close friends (*al-awliyāʾ*) chosen ones (*al-aṣfiyāhʾ*) and the exceptionally pious ones (*al-zuhhād*) and the exceedingly true worshippers (*al-ʿubbād*) and the extremely devout (*al-abdāl*) called upon You through, which You have imposed upon Yourself, O my [dear] Lord!

وَ أَسْأَلُكَ بِـحَقِّ الإِسْمِ الَّذِى قَامَتْ بِهِ السَّمَاوَاتُ السَّبْعُ وَ اسْتَقَرَّتْ بِهِ
الْأَرَضُونَ السَّبْعُ وَ اسْتَقَلَّتْ بِهِ الْجِبَالُ الرَّوَاسِى عَلَيْكَ يَا رَبِّ

And I ask You by the right of the name through which the seven heavens stand firm, and through which the seven earths are stabilized, and through which the firm mountains are made independent, which You have imposed upon Yourself, O my [dear] Lord!

وَ أَسْأَلُكَ بِـحَقِّ كُلِّ اسْمٍ لَهُ عِنْدَكَ حقا (حَقٌّ) عَلَيْكَ يَا رَبِّ

And I ask You by the right of every name which You truthfully have, which You have imposed upon Yourself, O my [dear] Lord!

وَ أَسْأَلُكَ بِـحَقِّ الإِسْمِ الَّذِى اصْطَفَيْتَهُ وَ لَمْ تُطْلِعْ عَلَيْهِ أَحَداً مِنَ الْمَلَائِكَةِ الْمُقَرَّبِينَ وَ الْأَنْبِيَاءِ وَ الْمُرْسَلِينَ عَلَيْكَ يَا رَبِّ

And I ask You by the right of the name through which You have chosen [for Yourself] and which You have not informed anyone from amongst the closest angels and the prophets and the messengers of, which You have imposed upon Yourself, O my [dear] Lord!

وَ أَسْأَلُكَ بِـحَقِّ الْبَيْتِ الْـحَرَامِ عَلَيْكَ يَا رَبِّ

And I ask You by the right of the Sacred House (*al-Bayt al-Ḥarām*), which You have imposed upon Yourself, O my [dear] Lord!

وَ أَسْأَلُكَ بِـحَقِّ الرُّكْنِ وَ الْمَقَامِ عَلَيْكَ يَا رَبِّ

And I ask You by the right of the Corner (*al-Rukn*) and the Station (*al-Maqām*), which You have imposed upon Yourself, O my [dear] Lord!

وَ أَسْأَلُكَ بِـحَقِّ الْبَيْتِ الْمَعْمُورِ عَلَيْكَ يَا رَبِّ

And I ask You by the right of the Ancient House (*al-Bayt al-Maʿmūr*), which You have imposed upon Yourself, O my [dear] Lord!

وَ أَسْأَلُكَ بِـحَقِّ الْمَشْعَرِ الْـحَرَامِ عَلَيْكَ يَا رَبِّ

And I ask You by the right of the Sacred Precinct (*al-Mashʿar al-Ḥarām*), which You have imposed upon Yourself, O my [dear] Lord!

وَ أَسْأَلُكَ بِـحَقِّ الصَّفَا وَ الْمَرْوَةِ عَلَيْكَ يَا رَبِّ

And I ask You by the right of [the two mountains of] *al-Ṣafā* and *al-Marwah*, which You have imposed upon Yourself, O my [dear] Lord!

وَ أَسْأَلُكَ بِـحَقِّ بِئْرِ زَمْزَمَ عَلَيْكَ يَا رَبِّ

And I ask You by the right of the well of *Zamzam*, which You have imposed on Yourself, O my dear Lord!

وَ أَسْأَلُكَ بِـحَقِّ الإِسْمِ الَّذِى دَعَاكَ بِهِ حُجَّاجُ بَيْتِكَ الْحَرَامِ عَلَيْكَ يَا رَبِّ

And I ask You by the right of the name through which the pilgrims *(ḥujjāj)* to Your Sacred House call You by, which You have imposed upon Yourself, O my [dear] Lord!

وَ أَسْأَلُكَ بِـحَقِّ الإِسْمِ الَّذِى تُحْيِي بِهِ الْأَمْوَاتَ وَ تُمِيتُ بِهِ الْأَحْيَآءَ عَلَيْكَ يَا رَبِّ

And I ask You by the right of the name through which You give life to the dead and through which You bring death to the living, which You have imposed upon Yourself, O my [dear] Lord!

وَ أَسْأَلُكَ بِـحَقِّ مُحَمَّدٍ الْمُصْطَفَى وَ أَهْلِ بَيْتِهِ عَلَيْهِمُ السَّلَامُ عَلَيْكَ يَا رَبِّ

And I ask You by the right of Muḥammad al-Muṣṭafā and his family, peace be upon them all, which You have imposed upon Yourself, O my [dear] Lord!

وَ أَسْأَلُكَ بِـحَقِّ سَعَةِ رَحْمَتِكَ عَلَيْكَ يَا رَبِّ

And I ask You by the right of the expanse of Your mercy, which You have imposed on Yourself, O my [dear] Lord!

وَ أَسْأَلُكَ بِـحَقِّ مَنْ حَقُّهُ عَلَيْكَ عَظِيمٌ عَلَيْكَ يَا رَبِّ

And I ask You by the right of the one who has the greatest of rights over You, which You have imposed upon Yourself, O my [dear] Lord!

وَ أَسْأَلُكَ بِـحَقِّ أَسْمَائِكَ الَّتِي إِذَا دُعِيتَ بِهَا أَجَبْتَ وَ إِذَا سُئِلْتَ بِهَا أَعْطَيْتَ عَلَيْكَ يَا رَبِّ

And I ask You by the right of those names through which if someone was to call upon You by them, You would reply to them and if someone was to ask You by them, You would grant them [what they ask for], which You have imposed upon Yourself, O my [dear] Lord!

وَ أَسْأَلُكَ بِـحَقِّ الرَّاغِبِينَ إِلَيْكَ عَلَيْكَ يَا رَبِّ

And I ask You by the right of those who are inclined towards You, which You have imposed upon Yourself, O my [dear] Lord!

وَ أَسْأَلُكَ بِـحَقِّ الْمُطِيعِينَ لَكَ وَ الْقَائِمِينَ بِأَمْرِكَ عَلَيْكَ يَا رَبِّ

And I ask You by the right of those who obey You and those who uphold Your orders, which You have imposed upon Yourself, O my [dear] Lord!

وَ أَسْأَلُكَ بِـحَقِّ الرُّوحَانِيِّينَ وَ الْمَلآئِكَةِ الْمُقَرَّبِينَ فِي السَّمَاوَاتِ وَ الْأَرَضِينَ عَلَيْكَ يَا رَبِّ

And I ask You by the right of the spiritual ones and the angels in close proximity [to You] who exist in the skies and the earths, which You have imposed upon Yourself, O my [dear] Lord!

صَلِّ عَلَىٰ مُحَمَّدٍ وَ آلِ مُحَمَّدٍ صَلَاةً كَثِيرَةً دَائِمَةً

Send [Your] many and continuous blessings upon Muḥammad and the family of Muḥammad.

وَ ارْحَمْنَا وَ عَافِنَا وَ اعْفُ عَنَّا وَ اغْفِرْ لَنَا وَ تُبْ عَلَيْنَا

And have mercy upon us and relieve us and forgive us and turn back towards us,

وَ أَصْلِحْ لَنَا شَأْنَنَا وَ اقْضِ حَوَائِجَنَا وَ حَقِّقْ آمَالَنَا وَ ارْضَ عَنَّا

And rectify for us our honour, and fulfill our requirements, and manifest our desires and make us pleased.

وَ انْظُرْ إِلَيْنَا بِعَيْنِ الرَّأْفَةِ وَ الرَّحْمَةِ

And cast a glance towards us with the eye of clemency and mercy.

وَ اغْفِرْ لَنَا وَ لِوَالِدَيْنَا وَ مَا وَلَدَا مِنَ الْمُؤْمِنِينَ وَ الْمُؤْمِنَاتِ

And forgive us and our parents and those who have brought us into this life from among the believing men and the believing women.

وَ ارْحَمْهُما كَما رَبَّيَانِي صَغِيراً

And have mercy upon them both [my mother and father] just as they brought me up with I was small.

وَ اجْزِهِمَا بِالْإِحْسَانِ إِحْسَاناً وَ بِالسَّيِّئَاتِ غُفْرَاناً

And reward them with goodness in return for the goodness [which they had previously shown] and forgiveness for the[ir] sins.

وَ عَافِنَا مِنَ الْآفَاتِ الدُّنْيَاوِيَّةِ مَا أَحْيَيْتَنَا

And relieve us from the tribulations of the temporal world for as long as we live.

وَ ادْفَعْ عَنَّا الْغَلَآءَ وَ الْوَبَآءَ وَ الْبَلَآءَ وَ الْأَوْجَاعَ وَ الْأَسْقَامَ وَ الْأَمْرَاضَ وَ الْقَحْطَ وَ الزَّلَازِلَ وَ الْفِتَنَ

And keep away from us the rising in prices, epidemics, hardships, soreness, sicknesses, illnesses, drought, earthquakes and seditions.

وَ جَوْرَ السُّلْطَانِ وَ كَيْدَ الشَّيْطَانِ وَ شَرَّ فَسَقَةِ الْجِنِّ وَ الْإِنْسِ

And [keep away from us the] injustices of the [unjust] governments, the plots of the Satan, and the evil of the maliciousness of the jinn and the human beings.

وَ شَرَّ فَسَقَةِ الْعَرَبِ وَ الْعَجَمِ

And from the evil of the lechery of the ʿArabs and the non-ʿArabs.

وَ أَهْلِكْ مَنْ فِي هَلَاكِهِ صَلَاحٌ لِلْمُؤْمِنِينَ

And destroy those whose destruction will improve [the condition] of the true believers.

وَ أَبْقِ مَنْ فِي بَقَائِهِ صَلَاحٌ لِلْمُؤْمِنِينَ

And preserve those whose preservation will improve [the condition] of the true believers.

أَللّٰهُمَّ وَ كُنْ لِوَلِيِّكَ فِي أَرْضِكَ وَ حُجَّتِكَ عَلٰى عِبادِكَ

O Allāh! And be for Your Guardian on Your earth, and for Your Proof over Your servants,

وَلِيّاً وَ حَافِظاً وَ قَائِداً وَ نَاصِراً وَ دَلِيلًا وَ عَيْناً حَتَّى تُسْكِنَهُ أَرْضَكَ طَوْعاً وَ تُمَتِّعَهُ فِيهَا طَوِيلًا

A friend, and a protector, and a leader, and a helper, and a guide, and an eye - until You determine to allow him to live on Your earth in obedience to You, and cause him to live in it for a long time.

وَ عَجِّلْ فَرَجَهُ وَ اجْعَلْنَا مِنْ شِيعَتِهِ وَ أَوْلِيَائِهِ وَ أَعْوَانِهِ وَ أَنْصَارِهِ وَ مُحِبِّيهِ وَ أَتْبَاعِهِ

And hasten his succour and allow us to be amongst his true followers and his close friends, and his helpers, and his assistants, and his lovers, and his disciples.

أَللّٰهُمَّ وَ أَحْيِنَا مَا كَانَتِ الْحَيَاةُ خَيْراً لَنَا

O Allāh! Allow us to live for as long as living is good for us [for our next life].

وَ أَخْرِجْنَا مِنَ الدُّنْيَا سَالِمِينَ

And cause us to leave from this transient world, spiritually sound.

وَ أَدْخِلْنَا الْـجَنَّةَ آمِنِينَ فِي جِوَارِ رَسُولِكَ مُحَمَّدٍ ﷺ الْمُصْطَفَى وَ الْأَئِمَّةِ مِنْ عِتْرَتِهِ صَلَوَاتُكَ عَلَيْهِمْ أَجْمَعِينَ

And enter us into Paradise, securely, in the presence of Your Messenger, Muḥammad al-Muṣṭafā and the leaders *(a'immah)* from his progeny, Your prayers be upon all of them.

أَللّٰهُمَّ وَ وَسِّعْ عَلَيْنَا مَعِيشَتَنَا

O Allāh! Expand the scope of our provisions;

وَ انْشُرْ عَلَيْنَا رَحْمَتَكَ وَ فَضْلَكَ

and spread out for us, Your mercy and Your grace;

وَ أَنْزِلْ عَلَيْنَا مِنْ بَرَكَاتِكَ

and send down upon us from Your blessings;

وَ ارْزُقْنَا رِزْقاً وَاسِعاً حَلَالًا طَيِّباً

and grant us sustenance that is ample, permissible and pure,

غَيْرَ مَمْنُونٍ وَ لَا مَحْظُورٍ

Neither something which we need to be obliged [to repay back to You], nor something which is prohibited;

بِفَضْلِكَ وَ رَحْمَتِكَ وَ كَرَمِكَ وَ جُودِكَ

By Your grace and Your mercy and Your nobility and Your liberality.

يَا ذَا الْفَضْلِ وَ الْمَنِّ وَ الْكَرَمِ وَ الْجُودِ وَ الْإِحْسَانِ الْقَدِيمِ

O the Possessor of Favour and Benevolence, and Nobility, and Liberality, and pre-eternal Goodness!

يَا ذَا الْجَلَالِ وَ الْإِكْرَامِ إِنَّكَ عَلَىٰ كُلِّ شَيْءٍ قَدِيرٌ

O the Possessor of Greatness and Majesty – indeed You have power over all things.

وَ الْحَمْدُ لِلّٰهِ رَبِّ الْعَالَمِينَ

And all praise belongs to Allāh, the Lord of all the Worlds.

وَ صَلَاتُهُ عَلَىٰ مُحَمَّدٍ خَاتَمِ النَّبِيِّينَ وَ آلِهِ الطَّيِّبِينَ الطَّاهِرِينَ

And His [Allāh's] prayers be upon Muḥammad, the finality of the prophets and upon His immaculate pure family,

وَ سَلَّمَ تَسْلِيماً

and may complete greetings be upon all of them!

15. Focus of Allāh ﷻ upon His Servants

Imam Jaʿfar al-Ṣādiq ؑ has said:

لَمَّا أَمَرَ اللّٰهُ عَزَّ وَ جَلَّ هٰذِهِ الْآيَاتِ أَنْ يَهْبِطْنَ إِلَىٰ الْأَرْضِ

تَعَلَّقْنَ بِالْعَرْشِ وَ قُلْنَ أَيْ رَبِّ إِلَىٰ أَيْنَ تُهْبِطُنَا إِلَىٰ أَهْلِ الْخَطَايَا

وَ الذُّنُوبِ فَأَوْحَى اللّٰهُ عَزَّ وَ جَلَّ إِلَيْهِنَّ أَنِ اهْبِطْنَ فَوَ عِزَّتِي

وَ جَلَالِي لَا يَتْلُوكُنَّ أَحَدٌ مِنْ آلِ مُحَمَّدٍ وَ شِيعَتِهِمْ فِي دُبُرِ
مَا افْتَرَضْتُ عَلَيْهِ مِنَ الْمَكْتُوبَةِ فِي كُلِّ يَوْمٍ إِلَّا نَظَرْتُ إِلَيْهِ
بِعَيْنِيَ الْمَكْنُونَةِ فِي كُلِّ يَوْمٍ سَبْعِينَ نَظْرَةً أَقْضِي لَهُ فِي كُلِّ
نَظْرَةٍ سَبْعِينَ حَاجَةً وَ قَبِلْتُهُ عَلَى مَا فِيهِ مِنَ الْمَعَاصِي وَ
هِيَ أُمُّ الْكِتَابِ وَ شَهِدَ اللهُ أَنَّهُ لاَ إِلٰهَ إِلَّا هُوَ وَ الْمَلائِكَةُ وَ أُولُوا
الْعِلْمِ وَ آيَةُ الْكُرْسِيِّ وَ آيَةُ الْمُلْكِ

When Allāh, the Noble and Grand, commanded the verse [mentioned at the end of this tradition] to descend upon the Earth, they (the verses) attached themselves to the Throne (of Allāh) and said: 'O Lord! Where are you sending us? Are you sending us to a place of [the people of] transgressions and sins?' Allāh, the Noble and Grand, revealed to them (the verses): 'Go down as I swear by My Greatness and My Majesty that not a single person from among the progeny of Muḥammad and their followers (*shīʿa*) who recite you - above that which I have made obligatory upon them [meaning the five canonical prayers] everyday - except that I will glance at them with a special glance with My [metaphorical] eyes seventy times every day [meaning multiple times]; and with every glance, I will fulfill seventy of their desires, and I will accept (their supplications) - even though they have sins (on their record). These verses are made up of the Basis of the Book (Umm al-Kitāb – meaning Sūrah al-Ḥamd[194]) and the verse ﴾Allāh bears witness that there is no other entity worthy of worship except for Him and so do the angels (bear witness to this) and so do those

[194] *Quran*, Sūrah al-Ḥamd (1), verses 1-7.

who possess knowledge﴾[195] and Āyatul Kursī[196] and the verse of dominion - ﴿Say: To Allāh belongs the Kingdom...﴾[197 and 198]

Therefore, based on this tradition, one should recite Sūrah al-Fātiḥa, followed by:

﴿شَهِدَ ٱللَّهُ أَنَّهُ لاَ إِلَـٰهَ إِلاَّ هُوَ وَٱلْمَلاَئِكَةُ وَأُوْلُواْ ٱلْعِلْمِ
قَآئِماً بِٱلْقِسْطِ لاَ إِلَـٰهَ إِلاَّ هُوَ ٱلْعَزِيزُ ٱلْحَكِيمُ ١٨﴾

Allāh bears witness that there is no god but He, and (so do) the angels and those possessed of knowledge, maintaining His creation with justice; there is no god but He, the Mighty, the Wise.

Then recite Āyatul Kursī followed by:

﴿قُلِ ٱللَّهُمَّ مَالِكَ ٱلْمُلْكِ تُؤْتِي ٱلْمُلْكَ مَن تَشَآءُ
وَتَنزِعُ ٱلْمُلْكَ مِمَّنْ تَشَآءُ وَتُعِزُّ مَن تَشَآءُ وَتُذِلُّ مَن
تَشَآءُ بِيَدِكَ ٱلْخَيْرُ إِنَّكَ عَلَىٰ كُلِّ شَيْءٍ قَدِيرٌ ٢٥٣﴾

Say: O Allāh, Master of the Kingdom! You give the kingdom to whomsoever You please and take away the kingdom from whomsoever You please, and You exalt whom You please and abase whom You please. In Your hand is all good; surely You have power over all things.

16. Waging Sacred Struggle Alongside the Prophets

It has been narrated from Thaʿlabī by his chain of narrators from

---

[195] *Quran*, Sūrah Āle ʿImrān (3), verse 18.

[196] *Quran*, Sūrah al-Baqarah (2), verse 255.

[197] Ibid., verse 26.

[198] *Al-Uṣūl min Al-Kāfī*, vol. 4, p. 426.

ʿAbdullāh b. ʿUmar that he narrates Prophet Muḥammad ﷺ as having said:

مَـنْ قَـرَءَ آيَـةَ الْكُـرْسِيِّ دُبُـرِ كُلِّ صَـلَاةٍ كَانَ الَّـذِي يَتَـوَلَّى قَبْـضَ نَفْسِـهِ ذُوالْـجَلَالِ وَ الإِكْـرَامِ وَ كَانَ كَمَـنْ قَاتَـلَ مَـعَ أَنْبِيَـآءِ اللّٰـهِ حَتّٰـى إِسْتَشْـهَدَ

A person who recites Āyatul Kursī after every *ṣalāt* will be one whom the Possessor of Greatness and Nobility (Allāh) will take his soul (directly), and that person will be like the one who fought alongside the prophets of Allāh until they attained martyrdom.

17. Leader of Sūrah al-Baqarah

The Messenger of Allāh ﷺ has said:

سَيِّدُ الْبَـشَرِ آدَمُ وَ سَـيِّدُ الْعَـرَبِ مُحَمَّـدٌ وَ لاَ فَخْـرَ وَ سَـيِّدُ الْفُـرْسِ سَـلْمَانٌ وَ سَـيِّدُ الـرُّوْمِ صُهَيـبٌ وَ سَـيِّدُ الْـحَبَشَةِ بِـلَالٌ وَ سَـيِّدُ الْـجِبَالُ الطُّـوْرٌ وَ سَـيِّدُ الشَّـجَرِ السِّـدْرُ وَ سَـيِّدُ الشُّـهُورِ الأَشْـهُوُر الْـحُرُمِ وَ سَـيِّدُ الأَيَّـامِ يُـومَ الْـجُمُعَةِ وَ سَـيِّدُ الْـكَلَامِ الْقُرَآنُ وَ سَـيِّدُ الْقُـرَآنِ الْبَقَـرَةِ وَ سَـيِّدُ الْبَقَـرَةِ آيَـةُ الْكُـرْسِيِّ.

The leader of all of the human beings is Ādam; and the leader of all of the ʿArabs is Muḥammad, however (I) do not boast or show pride in regards to this; and the leader of the Persians is Salmān; and the leader of the Romans is Ṣuhayb; and the leader of the Ethiopians is Bilāl; and the leader of all the mountains is (the mountain) of al-Ṭūr; and the leader of all of the trees is (the tree of) al-Sidr; and the leader of all of the months are the Inviolable Months [the four months namely:

Rajab, *Dhul Qa'dah*, *Dhūl Ḥijjah*, and *Muḥarram*]; and the leader of all of the days (of the week) is Friday; and the leader of all words is the Quran; and the leader of the Quran is (Sūrah) al-Baqarah; and the leader of (Sūrah) al-Baqarah is Āyatul Kursī.[199]

18. Intimate Friend of the Truthful and the True Worshippers

Imām ʿAlī ﷺ narrated that he heard the Messenger of Allāh ﷺ say:

لاَ يُوَاظِبُ عَلَيْهَا إِلاَّ صِدِّيقٌ أَوْ عَابِدٌ

No one will continuously recite it (Āyatul Kursī) except an extremely truthful person (*ṣiddīq*) or a true worshipper (*ʿābid*).[200]

19. Cure of Physical Ailments

It has been narrated from Ibn Nabāta in a lengthy tradition in which it is mentioned that a man stood up in the presence of the Commander of the Faithful, ʿAlī ﷺ and said:

إِنَّ فِي بَطْنِي مَاءً أَصْفَرَ فَهَلْ مِنْ شَفَآءٍ؟

I have jaundice – is there a cure for me?

The Imām replied:

قَالَ: نَعَمْ. تَكْتُبُ عَلىٰ بَطْنِكَ آيَةَ الْكُرْسِيِّ وَ تَكْتُبُهَا وَ تَشْرِبُهَا وَ تَجْعَلُهَا ذَخِيرَةٌ فِي بَطْنِكَ فَتَبْرَأُ بِإِذْنِ اللّٰهِ. فَفَعَلَ الرَّجُلُ فَبَرَأَ بِإِذْنِ اللّٰهِ تَعَالىٰ

Yes. Write Āyatul Kursī on your stomach and write it on a piece of paper, and tie it to your stomach and

[199] *Majmaʿ al-Bayān*, vol. 2, p. 360.
[200] Ibid.

you will be cured, by the permission of Allāh. The man did as he was told and he was cured, by the permission of Allāh, the Most High.[201]

20. Guarantee from an Infallible Imām

It has been narrated from Imām al-Ḥasan ﷺ that he said:

أَنَا ضَامِنٌ لِمَنْ قَرَأَ الْعِشْرِينَ آيَةً أَنْ يَعْصِمَهُ اللّٰهُ مِنْ كُلِّ سُلْطَانٍ ظَالِمٍ وَ مِنْ كُلِّ شَيْطَانٍ مَارِدٍ وَ مِنْ كُلِّ لِصٍّ عَادٍ وَ مِنْ كُلِّ سَبُعٍ ضَارٍ وَ هِيَ آيَةُ الْكُرْسِيِّ وَ ثَلَاثُ آيَاتٍ مِنَ الْأَعْرَافِ إِنَّ رَبَّكُمُ اللّٰهُ إِلَى الْمُحْسِنِينَ وَ عَشْرٌ مِنْ أَوَّلِ الصَّافَّاتِ وَ ثَلَاثٌ مِنَ الرَّحْمَنِ يا مَعْشَرَ الْجِنِّ وَ الْإِنْسِ إِلَى تَنْتَصِرانِ وَ ثَلَاثٌ مِنْ آخِرِ سُورَةِ الْحَشْرِ هُوَ اللّٰهُ إِلَى آخِرِهَا.

I am the guarantor for that person who recites twenty verses (from the Noble Quran) that Allāh will safeguard him from every oppressive regime, from the freed satan, from every sinner and from every harmful creature – and these [twenty verses] are: Āyatul Kursī, three verses from (Sūrah) al-Aʿrāf [verses 54 to 56]; the first ten verses from (Sūrah) al-Ṣaffāt, three verses from (Sūrah) al-Raḥmān[verses 34 and 35]; and three verses from the end of (Sūrah) al-Ḥashr.[202] [NOTE: The text of these verses is below in the order mentioned above – Tr.]

Sūrah al-Baqarah (2), verse 255:

﴿ٱللَّهُ لَآ إِلَـٰهَ إِلَّا هُوَ ٱلْحَىُّ ٱلْقَيُّومُ لَا تَأْخُذُهُۥ سِنَةٌ وَلَا

[201] *Biḥār al-Anwār*, vol. 89, p. 272.
[202] Ibid., p. 271.

نَـومٌ لَّهُ مَـا فِى ٱلسَّـمَاوَاتِ وَمَـا فِى ٱلأَرْضِ مَـن ذَا ٱلَّذِى يَشْـفَعُ عِنْـدَهُ إِلاَّ بِإِذْنِـهِ يَعْلَـمُ مَـا بَـيْنَ أَيْدِيهِـمْ وَمَـا خَلْفَهُـمْ وَلاَ يُحِيطُـونَ بِشَىْءٍ مِّـنْ عِلْمِـهِ إِلاَّ بِمَـا شَـآءَ وَسِـعَ كُرْسِـيُّهُ ٱلسَّـمَاوَاتِ وَٱلأَرْضَ وَلاَ يَـؤُودُهُ حِفْظُهُمَـا وَهُـوَ ٱلْعَـلِىُّ ٱلْعَظِيـمُ ﴿٢٥٥﴾

Allāh is He besides Whom there is no god, the Ever-Living, the Self-Subsisting by Whom all subsist; slumber does not overtake Him nor sleep; whatever is in the heavens and whatever is in the earth is His; who is he that can intercede with Him but by His permission? He knows what is before them and what is behind them, and they cannot comprehend anything out of His knowledge except what He pleases, His knowledge extends over the heavens and the earth, and the preservation of them both tires Him not, and He is the Most High, the Great.

Sūrah al-Aʿrāf (7), verses 54-56:

﴿إِنَّ رَبَّكُـمُ ٱللهُ ٱلَّذِى خَلَـقَ ٱلسَمَاوَاتِ وَٱلأَرْضَ فِى سِـتَّةِ أَيَّـامٍ ثُـمَّ ٱسْـتَوَىٰ عَلَى ٱلْعَـرْشِ يُغْـشِى ٱللَّيْـلَ ٱلنَّهَـارَ يَطْلُبُـهُ حَثِيثـاً وَٱلشَّـمْسَ وَٱلْقَمَـرَ وَٱلنُّجُـومَ مُسَـخَّرَاتٍ بِأَمْـرِهِ أَلاَ لَهُ ٱلْخَلْـقُ وَٱلأَمْـرُ تَبَـارَكَ ٱللهُ رَبُّ ٱلْعَالَمِـينَ ﴿٥٤﴾ ٱدْعُـواْ رَبَّكُـمْ تَـضَرُّعاً وَخُفْيَـةً إِنَّـهُ لاَ يُحِبُّ ٱلْمُعْتَدِيـنَ ﴿٥٥﴾ وَلاَ تُفْسِـدُواْ فِى ٱلأَرْضِ بَعْـدَ إِصْلاَحِهَـا وَٱدْعُـوهُ خَوْفـاً وَطَمَعـاً إِنَّ رَحْمَـةَ ٱللهِ قَرِيـبٌ مِّـنَ ٱلْمُحْسِـنِينَ ﴿٥٦﴾

Surely your Lord is Allāh, Who created the heavens and the earth in six periods of time, and He is firm in power; He throws the veil of night over the day, which it pursues incessantly; and (He created) the sun and the moon and the stars, made subservient by His command; surely His is the creation and the command; blessed is Allāh, the Lord of the worlds. Call on your Lord humbly and secretly; surely He does not love those who exceed the limits. And do not make mischief in the earth after its reformation, and call on Him fearing and hoping; surely the mercy of Allāh is close to those who do good (to others).

Sūrah al-Ṣāffāt (37), verses 1-10:

﴿وَٱلصَّافَّاتِ صَفًّا ۝١ فَٱلزَّاجِرَاتِ زَجْراً ۝٢ فَٱلتَّالِيَاتِ
ذِكْراً ۝٣ إِنَّ إِلَـٰهَكُمْ لَوَاحِدٌ ۝٤ رَّبُّ ٱلسَّمَاوَاتِ وَٱلأَرْضِ
وَمَا بَيْنَهُمَا وَرَبُّ ٱلْمَشَارِقِ ۝٥ إِنَّا زَيَّنَّا ٱلسَّمَآءَ ٱلدُّنْيَا
بِزِينَةٍ ٱلْكَوَاكِبِ ۝٦ وَحِفْظاً مِّن كُلِّ شَيْطَانٍ مَّارِدٍ ۝٧
لاَّ يَسَّمَّعُونَ إِلَىٰ ٱلْمَلإِ ٱلأَعْلَىٰ وَيُقْذَفُونَ مِن كُلِّ جَانِبٍ
۝٨ دُحُوراً وَلَهُمْ عَذَابٌ وَاصِبٌ ۝٩ إِلاَّ مَنْ خَطِفَ
ٱلْخَطْفَةَ فَأَتْبَعَهُ شِهَابٌ ثَاقِبٌ ۝١٠﴾

I swear by those who draw themselves out in ranks. Then those who drive away with reproof. Then those who recite, being mindful, most surely your Allāh is One: The Lord of the heavens and the earth and what is between them, and Lord of the easts. Surely We have adorned the nearest heaven with an adornment, the stars; and (there is) a safeguard against every rebellious

Shaitan. They cannot listen to the exalted assembly and they are thrown at from every side, being driven off, and for them is a perpetual chastisement; except him who snatches off but once, then there follows him a brightly shining flame.

Sūrah al-Raḥmān (55), verses 34-35:

﴿فَبِأَيِّ آلَاءِ رَبِّكُمَا تُكَذِّبَانِ ﴿٣٤﴾ يُرْسَلُ عَلَيْكُمَا
شُوَاظٌ مِّن نَّارٍ وَنُحَاسٌ فَلَا تَنتَصِرَانِ ﴿٣٥﴾﴾

Which then of the bounties of your Lord will you deny? The flames of fire and smoke will be sent on you two, then you will not be able to defend yourselves.

Sūrah al-Ḥashr (59), verses 22-24:

﴿هُوَ ٱللَّهُ ٱلَّذِى لَآ إِلَٰهَ إِلَّا هُوَ عَالِمُ ٱلْغَيْبِ وَٱلشَّهَادَةِ
هُوَ ٱلرَّحْمَٰنُ ٱلرَّحِيمُ ﴿٢٢﴾ هُوَ ٱللَّهُ ٱلَّذِى لَآ إِلَٰهَ إِلَّا هُوَ
ٱلْمَلِكُ ٱلْقُدُّوسُ ٱلسَّلَامُ ٱلْمُؤْمِنُ ٱلْمُهَيْمِنُ ٱلْعَزِيزُ
ٱلْجَبَّارُ ٱلْمُتَكَبِّرُ سُبْحَانَ ٱللَّهِ عَمَّا يُشْرِكُونَ ﴿٢٣﴾ هُوَ ٱللَّهُ
ٱلْخَالِقُ ٱلْبَارِئُ ٱلْمُصَوِّرُ لَهُ ٱلْأَسْمَآءُ ٱلْحُسْنَىٰ يُسَبِّحُ لَهُ مَا
فِى ٱلسَّمَاوَاتِ وَٱلْأَرْضِ وَهُوَ ٱلْعَزِيزُ ٱلْحَكِيمُ ﴿٢٤﴾﴾

He is Allāh besides Whom there is no god; the Knower of the unseen and the seen; He is the Beneficent, the Merciful. He is Allāh, besides Whom there is no god; the King, the Holy, the Giver of peace, the Granter of security, Guardian over all, the Mighty, the Supreme, the Possessor of every greatness. Glory be to Allāh from what they set up (with Him). He is Allāh, the

Creator, the Maker, the Fashioner; His are the most excellent names; whatever is in the heavens and the earth declares His glory; and He is the Mighty, the Wise.

21. Recitation in the State of Prostration (Sajdah)

It has been narrated by Imam Muḥammad al-Bāqir ﵇ that he said:

مَنْ قَرَأَ آيَةَ الْكُرْسِيِّ وَ هُوَ سَاجِدٌ لَمْ يَدْخُلِ النَّارَ أَبَداً

A person who recites Āyatul Kursī while in the state of sajdah (prostration) will never enter into the fire of hell.[203]

22. How to Enter into Paradise

It has been narrated that the Noble Prophet ﷺ said:

مَنْ قَرَأَ آيَةَ الْكُرْسِيِّ فِي دُبُرِ كُلِّ صَلاَةٍ لَمْ يَمْنَعْهُ دُخُولَ الْجَنَّةِ إِلاَّ الْمَوْتَ

A person who recites Āyatul Kursī after every *ṣalāt* will find that nothing will prevent him from entering into Paradise except for death.[204]

23. Protection for One's Neighbours

It has been narrated that the Noble Prophet ﷺ said:

مَنْ قَرَأَهَا حِينَ نَامَ آمَنَهُ اللّهُ تَعَالي جَارَهُ وَ أَهْلَ الدُّوَيرَاتِ حَوْلَهُ

A person who recites it (Āyatul Kursī) at the time of sleep, Allāh the Most High, will safeguard the

---

[203] Ibid., p. 269.

[204] Ibid.

neighbour of that person, and will also protect the others who live around him (in his neighbourhood).[205]

24. Cure for Eye Pain

It has been narrated that the Commander of the Faithful, Imām ʿAlī said:

إِذَا اشْتَكَى أَحَدُكُمْ عَيْنَهُ فَلْيَقْرَأْ آيَةَ الْكُرْسِيِّ وَلْيُضْمِرْ فِي نَفْسِهِ أَنَّهَا تَبْرَأُ فَإِنَّهُ يُعَافَى إِنْشَاءَ اللَّهُ

Whenever one of you complains about pain in the eyes, then him recite Āyatul Kursī, and have deep certainty within your heart that it will cure you, and indeed, the pain in your eyes will get better - God Willing.[206]

25. Recite it Before One Leaves the House

It has been narrated that the Commander of the Faithful, Imām ʿAlī said:

وَ لْيَقْرَأْ إِذَا خَرَجَ مِنْ بَيْتِهِ الْآيَاتِ مِنْ آخِرِ آلِ عِمْرَانَ وَ آيَةَ الْكُرْسِيِّ وَ إِنَّا أَنْزَلْنَاهُ وَ أُمَّ الْكِتَابِ فَإِنَّ فِيهَا قَضَاءً لِحَوَائِجِ الدُّنْيَا وَ الْآخِرَةِ

When you leave your house, each one of you should recite verses from the end of (Sūrah) Āle ʿImrān[207], Āyatul Kursī, Sūrah al-Qadr and Ummul Kitāb (Sūrah al-Fātiḥa) because in this lies the attainment of one's desires in this world and in the next.[208]

---

[205] Ibid.

[206] Ibid., p. 263.

[207] *Quran*, Sūrah Āle ʿImrān (3), verses 190-200. These are mentioned in Appendix I in this book. (Tr.)

[208] *Al-Khiṣāl*, vol. 2, p. 162.

26. Amazing Anecdote

It has been narrated by Imām Jaʿfar al-Ṣādiq ﷺ that one day, two brothers came to the Noble Prophet ﷺ and said to him: "We want to go to the Levant for business – can you please teach us something that we can recite if we are confronted by any dangers or enemies?" The Prophet of Islam ﷺ replied: "When you arrive to a location [where you want to set up a tent] and have completed your *ʿIshā* prayers and want to go and rest, then go near your belongings and start by reciting the *tasbīḥ* of Lady Fāṭima ﷺ, followed by Āyatul Kursī, as this will safeguard you and your wealth." The two people did as they were ordered (by the Prophet) and camped at a location. That evening, a spy was sent from among a band of thieves to see if the brothers were awake or sleeping. When the spy approached their location, he only saw a wall and nothing else! He returned back to his camp and told his cohorts what he saw – they immediately began to mock him and say that he was scared and that is why he was saying what he was! The band of thieves went to see the two people (whom they hoped to rob from) and when they reached to the place they were supposed to be, they saw exactly what their accomplice had seen. When morning came, they saw that the scene around the entire area had changed – not only was there no wall, but they actually saw the traders and all of their belongings which they were carrying to trade in the Levant! They became surprised and approached the brothers and explained to them what transpired that previous night, and asked them what had happened. The brothers replied that: "The Prophet of Islam ﷺ had taught us something to recite to save ourselves from the thieves!" The thieves promised the brothers that they were free to leave and that they would never be troubled again by them and they affirmed that not a single thief would ever be able to cause them any harm [due to what they had been taught by the

Prophet ﷺ].[209]

27. Way of Imam al-Sajjād ‎(ع)

It has been narrated that on Friday, just after sunrise, Imām al-Sajjād ‎(ع) would continuously recite Āyatul Kursī until *ḍhuhr* time and when he finished his (afternoon) prayers, he would be busy reciting *Sūrah al-Qadr*.[210]

28. Reward of Worship for Forty Years

One of the acts of worship to be performed on the night of *ʿEid al-Fiṭr* is a special *ṣalāt* which has been mentioned by the late scholar, Shaykh ʿAbbās al-Qummī in which a total of fourteen *rakʿat* are to be performed. In each *rakʿat*, Sūrah al-Fātiḥa and Āyatul Kursī are read once, and Sūrah al-Ikhlāṣ is recited three times. He has stated (based on traditions) that such a prayer will be rewarded with the worship of forty years for each *rakʿat* performed, and also one will get the reward of all of those who have fasted and prayed during that particular month.[211]

29. Reciting it During a Journey

It has been narrated from Imām Jaʿfar al-Ṣādiq ‎(ع) that: "Whoever recites Āyatul Kursī every night while on a journey will remain safe, and anything that is with him will also be safeguarded."[212]

30. Etiquette of Travelling

It has been mentioned in regards to the etiquette of travelling that one should begin any trip by saying farewell to one's family, and then while standing in one's house, one should recite the *tasbīḥ* of Fāṭima al-Zahrā ‎(ع); then recite Sūrah al-Ḥamd once towards

---

[209] *Biḥār al-Anwār*, vol. 89, p. 266.

[210] *Mafātīḥ al-Jinān*.

[211] Ibid.

[212] Ibid.

his front, once towards his right side, once towards his left side, and then recite Āyatul Kursī in the same three directions and then begin one's journey.[213]

31. First Rains in Spring

The venerated scholar, Sayyid ʿAlī ibn Ṭāwūs has narrated a tradition which states: "One day, a group of companions were sitting with one another when Prophet Muḥammad ﷺ entered into the gathering and greeted those who were present. They all replied to his greeting and the Prophet then said: 'Shall I teach you a medication which [angel] Jibrāʾīl taught to me for which you will not require any medicine from a doctor?' ʿAlī and Salmān and a host of others asked: 'What medication is this' The Prophet replied: 'In the month of *Nisān* of the Roman calendar [mid-March until mid-April], collect the rain water and recite upon it: Sūrah al-Fātiḥa, Āyatul Kursī, Sūrah al-Ikhlāṣ, Sūrah al-Falaq, Sūrah al-Nās and Sūrah al-Kāfirūn seventy times each over it. (In other narrations it has been mentioned that Sūrah al-Qadr should be recited seventy times, while Āyatul Kursī should be recited seventy times followed by '*Lā Ilāha Illallāh*' seventy times and then *ṣalawāt* upon the Prophet and his family seventy times, and that this should be performed for seven days straight – in the morning and afternoon and then the water should be consumed.)' The Prophet ﷺ then said: 'By the right of the Creator who raised me up as a Prophet, I swear that whatever ailments your body is facing will be relieved, and all of the pains which are in your body and bones will be removed from you, and if there were some illness which is written in your tablet (of what will happen to you), then it will be removed, and I swear by the Lord that if a person does not have a child and wants one and performs the above actions, then they will

[213] Ibid.

be granted a child...'"[214]

32. Ṣalāt for the Deceased

As our religious heritage states, on the first night after a believer passes away, other people should perform a two *rakʿat ṣalāt* for the safety of the deceased one - and this is known as *ṣalāt* for the first night after death (*Laylat al-Dafan* – also known as *Ṣalāt al-Wahshat.*) It is performed in the following manner: In the first *rakʿat,* one should recite Sūrah al-Ḥamd and then Āyatul Kursī one time; and in the second *rakʿat,* one should recite Sūrah al-Ḥamd followed by Sūrah al-Qadr ten times; and once the prayer is finished, then the following supplication should be recited to "complete" the *ṣalāt*:

أَللّٰهُمَّ صَلِّ عَلىٰ مُحَمَّدٍ وَ آلِ مُحَمَّدٍ وَ ابْعَثْ ثَوَابَهَا إِلىٰ قَبْرِ فُلاَنِ ابْنِ فُلاَنٍ.

> O' Allāh! Send down blessings upon Muḥammad and the family of Muḥammad and grant the reward of this prayer to the grave of **so-and-so**. [In the place of **so-and-so**, you should take the name of the deceased and his/her father].

Sayyid ibn Ṭāwūs has narrated a tradition from the Noble Prophet ﷺ in which he said: "There is no other time which is more difficult for a deceased person than the first night in the grave. Therefore, show mercy upon your deceased one by offering charity in their honour, and if you do not have anything to offer as charity, then one of you should perform a two *rakʿat ṣalāt* in the following manner." The Prophet then narrated the method of this prayer, as we have mentioned above.[215]

---

[214] Ibid. For further details, refer to the section detailing the benefits of the spring rain fall in *Mafātīḥ al-Jinān*.

[215] Ibid., Section on the *ṣalāt* for the first night after burial.

33. Advice from the Prophet to Imām ʿAlī

The Prophet of Islam said to Imām ʿAlī the following: "O ʿAlī! I advise you to recite Āyatul Kursī after every obligatory prayer. Indeed, no one can enact this except a prophet, a truthful person or a witness."

In another tradition it has been mentioned that: "Whoever recites Āyatul Kursī after every obligatory prayer will have one's prayer accepted, will be in the protection of Allāh, and Allāh will safeguard that person from any physical ailments and from the performance of sins."[216]

34. Ṣalāt to Repay a Debt

Shaykh al-Ṭūsī has narrated that a man once came to Imam Jaʿfar al-Ṣādiq and said: "I complain to you, O my master that I am drowning in debt and [I also complain to you about] an oppressive regime that is over me. Can you teach me a supplication through which I will be able to acquire such wealth that I will be able to pay back my debts and through which I can be protected from the oppressive ruler?" The Imām replied: "Once the night falls, perform a two *rakʿat ṣalāt* and in the first *rakʿat*, recite Sūrah al-Ḥamd followed by Āyatul Kursī and in the second *rakʿat* recite Sūrah al-Ḥamd followed by the last verses of Sūrah al-Ḥashr until the end of the chapter [as mentioned below]:

﴿لَوْ أَنزَلْنَا هَٰذَا ٱلْقُرْءَانَ عَلَىٰ جَبَلٍ لَّرَأَيْتَهُۥ خَٰشِعًا
مُّتَصَدِّعًا مِّنْ خَشْيَةِ ٱللَّهِ وَتِلْكَ ٱلْأَمْثَٰلُ نَضْرِبُهَا
لِلنَّاسِ لَعَلَّهُمْ يَتَفَكَّرُونَ ﴿٢١﴾ هُوَ ٱللَّهُ ٱلَّذِى لَآ إِلَٰهَ إِلَّا
هُوَ عَٰلِمُ ٱلْغَيْبِ وَٱلشَّهَٰدَةِ هُوَ ٱلرَّحْمَٰنُ ٱلرَّحِيمُ ﴿٢٢﴾

[216] Ibid., Section on the general recommended supplications after the *ṣalāt*.

هُوَ ٱللَّهُ ٱلَّذِى لَآ إِلَٰهَ إِلَّا هُوَ ٱلْمَلِكُ ٱلْقُدُّوسُ ٱلسَّلَٰمُ ٱلْمُؤْمِنُ ٱلْمُهَيْمِنُ ٱلْعَزِيزُ ٱلْجَبَّارُ ٱلْمُتَكَبِّرُ سُبْحَٰنَ ٱللَّهِ عَمَّا يُشْرِكُونَ ﴿٢٣﴾ هُوَ ٱللَّهُ ٱلْخَٰلِقُ ٱلْبَارِئُ ٱلْمُصَوِّرُ لَهُ ٱلْأَسْمَآءُ ٱلْحُسْنَىٰ يُسَبِّحُ لَهُ مَا فِى ٱلسَّمَٰوَٰتِ وَٱلْأَرْضِ وَهُوَ ٱلْعَزِيزُ ٱلْحَكِيمُ ﴿٢٤﴾

Had We sent down this Quran on a mountain, you would certainly have seen it falling down, splitting asunder because of the fear of Allāh, and We set forth these parables to men that they may reflect. He is Allāh besides Whom there is no god; the Knower of the unseen and the seen; He is the Beneficent, the Merciful. He is Allāh, besides Whom there is no god; the King, the Holy, the Giver of peace, the Granter of security, Guardian over all, the Mighty, the Supreme, the Possessor of every greatness. Glory be to Allah from what they set up (with Him). He is Allāh the Creator, the Maker, the Fashioner; His are the most excellent names; whatever is in the heavens and the earth declares His glory; and He is the Mighty, the Wise.

Once the *ṣalāt* is complete, take the Quran, place it on your head and recite:

بِحَقِّ هٰذَا الْقُرآنِ وَ بِحَقِّ مَنْ أَرْسَلْتَهُ بِهِ وَ بِحَقِّ كُلِّ مُؤْمِنٍ مَدَحْتَهُ فِيهِ وَ بِحَقِّكَ عَلَيْهِمْ فَلاَ أَحَدٌ أَعْرَفُ بِحَقِّكَ مِنْكَ

[O Allāh!] For the sake of this Quran and for the sake of the one whom You sent it to and for the sake of every single believer whom You have praised therein and for Your rights upon them all indeed there is not a single person who is more knowing of Your rights than You Yourself.

Then say each of the following ten times each:

بِكَ يَا اللهُ

For Your sake, O Allāh!

بِكَ يَا مُحَمَّدُ

For your sake, O Muḥammad

بِكَ يَا عَلِيُّ

For your sake, O ʿAlī

بِكِ يَا فَاطِمَةُ

For your sake, O Fāṭima

بِكَ يَا حَسَنُ

For your sake, O Ḥasan

بِكَ يَا حُسَيْنُ

For your sake, O Ḥusayn

بِكَ يَا عَلِيِّ بْنِ الْحُسَيْنِ

For your sake, O ʿAlī the son of al-Ḥusayn

بِكَ يَا مُحَمَّدَ بْنَ عَلِيٍّ

For your sake, O Muḥammad the son of ʿAlī

بِكَ يَا جَعْفَرَ بْنَ مُحَمَّدٍ

For your sake, O Jaʿfar the son of Muḥammad

بِكَ يَا مُوسَى بْنِ جَعْفَرٍ

For your sake, O Mūsā the son of Jaʿfar

بِكَ يَا عَلِيُّ بْنُ مُوسَى

For your sake, O ʿAlī the son of Mūsā

بِكَ يَا مُحَمَّدُ بْنُ عَلِيٍّ

For your sake, O Muḥammad the son of ʿAlī

بِكَ يَا عَلِيُّ بْنُ مُحَمَّدٍ

For your sake, O ʿAlī the son of Muḥammad

بِكَ يَا حَسَنَ بْنَ عَلِيٍّ

For your sake, O Ḥasan the son of ʿAlī

بِالْحُجَّةِ

For [your sake O] al-Ḥujjah (Proof)

Then request your desires (from Allāh ﷻ)."

The man performed this action just as he was taught and after some time, he was finally able to pay back his debt and his complications with the government were also rectified, and to top it off, his wealth and prosperity also increased.[217]

35. Special Ṣalāt for Saturday

Sayyid ibn Ṭāwūs has narrated from Imām Ḥasan b. ʿAlī al-ʿAskarī (a) that: "I read in the books of my father that whoever performs [every Saturday], two *ṣalāt* of two *rakʿat* each and in each *rakʿat* recites Ṣurah al-Ḥamd and Ṣurah al-Ikhlāṣ, followed by Āyatul

[217] Ibid., Section of the Recommended Prayers for the Fulfillment of One's Legitimate Desires.

Kursī, Allāh ﷻ will record that person's rank to be that of the prophets, martyrs and the doers of good."[218]

36. Accompaniment of 30,000 Angels

It has been narrated in a tradition that:

آيَةُ الْكُرْسِيِّ نُزِلَتْ وَ مَعَهَا ثَلاَثُونَ أَلْفَ مَلَكٍ

Āyatul Kursī was sent down along with 30,000 angels (with it) alongside [the angel] Jibrā'īl.[219]

37. Lofty Fortress of the Quran

The Messenger of Allāh ﷺ has said:

أَلْبَقَرَةُ سِنَامُ الْقُرَآنِ وَ ذِرْوَتُهُ نُزِلَ مَعَ كُلِّ آيَةٍ مِنْهَا ثَمَانُونَ مَلِكاً وَ اسْتَخْرَجَتِ اللّٰهُ لاَ إِلٰهَ إِلاَّ هُوَ الْحَيُّ الْقَيُّومُ مِنْ تَحْتِ الْعَرْشِ فَوَصَلَتْ بِهَا.

Sūrah al-Baqarah is the lofty pinnacle of the Quran and its peak; and eighty angels accompanied each verse which was revealed (from this chapter) while ﴾Allāh! There is no entity worthy of worship except for Him, the All-Living, the Self-Subsisting﴿ [Āyatul Kursī] was extracted from under the Throne (of Allāh) and was included within it (al-Baqarah).[220]

38. Joy of the Noble Prophet ﷺ

It has been narrated from Ibn ʿAbbās that he said:

كَانَ رَسُولِ اللّٰهِ إِذَا قَرَأَ آيَةَ الْكُرْسِيِّ ضَحِكَ وَ قَالَ: إِنَّمَا مِنْ

[218] Ibid., Section of the Recommended Prayers for Each of the Days of the Week.

[219] *Al-Itqān fī ʿUlūm al-Qur'ān*, vol. 1, p. 138.

[220] Ibid., vol. 1, p. 139.

كَنْـزِ الرَّحْمَـنِ تَحْـتَ الْعَـرْشِ.

Whenever the Messenger of Allāh ﷺ would recite Āyatul Kursī, he would laugh and say: Indeed this is a treasure of the All-Merciful from beneath the Throne.[221]

39. Greatest Verse of the Quran

It has been narrated that the Messenger of Allāh ﷺ said:

إِنَّ أَعْظَمَ آيَةٍ فِي الْقُرآنِ آيَةُ الْكُرْسِيِّ

Indeed the greatest verse in the Quran is Āyatul Kursī.[222]

40. Treasure from the Heavens

It has been narrated that Imām ʿAlī ﷷ said:

لَـوْ تَعْلَمُـونَ مَـا فِيهَـا لَـمَا تَرَكْتُمُوهَـا عَـلَىٰ حَـالٍ إِنَّ رَسُـولَ اللّٰـهِ قَـالَ: أُعْطِيـتُ آيَـةَ الْكُـرْسِيِّ مِـنْ كَنْـزِ تَحْـتِ الْعَـرْشِ لَـمْ يُؤْتَهَـا نَبِـيٌّ قَبْـلِي

If you all knew what is contained within this [verse], you would never leave its recitation regardless of the state that you find yourself in. Indeed the Messenger of Allāh said: 'I have been given Āyatul Kursī, which is one of the treasures from beneath the Throne (of Allāh), and no other Prophet before me has been given anything like it.'[223]

41. When this Passage was Named 'Āyatul Kursī'

Since the time it was sent down, Āyatul Kursī holds a special place and from the time of its revelation, it has been known by this title

[221] Ibid., vol. 1, p. 141.

[222] *Rūḥ al-Maʿānī*, vol. 3, p. 10.

[223] Ibid.

(Āyatul Kursī); and it is the Noble Prophet of Islam ﷺ and the infallible leaders after him who have spoken about its importance.

In his seminal work of the exegesis of the Noble Quran, the late scholar, ʿAllāmah Ṭabāʾṭabāʾī has narrated the following in regards to the naming of this passage: This verse was named Āyatul Kursī in the early period of Islam during the lifetime of the Prophet; and was thus described by the Prophet himself and the traditions quoted from him and the Imāms of Ahlul Bayt and the companions all proved this point. The fact that this verse was given a special name shows how much importance was attached to it and it could only be because of the highest nobility of its meaning and the elegance and grace of its style.[224]

42. Repelling an Animal

ʿAbdullāh b. Yaḥyā b. al-Kāhilī has been quoted as saying: Imām al-Ṣādiq (a) said:

> When you see an animal running towards you, stand towards it, recite Āyatul Kursī and then say:
>
> عَزَمْتُ عَلَيْكَ بِعَزِيمَةِ اللهِ وَ عَزِيمَةِ مُحَمَّدٍ وَ عَزِيمَةِ سُلَيْمَانَ بْنَ دَاوُدَ وَ عَزِيمَةِ أَمِيرِ الْمُؤْمِنِينَ عَلِيٍّ بْنَ أَبِي طَالِبٍ وَ الأَئِمَّةِ الطَّاهِرِينَ مِنْ بَعْدِهِ.
>
> I stand with fortitude [against you], through the determination of Allāh, and the determination of Muḥammad, the determination of Sulaymān b. Dāwūd, and the determination of the Commander of the Faithful, ʿAlī b. Abī Ṭālib and the pure leaders after him.
>
> After saying this, God Willing, the animal will flee

---

[224] *Al-Mizān*, vol. 2, p. 515.

> from you.

ʿAbdullāh b. Yaḥyā then stated:

> I left the Imām and anytime I saw an animal approaching me, I recited this supplication and noticed that the animal always moved away from me and did not cause me any difficulty. He then said: When I looked at the animal, I would notice that it would always lower its head and would turn away with its tail between its legs.[225]

The great scholar, Sayyid ibn Ṭāwūs narrated in his book, *Dalāʾīl al-Nuʿmānī* that he tried this supplication, and it proved to work for him.[226]

43. Supplication to Read Whenever Alone

Imām al-Ṣādiq ﷺ has stated:

> Whoever sleeps alone at home should recite Āyatul Kursī and then say the following supplication:
>
> أَللّٰهُمَّ آيِسْ وَحْشَتِي وَ آمِنْ رَوْعَتِي وَ أَعِنِّي عَلىٰ وَحْدَتِي
>
> O Allāh! Calm my fear; and safeguard me from my fear and assist me in my state of loneliness.[227]

44. Being Cured of Bile

Aṣbagh b. Nabāta has stated that the Commander of the Faithful ﷺ said:

> وَ الَّـذِي بَعَـثَ مُحَمَّـداً ﷺ بِالْحَـقِّ وَ أَكْـرَمَ أَهْـلَ بَيْتِـهِ مَـا مِـنْ
>
> شَيْءٍ تَطْلُبُونَـهُ مِـنْ حِـرْزٍ مِـنْ حَـرَقٍ أَوْ غَـرَقٍ أَوْ سَرَقٍ أَوْ إِفْلَاتِ

---

225 *Al-Kāfī*, vol. 2, p. 572.

226 *Al-Amān*, p. 131.

227 *Al-Kāfī*, vol. 2, p. 573.

دَابَّـةٍ مِـنْ صَاحِبِهَـا أَوْ ضَالَّـةٍ أَوْ آبِـقٍ إِلَّا وَ هُـوَ فِي الْقُـرْآنِ فَمَـنْ أَرَادَ ذَلِـكَ فَلْيَسْـأَلْنِي عَنْـهُ

I take an oath by the One who sent Muḥammad with the truth, and who ennobled his family (the Ahlul Bayt) that there is nothing which the people can ask from being protected such as: from being burnt (alive), drowning, having their possessions stolen, an animal running away from its owner, losing something, or their slave abandoning them - except that its remedy is found in the Quran. Therefore, whosoever wants to know where this is, should ask me.

قَـالَ فَقَـامَ إِلَيْـهِ رَجُـلٌ فَقَـالَ يَـا أَمِـيرَ الْمُؤْمِنِـينَ أَخْـبِرْنِي عَـمَّا يُؤْمِـنُ مِـنَ الْحَـرَقِ وَ الْغَـرَقِ

He [Aṣbagh] stated: A man stood up and said: 'O Commander of the Faithful! Inform us about that which will safeguard us from being burnt (alive) or being drowned!'

فَقَالَ اقْرَأْ هَذِهِ الْآيَاتِ

He [the Imām ﷺ] said: 'Recite these verses [of the Quran]:

﴿ٱللَّهُ ٱلَّذِى نَـزَّلَ ٱلْكِتَـٰبَ وَهُـوَ يَتَـوَلَّى ٱلصَّـٰلِحِـينَ ... وَمَـا قَـدَرُوا۟ ٱللَّهَ حَـقَّ قَـدْرِهِ... سُـبْحَـٰنَهُۥ وَتَعَـٰلَىٰ عَمَّـا يُشْرِكُونَ﴾

It is Allāh who is the One who revealed the Book and He befriends the righteous doers ... and they did not estimate Allāh with the estimation which is due to Him ... Glory be to Him, and exalted is He above what they associate (with Him).

فَمَنْ قَرَأَهَا فَقَدْ أَمِنَ الْحَرَقَ وَ الْغَرَقَ

Whosoever recites this [collection of three separate verses] will be protected from being burnt (alive) and from drowning.'

قَالَ فَقَرَأَهَا رَجُلٌ وَ اضْطَرَمَتِ النَّارُ فِي بُيُوتِ جِيرَانِهِ وَ بَيْتُهُ وَسَطَهَا فَلَمْ يُصِبْهُ شَيْءٌ

He [Asbagh] then said the person [who asked the question followed this guidance] and continuously read these verses, and one day his [two] neighbours' houses caught fire, but his own house which was between them was saved [from being destroyed].

ثُمَّ قَامَ إِلَيْهِ رَجُلٌ آخَرُ فَقَالَ يَا أَمِيرَ الْمُؤْمِنِينَ إِنَّ دَابَّتِيَ اسْتَصْعَبَتْ عَلَيَّ وَ أَنَا مِنْهَا عَلَى وَجَلٍ

At this point, another man stood up and said: 'O Commander of the Faithful! My animal continuously wails and this sound frightens me [what can be done about this]?'

فَقَالَ اقْرَأْ فِي أُذُنِهَا الْيُمْنَى

He [the Imām ﷺ] replied: 'Recite the following in its [the animal's] right ear:

﴿وَلَهُ أَسْلَمَ مَنْ فِي السَّمَاوَاتِ وَالأَرْضِ طَوْعًا وَكَرْهًا وَإِلَيْهِ يُرْجَعُونَ ﴿٨٣﴾﴾

And whatsoever is in the heavens and the earth submit to Him voluntarily or by force and indeed all of you shall be returned back to Him.'[228]

فَقَرَأَهَا فَذَلَّتْ لَهُ دَابَّتُهُ

The man did as he was told and his animal regained its composure.

وَ قَامَ إِلَيْهِ رَجُلٌ آخَرُ فَقَالَ يَا أَمِيرَ الْمُؤْمِنِينَ إِنَّ أَرْضِي أَرْضٌ مَسْبَعَةٌ وَ إِنَّ السِّبَاعَ تَغْشَى مَنْزِلِي وَ لَا تَجُوزُ حَتَّى تَأْخُذَ فَرِيسَتَهَا

Then another man stood up and said: 'O Commander of the Faithful! My land is located in an area in which there are many wild animals around there, and sometimes they surround my house and don't leave until they capture their prey [and because of this, I am not able to make my way home]!'

فَقَالَ اقْرَأْ

He [the Imām ﷺ] said to that man: 'Recite the following:

﴿لَقَدْ جَآءَكُمْ رَسُولٌ مِنْ أَنفُسِكُمْ عَزِيزٌ عَلَيْهِ مَا عَنِتُّمْ حَرِيصٌ عَلَيْكُم بِالْمُؤْمِنِينَ رَءُوفٌ رَحِيمٌ ﴿١٢٨﴾ فَإِنْ تَوَلَّوْا فَقُلْ حَسْبِيَ اللهُ لَآ إِلٰهَ إِلَّا هُوَ عَلَيْهِ تَوَكَّلْتُ وَهُوَ رَبُّ الْعَرْشِ الْعَظِيمِ﴿١٢٩﴾﴾

There has certainly come to you an apostle from among yourselves. Grievous to him is your distress; he has deep concern for you, and he is most kind and merciful to the faithful. But if they turn their backs [on

[228] *Quran*, Sūrah Āle 'Imrān (3), verse 83.

you], say: 'God is sufficient for me. There is no god except Him. In Him I have put my trust and He is the Lord of the Great Throne.''[229]

فَقَرَأَهُمَا الرَّجُلُ فَاجْتَنَبَتْهُ السِّبَاعُ

This man also acted as he was told and continuously recited these two verses, and the wild animals were kept away from him.

ثُمَّ قَامَ إِلَيْهِ آخَرُ فَقَالَ يَا أَمِيرَ الْمُؤْمِنِينَ إِنَّ فِي بَطْنِي مَاءً أَصْفَرَ فَهَلْ مِنْ شِفَاءٍ

Then another man stood up and said: 'O Commander of the Faithful! I have some bile built up in my stomach – is there any cure for me?'

فَقَالَ نَعَمْ بِلَا دِرْهَمٍ وَ لَا دِينَارٍ وَ لَكِنِ اكْتُبْ عَلَى بَطْنِكَ- آيَةَ الْكُرْسِيِّ وَ تَغْسِلُهَا وَ تَشْرَبُهَا وَ تَجْعَلُهَا ذَخِيرَةً فِي بَطْنِكَ فَتَبْرَأُ بِإِذْنِ اللّٰهِ عَزَّ وَ جَلَّ فَفَعَلَ الرَّجُلُ فَبَرَأَ بِإِذْنِ اللّٰهِ

The Imām ﷺ said to him: 'Yes there is and you don't have to spend any money on the cure. Rather, write Āyatul Kursī on your stomach, wash it off (with water), then drink this water, and then keep some of this water on your stomach, and with the permission of Allāh, the Noble and Grand, this problem will go away.'

This man acted as he was instructed and found that he was cured of his sickness, by the permission of Allāh.

ثُمَّ قَامَ إِلَيْهِ آخَرُ فَقَالَ يَا أَمِيرَ الْمُؤْمِنِينَ أَخْبِرْنِي عَنِ الضَّالَّةِ

[229] *Quran*, Sūrah al-Tawbah (9), verses 128-129.

Another man then stood up and said: 'O Commander of the Faithful! Inform me of how I can find the thing which I have lost [through the Qurān].'

فَقَالَ اقْرَأْ يس فِي رَكْعَتَيْنِ

He (the Imām ﷺ) said to him: 'Recite a two *rakʿat* prayer with Sūrah Yāsīn [in both *rakʿat*] and then after the *ṣalāt*, say the following:

يَا هَادِيَ الضَّالَّةِ رُدَّ عَلَيَّ ضَالَّتِي

O the Guide to that which is lost, return back to me that which I have lost.'

فَفَعَلَ فَرَدَّ اللَّهُ عَزَّ وَ جَلَّ عَلَيْهِ ضَالَّتَهُ

The man did as he was instructed and Allāh, the Noble and Grand, returned that thing back to him.

ثُمَّ قَامَ إِلَيْهِ آخَرُ فَقَالَ يَا أَمِيرَ الْمُؤْمِنِينَ أَخْبِرْنِي عَنِ الْآبِقِ

Then a man stood up and said: 'Commander of the Faithful! Inform me what I should recite if my slave runs away from me."'

فَقَالَ اقْرَأْ

He ﷺ replied: 'Recite the following:

﴿أَوْ كَظُلُمَاتٍ فِي بَحْرٍ لُّجِّيٍّ يَغْشَاهُ مَوْجٌ مِّن فَوْقِهِ مَوْجٌ مِّن فَوْقِهِ سَحَابٌ ظُلُمَاتٌ بَعْضُهَا فَوْقَ بَعْضٍ إِذَآ أَخْرَجَ يَدَهُ لَمْ يَكَدْ يَرَاهَا وَمَن لَّمْ يَجْعَلِ ٱللَّهُ لَهُ نُوراً فَمَا لَهُ مِن نُورٍ ﴿٤١﴾﴾

Or like utter darkness in the deep sea: there covers

it a wave above which is another wave, above which is a cloud, (layers of) utter darkness one above another; when he holds out his hand, he is almost unable to see it; and to whomsoever Allāh does not give light, he has no light.'[230]

فَقَالَهَا الرَّجُلُ فَرَجَعَ إِلَيْهِ الْآبِقُ

The man recited this and his slave returned back to him.

ثُمَّ قَامَ إِلَيْهِ آخَرُ فَقَالَ يَا أَمِيرَ الْمُؤْمِنِينَ أَخْبِرْنِي عَنِ السَّرَقِ فَإِنَّهُ لَا يَزَالُ قَدْ يُسْرَقُ لِيَ الشَّيْءُ بَعْدَ الشَّيْءِ لَيْلًا

Then another man stood up and said: 'O Commander of the Faithful! Teach me something which will protect me from thieves as things are continuously being stolen from me at night.'

He ﷺ said: 'When you get to bed, recite the following:

﴿قُلِ ٱدْعُواْ ٱللَّهَ أَوِ ٱدْعُواْ ٱلرَّحْمَـٰنَ أَيّاً مَّا تَدْعُواْ فَلَهُ ٱلأَسْمَآءُ ٱلْحُسْنَىٰ وَلاَ تَجْهَرْ بِصَلاَتِكَ وَلاَ تُخَافِتْ بِهَا وَٱبْتَغِ بَيْنَ ذٰلِكَ سَبِيلاً ۝١١٠ وَقُلِ ٱلْحَمْدُ لِلَّهِ ٱلَّذِى لَمْ يَتَّخِذْ وَلَداً وَلَم يَكُنْ لَّهُ شَرِيكٌ فِى ٱلْمُلْكِ وَلَمْ يَكُنْ لَّهُ وَلِيٌّ مِّنَ ٱلذُّلِّ وَكَبِّرْهُ تَكْبِيراً ۝١١١﴾

Say: 'Call upon Allāh, or call upon the Beneficent Allāh; whichever you call upon, He has the best of names; and do not utter your prayer with a very raised voice, nor be silent with regard to it, and seek

---

[230] *Quran*, Sūrah al-Nūr (24), verse 41.

a way between these.' And say: '(All) praise is due to Allāh, Who has not taken a son and Who has not a partner in the kingdom, and Who has not a helper to save Him from disgrace; and proclaim His greatness magnifying (Him).''[231]

ثُمَّ قَالَ أَمِيرُ الْمُؤْمِنِينَ عَلَيْهِ السَّلَامُ مَنْ بَاتَ بِأَرْضٍ قَفْرٍ فَقَرَأَ هَذِهِ الْآيَةَ حَرَسَتْهُ الْمَلَائِكَةُ وَ تَبَاعَدَتْ عَنْهُ الشَّيَاطِينُ

The Commander of the Faithful ﷺ then said: 'A person who goes to sleep on the ground in the wilderness and recites the following verse will find that the angels will safeguard [him] and that the devils will be distanced from him:

﴿إِنَّ رَبَّكُمُ ٱللَّهُ ٱلَّذِى خَلَقَ ٱلسَّمَاوَاتِ وَٱلْأَرْضَ فِى سِتَّةِ أَيَّامٍ ثُمَّ ٱسْتَوَىٰ عَلَى ٱلْعَرْشِ يُغْشِى ٱلَّيْلَ ٱلنَّهَارَ يَطْلُبُهُ حَثِيثًا وَٱلشَّمْسَ وَٱلْقَمَرَ وَٱلنُّجُومَ مُسَخَّرَاتٍۭ بِأَمْرِهِۦٓ أَلَا لَهُ ٱلْخَلْقُ وَٱلْأَمْرُ تَبَارَكَ ٱللَّهُ رَبُّ ٱلْعَالَمِينَ ۝٥٤﴾

Surely your Lord is Allāh, Who created the heavens and the earth in six periods of time, and He is firm in power; He throws the veil of night over the day, which it pursues incessantly; and (He created) the sun and the moon and the stars, made subservient by His command; surely His is the creation and the command; blessed is Allāh, Lord of the Worlds.'[232]

قَالَ فَمَضَى الرَّجُلُ فَإِذَا هُوَ بِقَرْيَةٍ خَرَابٍ فَبَاتَ فِيهَا وَ لَمْ

[231] *Quran*, Sūrah al-Isrā (17), verses 110-111.
[232] *Quran*, Sūrah al-Aʿrāf (17), verse 54.

يَقْـرَأْ هٰـذِهِ الْآيَـةَ فَتَغَشَّـاهُ الشَّـيْطَانُ وَ إِذَا هُـوَ آخِـذٌ بِخَطْمِـهِ فَقَـالَ لَـهُ صَاحِبُـهُ أَنْظِـرْهُ وَ اسْـتَيْقَظَ الرَّجُـلُ فَقَـرَأَ الْآيَـةَ فَقَـالَ الشَّـيْطَانُ لِصَاحِبِـهِ أَرْغَـمَ اللّٰـهُ أَنْفَـكَ احْرُسْـهُ الْآنَ حَتَّـى يُصْبِـحَ فَلَـمَّا أَصْبَـحَ رَجَـعَ إِلَى أَمِـيرِ الْمُؤْمِنِـينَ ﵇ فَأَخْـبَرَهُ وَ قَـالَ لَـهُ رَأَيْـتُ فِي كَلَامِـكَ الشِّـفَاءَ وَ الصِّـدْقَ وَ مَـضَى بَعْـدَ طُلُـوعِ الشَّـمْسِ فَـإِذَا هُـوَ بِأَثَـرِ شَـعْرِ الشَّـيْطَانِ مُجْتَمِعـاً فِي الْأَرْضِ

The narrator [of the *ḥadīth*] then says: 'Then, that man (either the man who had asked the question about seeking protection from the thieves or another one) left, he reached back to the ruins of the village [where he stayed], and spent the night there sleeping however he did not recite the verses [which he was told to recite] so the Satan went towards him and took him by the nose. The man's friend who was with him said to Satan: 'Give him some respite' [the man woke up when he heard this conversation happening] and began to recite the verses [which the Commander of the Faithful ﵇ had taught him] and at this point, Satan said to the friend of this man: 'May Allāh rub your nose in the dirt! You now need to safeguard and stay watch over this man until the morning time.' When the morning came, these two people went to the Commander of the Faithful ﵇ and explained to him what had happened and said to him: 'We have found a cure and truthfulness [for our problems] in your words [to us].' Once the sun rose they all went back to that ruined place and found some of Satan's hair on the ground.'[233]

[233] Ibid., p. 624.

45. Travelling on Not Good Days

Ḥammād b. ʿUthmān stated:

أَ يُكْـرَهُ السَّـفَرُ فِي شَيْءٍ مِـنَ الْأَيَّـامِ الْمَكْرُوهَـةِ الْأَرْبِعَـاءِ وَ غَـيْرِهِ

فَقَـالَ افْتَتِـحْ سَـفَرَكَ بِالصَّدَقَـةِ وَ اقْـرَأْ آيَـةَ الْكُـرْسِيِّ إِذَا بَـدَا لَـكَ.

I asked Imām al-Ṣādiq: 'Is it actually reprehensible to travel on those days which are known to be days that one should not travel on and on Wednesdays as well?' The Imām replied: 'Start your journey by offering some charity (*ṣadaqah*), and when you embark, begin by reciting Āyatul Kursī.'[234]

46. 1,000 Blessings Contained in Each Letter

Imām ʿAlī said: 'The Messenger of Allāh called me towards him and said:

يَـا عَـلِيُّ إِذَا أَخَـذْتَ مَضْجَعَـكَ فَعَلَيْـكَ بِالاسْـتِغْفَارِ وَ الصَّـلَاةِ عَـلَيَّ

وَ قُـلْ:

O ʿAlī! Whenever you are faced with calamities, seek forgiveness (from Allāh), send prayers upon me and then say:

سُبْحَانَ اللّٰهِ وَ الْـحَمْدُ لِلّٰـهِ وَ لَا إِلٰـهَ إِلَّا اللّٰـهُ وَ اللّٰهُ أَكْـبَرُ وَ لَا حَوْلَ

وَ لَا قُـوَّةَ إِلَّا بِاللّٰـهِ الْعَـلِيِّ الْعَظِيمِ

Glory be to Allāh; and all of the Praise belongs to Allāh and there is no god except for Allāh and Allāh is the greatest and there is no power nor strength save with Allāh, the Elevated, the Grand.

---

[234] Ibid., vol. 4, p. 283.

وَ أَكْثِرْ مِنْ قِرَاءَةِ قُلْ هُوَ اللَّهُ أَحَدٌ فَإِنَّهَا نُورُ الْقُرْآنِ وَ عَلَيْكَ بِقِرَاءَةِ آيَةِ الْكُرْسِي فَإِنَّ فِي كُلِّ حَرْفٍ مِنْهَا أَلْفَ بَرَكَةٍ وَ أَلْفَ رَحْمَة

Then recite Sūrah al-Ikhlāṣ profusely as this verse is the Divine light of the Quran; and recite Āyatul Kursī for in each letter contained within it, there are 1,000 blessings and 1,000 mercies.'[235]

47. Recovering Lost or Stolen Goods

It has been narrated from Imam ʿAli ﷺ that to find something which has been lost, or an animal which has run away, the following supplication should be written:

أَللّٰهُمَّ إِنَّ السَّمَآءَ سَمَآؤُكَ وَ الأَرْضَ أَرْضُكَ وَ الْبَرَّ بَرُّكَ وَ الْبَحْرَ بَحْرُكَ وَ مَا بَيْنَهُمَا فِي الدُّنْيَا وَ الآخِرَةِ لَكَ. أَللّٰهُمَّ فَاجْعَلِ الْأَرْضَ بِمَا رَحُبَتْ عَلىٰ فُلاَنِ بْنِ فُلاَنٍ أَضْيَقُ مِنْ مِسْكِ جَمَلٍ وَ خُذْ بِسَمْعِهِ وَ بَصَرِهِ وَ قَلْبِهِ أَوْ كَظُلُمَاتٍ فِي بَحْرٍ لُجِيٍّ يَغْشٰيهُ مَوْجٌ مِنْ فَوْقِهِ مَوْجٌ مِنْ فَوْقِهِ سَحَابٌ ظُلُمَاتٌ بَعْضُهَا فَوْقَ بَعْضٍ إِذَا خَرَجَ يَدَهُ لَمْ يَكَدْ يَرٰيهَا وَ مَنْ لَمْ يَجْعَلِ اللّٰهُ لَهُ نُوْراً فَمَا لَهُ مِنْ نُورٍ.

O Allāh! Indeed the skies are Your skies and the earth is Your earth, and the land is Your land, and the ocean is Your ocean, and all that which is between them (the skies and the Earth) in the transient world and the next world [are all Yours]. O Allāh! So then make the Earth, despite its spaciousness, confined for so-and-so person even more than the musk of a camel; and take away his

[235] *Al-Daʿwāt*, p. 84.

> hearing and sight and insight [spiritual heart] or like utter darkness in the deep sea: there covers it a wave above which is another wave, above which is a cloud, (layers of) utter darkness one above another; when he holds out his hand, he is almost unable to see it; and to whomsoever Allāh does not give light, he has no light.

One should also write Āyatul Kursī around this supplication and hang this supplication outside and then after three days, take it down and God Willing, that thing which was lost or had gone away will be found.[236]

48. Distancing Satan from a Person

The Noble Prophet ﷺ has said: "Āyatul Kursī is not recited in any house except that Satan is repelled from that place for thirty days. After stating this, the Prophet then addressed the Commander of the Faithful ʿAli ﷺ and said to him: 'O ʿAli! Teach this grand verse to your children; teach this to your (other) family members; and to your neighbours, as the Most High (Allāh) has not sent any other verse which is as great as this one.'"[237]

49. Protection of Two Angels

The Noble Prophet ﷺ has said: "The greatest verse which exists in the Noble Quran is Āyatul Kursī and whoever recites it, Allāh will appoint two angels to record all of their good deeds in their book of records, and (will instruct them) not to write any of their bad deeds in the book of records - until the next day in which one recites Āyatul Kursī (again)."[238]

---

[236] *Al-Miṣbāḥ* of al-Kafʿamī, p. 181.

[237] *Talkhīṣ Manhaj al-Ṣādiqīn*, vol. 1, p. 155.

[238] Ibid.

50. Reciting it in Kerbalāʾ

Imam Jaʿfar al-Ṣādiq ﷺ said: "Whoever recites Āyatul Kursī on the night of the 15th of Shaʿbān while in Kerbalā', then recites Sūrah al-Ikhlāṣ 1,000 times and says *'astaghfirullāh'* 1,000 times, then praises Allāh, and gets up and performs a four *rakʿat* prayer in which in each *rakʿat*, one recites (after Sūrah al-Ḥamd), Āyatul Kursī 1,000 times, Allāh, the Most High, will appoint two angels to protect this person from every evil and bad thing, and one will also be protected from despicable rulers, and in addition, good deeds will be written for that person and no sins will be recorded, and as long as these angels are with that individual, they will continue to ask for forgiveness for them."[239]

NOTE: The meaning of this tradition is that whoever performs this act of worship, and then following this goes to sleep and then wakes up, and performs the four *rakʿat* prayer as mentioned above.

51. Writing Your Pleas to Allāh ﷻ

Imam ʿAli b. Abi Talib ﷺ said: "Anytime one of you begins to write down your desires and wishes (that you want Allāh to fulfill), then recites Āyatul Kursī and the last verse of Sūrah Banī Isrāʾīl [as shown below] will have your wishes will be fulfilled.[240]

﴿وَقُلِ ٱلْحَمْدُ لِلَّهِ ٱلَّذِى لَمْ يَتَّخِذْ وَلَدًا وَلَمْ يَكُن لَّهُۥ شَرِيكٌ فِى ٱلْمُلْكِ وَلَمْ يَكُن لَّهُۥ وَلِىٌّ مِّنَ ٱلذُّلِّ وَكَبِّرْهُ تَكْبِيرًا ١١١﴾

And say: 'All the praise belongs to Allāh Who has not taken to Himself a son, and Who has no associate-partner in His kingdom, nor has He any helper because

[239] *Miṣbāḥ al-Mutahajjid*, p. 853.

[240] *Mishkāt al-Anwār*, p. 143.

of any weakness. And extol His glory with repeated glorification."[241]

52. Removing Fear from a Person

Wālid b. Sabīḥ said: Shahab b. ʿAbdurabbah said to me: "Convey my regards to Imām Jaʿfar al-Ṣādiq ﷺ and say to him that when I am about to go to sleep, I feel fear in my heart in regards to a certain person. So I conveyed this information to the Imām and the Imām ﷺ said to me: 'Tell him that when he is ready to go to sleep, he should recite the 'two chapters of seeking refuge' (Sūrah al-Falaq and Sūrah al-Nās) and Āyatul Kursī - and Āyatul Kursī is even better (to recite).'"[242]

53. Greatest Name of Allāh ﷻ

Imam Jaʿfar al-Ṣādiq ﷺ said the following to a group of his companions: "Should I not inform you about the greatest name of Allāh?' His companions replied that they wanted to know what it was, and the Imām informed them: 'Recite Sūrah al-Ḥamd, Sūrah al-Ikhlāṣ, Āyatul Kursī and Sūrah al-Qadr and then face towards the direction of the *qiblah* and ask Allāh for whatever it is that you desire.'"[243]

54. Opening of the Seven Doors of Heaven

Jābir b. ʿAbdullāh al-Anṣārī has related that the Noble Messenger ﷺ said: "Whoever recites Āyatul Kursī after every obligatory *ṣalāt* will have the seven doors of heaven open up (for them) and these doors will not close until the Most High looks towards His servant with His grace and forgiveness, pardons his sins; and anytime Āyatul Kursī is recited and the reciter asks for its reward to be given to the deceased Muslims, the Most High will bless the graves

---

[241] *Quran*, Sūrah al-Isrā (17), verse 111.
[242] *Falāḥ al-Sā'il*, p. 281.
[243] *Mahj al-Daʿwāt*, p. 316; *al-Miṣbāḥ* of al-Kafʿamī, p. 308.

of the deceased with forty lights which stretch from the east to the west, and their graves will be expanded and filled with light. The person who recited Āyatul Kursī will be given the reward [which has been given] to sixty prophets and for every letter contained within it (Āyatul Kursī), an angel will be created who will perform the glorification of Allāh on that person's behalf."[244]

55. At the Time of Facing Fear

Ibrāhīm b. Naʿīm has narrated from Imām Jaʿfar al-Ṣādiq ﵇ that he said: "Anytime something happens that instills fear into your hearts, recite the following:

﴿رَبِّ أَدْخِلْنِي مُدْخَلَ صِدْقٍ وَأَخْرِجْنِي مُخْرَجَ صِدْقٍ وَاجْعَل لِي مِن لَدُنْكَ سُلْطَاناً نَصِيراً ﴿٨٠﴾﴾

> My Lord! make me to enter a goodly entering, and cause me to go forth a goodly going forth, and grant me from near Thee power to assist (me).[245]

If the feeling of fear intensifies, then recite Āyatul Kursī."[246]

56. In the House of Imām Jaʿfar al-Ṣādiq ﵇

Abī Khadījah said: "I saw Āyatul Kursī written (on something) and it was kept in a corner of the house of Imām al-Ṣādiq, and I also saw Āyatul Kursī written and kept in the direction of *qiblah* in the area where the Imām was engaged in worship."[247]

57. Removal of Poverty and Growth in Sustenance

It has been mentioned in the traditions that whoever recites Āyatul Kursī after every obligatory *ṣalāt* and persists in this action will be

---

[244] *Summary of Manhaj al-Ṣādiqīn*, vol. 1, p. 155.
[245] *Quran*, Sūrah al-Isrā (17), verse 80.
[246] *Al-Maḥāsin* of al-Barqī, vol. 2, p. 67.
[247] Ibid., vol. 2, p. 609.

protected from poverty, and the Most High will grant that person ample wealth.

Whoever recites Āyatul Kursī in the morning and the evening will be protected from thieves, safeguarded from fire, and one's personal property will be secured from being burned. In addition, that person will also be protected from the hazards of snakes, scorpions and other such things, and neither the Jinn nor the human beings will be able to enact any kind of evil upon them.

If Āyatul Kursī is written and buried on the farm land, then the person (and his farm land) will be safeguarded from loss and there will be great blessings in whatever is grown.

If Āyatul Kursī is written and kept in a person's store, then one will see an increase in one's profits.

If Āyatul Kursī is written and kept in one's house, then a thief will never enter into that house; and finally if it is continuously recited, then a person will see one's own station in the next life in paradise.[248]

58. Reward for the Deceased

The Noble Messenger ﷺ has said: "When a faithful believer recites Āyatul Kursī and dedicates the reward of it to the deceased in the graveyard, then Allāh, the Noble and Grand will create an angel for every letter recited and up until the Day of Resurrection, those angels will glorify Allāh [and the reward of that glorification] will go to the person who recited the Āyatul Kursī."[249]

59. Gaining Power and Prestige

It has been stated that if a person wants to attain power and prestige, then one should: keep away from eating meat for twelve days; fast for those twelve days and break the fast with only permissible

---

[248] *Summary of Manhaj al-Ṣādiqīn*, vol. 1, p. 156.

[249] *Man lā Yaḥḍhuruhu al-Faqīh*, vol. 1, p. 470.

food. Each day, one should perform a *ghusl* and afterwards, put on the purest of clothes. After the *ghusl* and wearing one's best clothes, the person should, before talking to anyone, perform a two *rakʿat ṣalāt*, and once complete while still sitting on the prayer mat, recite Āyatul Kursī 1,000 times. If a person performs this by strictly adhering to all of the conditions laid down and does this with a true and sincere intention, then one will attain the desired goal.

60. Helping to Repay Debts and Increase Sustenance

In order to be able to pay back one's debts and have an increase in one's sustenance, one should fast every Friday (or as mentioned in other traditions, one should fast on Thursday) and perform a two *rakʿat ṣalāt* (like the *fajr ṣalāt*).

After the *ṣalāt* is complete, one should send blessings upon Muḥammad and his family [by saying أَللّٰهُمَّ صَلِّ عَلٰى مُحَمَّدٍ وَ آلِ مُحَمَّدٍ] and then with whatever intention one has in mind, one should perform another *ṣalāt* (of two *rakʿat*). In this prayer, in each *rakʿat*, after the recitation of Sūrah al-Fātiha, one should recite Āyatul Kursī eleven times and then recite Sūrah al-Ikhlāṣ twenty-five times. Once this *ṣalāt* is complete, the person should say the following 41,000 times: "يَا وَهَّابُ".

While performing this entire act of worship, one should try to ensure that from the beginning to the end, one does not speak anything at all, and once complete, the person should specify one's desires which will be granted, God Willing.

61. Mounting One's Ride

Aṣbagh b. Nabāta has stated: "I was standing beside the Commander of the Faithful when I saw that he wanted to mount his riding animal. He raised his head towards the sky and then smiled. I said to him: 'O Commander of the Faithful! I just saw you raise your head and then smile?!' He replied: 'Yes Aṣbagh. I was once standing beside the Messenger of Allāh and his horse when he raised his head to the sky and smiled.' I asked him: 'O Messenger of Allāh! Why did you raise your head to the sky?' He smiled and said to me: "ʿAlī! There is not a single person who mounts his ride and recites Āyatul Kursī and then says [the following] except that the Supreme Master (Allāh) replies: 'Angels! This servant of mine knows that there is no one other than I who can forgive his sins! Thus, you bear witness that I have forgiven him his sins.'"[250]:

أَسْتَغْفِرُ اللّٰهَ الَّذِي لاَ إِلٰهَ إِلاَّ هُوَ الْحَيُّ الْقَيُّومُ وَ أَتُوبُ إِلَيْهِ.
أَللّٰهُمَّ اغْفِرْلِي ذُنُوبِي إِنَّهُ لاَ يَغْفِرُ الذُّنُوبَ إِلاَّ أَنْتَ

I seek forgiveness from Allāh – the One whom there is no other god except for Him, the Ever-Living, the Self Sustaining and I turn towards Him (in repentance). O Allāh! Forigve my sins as indeed there is no one who can forgive the sins except for You.

62. Immunity from the Fire of Hell

Imām Mūsā al-Kādhim ﷺ said: "I heard from some of my noble ancestors that a man recited *Umm al-Quran* (Sūrah al-Fātiḥa) and then said that he has fulfilled his obligation of thanking (God) and received his reward. I then heard him recite Sūrah al-Ikhlāṣ and say: 'I have gained faith and am now protected (from gravitating towards disbelief).' I then heard him recite Sūrah al-Qadr and say: 'The truth has been spoken and I have been forgiven.' I then heard him recite Āyatul Kursī and say: 'Congratulations! This is a protection for you from the fire of hell.'"[251]

63. Alleviating Eye Pain

Imām ʿAlī ﷺ said: "Whenever one of you has pain in the eyes, then recite Āyatul Kursī, but do not disclose that you have eye pain;

---

[250] *Al-Amālī* of Shaykh al-Ṣādūq, p. 507.
[251] Ibid.

God Willing, the pain will be alleviated and you will find blessings in that (the recitation of Āyatul Kursī)."[252]

64. Raising One's Rank

Imām al-Ṣādiq ﷺ said: "Indeed it is through the recitation of Āyatul Kursī that I elevate (my) rank and through which I seek help and assistance (from God)."[253] (Meaning that it is through the recitation of Āyatul Kursī that one's spiritual status is elevated)."

65. Āyatul Kursī is not Recited after the Salāt Except That...

The Prophet of Islam ﷺ has said: "*Fātiḥa al-Kitāb* (Sūrah al-Ḥamd) and Āyatul Kursī and two verses of [Sūrah] Āle ʿImrān until the end of these verses are 'suspended verses' and between these verses and Allāh, the Blessed and Most High, there are no veils, and they [these verses] say: 'O Allāh! Send us to the earth and to those individuals who have sinned!'"

Allāh, the Blessed and the Most High, then says: "No one from among the people of My servants recites this after their *ṣalāt* except that I make a place in paradise for them and I grant them a sublime location in [that] place and every day, I will glance towards them seventy times."[254]

Sūrah Āle ʿImrān (3), verse 18:

﴿شَهِدَ اللَّهُ أَنَّهُ لَا إِلَٰهَ إِلَّا هُوَ وَالْمَلَائِكَةُ وَأُولُوا الْعِلْمِ
قَائِمًا بِالْقِسْطِ لَا إِلَٰهَ إِلَّا هُوَ الْعَزِيزُ الْحَكِيمُ ﴿١٨﴾﴾

Allāh bears witness that there is no god but He, and (so do) the angels and those possessed of knowledge, maintaining His creation with justice; there is no god

[252] *Tuḥf al-ʿUqūl*, p. 106; *al-Khiṣāl*, vol. 2, p. 616.
[253] *Tafsīr* of al-ʿAyyāshī, vol. 1, p. 136.
[254] *Jāmiʿ al-Akhbār*, p. 45.

but He, the Mighty, the Wise.

Sūrah Āle ʿImrān (3), verse 26:

﴿قُلِ اللَّهُمَّ مَالِكَ الْمُلْكِ تُؤْتِي الْمُلْكَ مَنْ تَشَاءُ وَتَنْزِعُ الْمُلْكَ مِمَّنْ تَشَاءُ وَتُعِزُّ مَنْ تَشَاءُ وَتُذِلُّ مَنْ تَشَاءُ بِيَدِكَ الْخَيْرُ إِنَّكَ عَلَىٰ كُلِّ شَيْءٍ قَدِيرٌ ﴿٢٦﴾﴾

Say: O Allāh, Master of the Kingdom! You give the kingdom to whomsoever You please and take away the kingdom from whomsoever You please, and You exalt whom You pleas and abase whom You please in Your hand is the good; surely, You have power over all things.

[**Explanation**: It must be noted that merely reciting this and not paying any focus or attention to what is being recited and not knowing or understanding the contents of these verses is merely an exercise in verbally articulating something; so this grand reward is not for those people who only engage in this superficial level of action. Indeed, that noble place in paradise will be given to the person who thinks and ponders upon what one is reciting and acts according to what is contained within it, God Willing.]

66. After Every Obligatory Prayer

Imām ʿAlī ﷺ has said: "Whoever recites Āyatul Kursī after every obligatory *ṣalāt* will have one's *ṣalāt* accepted, will be in the special protection of Allāh, and Allāh will safeguard that person."[255]

67. If Someone Recites it One Hundred Times...

Imām ʿAlī ﷺ has said: "The Noble Prophet ﷺ said: 'Whoever recites Āyatul Kursī one hundred times is like a person who

[255] *Al-Daʿwāt*, p. 84.

worshipped Allāh for an entire lifetime.'"[256]

68. Repelling the Devils

It was once asked from Ayatullāh Kashmirī that in order to drive away the devils, which verses and chapters of the Quran are beneficial to recite, to which he replied: "If you recite Āyatul Kursī and the *muʿawidhtayn* (Sūrah al-Falaq and Sūrah al-Nās), then you will be able to repel the devils away."[257]

69. Depondency of the Devils

Imām Jaʿfar al-Ṣādiq ﷺ has narrated from his noble forefathers that the Commander of the Faithful ﷺ said: "When Āyatul Kursī was revealed, the Leader of the Universe [Prophet Muḥammad ﷺ] would say: 'Verses have been revealed from the treasure of the Grand Emperion (Throne) which are better than whatever exists, and every idol which was between the East to the West fell into submission." At this point, *Iblīs* (the chief devil) became frightened and said to his nation: 'Tonight, something great has taken place. Allow me to travel from the East to the West and see what has transpired.' He began his journey throughout the universe until he reached the city of Medina. He asked someone (in Medina): 'What happened here last night?' The person replied: 'The Messenger of God informed us that a grand verse from the treasures of the Grand Emperion of God was revealed yesterday and as a sign of their awe, all of the idols which were around fell into the state of submission.' *Iblīs* returned back to his community and told them about what had transpired and after hearing this, all of them became sad with grief."[258]

---

[256] *ʿUyūn al-Akhbār al-Riḍā*, vol. 2, p. 65.

[257] *Rūḥ wa Rayḥān*, p. 137.

[258] *Summary of Manhaj al-Ṣādiqīn*, vol. 1, p. 156.

70. Means of Entering into Paradise

ʿAbdullah b. ʿAwf has narrated that: "One night I saw in my sleep that the Day of Resurrection was taking place and everyone was lined up in a single file. I too was brought into the line and my actions were then taking account of, after which I was lead into Paradise. After entering into Paradise, large and beautiful mansions were presented to me and I was told to count the number of doors of the mansion. I began to count the number of doors and enumerated fifty. I was then told to count the number of houses, and when I counted them, I saw that there were 155 homes. I was then told that all of these were for me! I woke up from my dream, elated, and went to Muḥammad b. Sirīn – a person who had complete skills in the interpreration of dreams and explained my dream to him. He said to me, 'Is it true that you recite Āyatul Kursī frequently?' I replied, 'Yes it is – how do you know?' He said to me, 'I realized this as Āyatul Kursī has fifty words and 155 letters.' He then said to me, 'O ʿAbdullāh! Whosoever recites Āyatul Kursī frequently will find the pangs of death (*sakratul mawt*) will be made easy for him.'"[259]

71. Protection during Pregnancy and Delivery

It has been narrated from Fāṭima al-Zahrā' ﷺ that when she was pregnant and about to deliver her child, the Messenger of Allāh ﷺ told Umm Salama and Zaynab, the daughter of Jaḥsh, to go to her and protect her through the recitation of Āyatul Kursī, and verse 54 from Sūrah al-Aʿrāf which is as follows:

﴿إِنَّ رَبَّكُمْ اللهُ الَّذِى خَلَقَ السَّمَاوَاتِ وَالأَرْضَ فِى سِتَّةِ
أَيَّامٍ ثُمَّ اسْتَوَى عَلَى الْعَرْشِ يُغْشِى اللَّيْلَ النَّهَارَ
يَطْلُبُهُ حَثِيثًا وَالشَّمْسَ وَالْقَمَرَ وَالنُّجُومَ مُسَخَّرَاتٍ

[259] Ibid., vol. 1, p. 157.

بِأَمْـرِهِ أَلاَ لَهُ الْـخَلْقُ وَالأَمْـرُ تَبَـارَكَ اللهُ رَبُّ الْعَالَمِـينَ ﴿٥٤﴾

Surely your Lord is Allāh, Who created the heavens and the earth in six periods of time, and He is firm in power; He throws the veil of night over the day, which it pursues incessantly; and (He created) the sun and the moon and the stars (and they are) made subservient by His command; surely His is the creation and the command; blessed is Allāh, the Lord of the Worlds.[260]

72. Alleviation from Headaches

A man once complained to Imām al-Sādiq ﷺ about headaches that he was having, and in reply the Imām said: "Place your hand on the part of your head which is hurting and recite Āyatul Kursī and Sūrah al-Fātiḥa and then recite the following supplication."

أَللّٰهُ أَكْبَرُ أَللّٰهُ أَكْبَرُ لاَ إِلٰهَ إِلاَّ اللّٰهُ وَ اللّٰهُ أَكْبَرُ أَللّٰهُ أَجَلُّ وَ أَكْبَرُ مِمَّا أَخَافُ وَ أَحْذَرُ أَعُوذُ بِاللّٰهِ مِنْ عِرْقٍ نِعَارٍ وَ أَعُوذُ بِاللّٰهِ مِنْ حَرِّ النَّارِ

Allāh is greater [than anything else]; Allāh is greater [than anything else]. There is no god worthy of worship except for Allāh and Allāh is greater [than anything else]. Allāh is more glorious and much greater than that which I fear [from other things] and I am careful from. I seek refuge in Allāh from excessive blood flow from the veins and I seek refuge in Allāh from the burning of the fire of hell.

73. Relief from the "Evil Eye"

Muʿamar b. Khilād said: "I was with Imām ʿAlī al-Riḍā ﷺ in one

[260] *Quran*, Sūrah al-Aʿrāf (7), verse 54; *Musnad Fāṭima*, p. 336.

of the markets of Khorāsān [present day Mashad] when the Imām asked me to purchase some perfume for him. When I got the perfume, I looked at it with amazement to which the Imām replied to me, 'O Muʿamar! Indeed the 'evil eye' is a reality – thus on a piece of paper, write Sūrah al-Ḥamd, [Sūrah] al-Ikhlāṣ, the *muʿawīdhatayn* (Sūrah al-Falaq and Sūrah al-Nās) and Āyatul Kursī and place them in a pot or glass [and keep it with you].'"

74. When Wearing New Clothing

Anytime Imām ʿAlī al-Riḍā ﷺ would put on new clothing, he would start off by first putting on the right side; but before that, he would ask for a glass of water and recite Sūrah al-Ikhlāṣ, Āyatul Kursī and Sūrah al-Kāfirūn each ten times over the glass of water and then sprinkle the water over the clothes; and he would say: "Whoever does this will continuously have ample sustenance as long as the fibres of that clothing remain."

75. Strengthening One's Memory

In his final treatise entitled *Ādāb al-Mutaʿalimīn*, the late Muḥaqqiq al-Ṭūsī states the following in the 11th section: "Some of the best things which can be used to strengthen one's memory are: always exerting efforts (in one's work), taking care of one's self (spiritually), eating less, performing the night prayers with complete humility and humbleness, and reciting the Quran. It has also been stated that there is nothing better to help in strengthening one's memory than reciting the Quran - and specifically Āyatul Kursī."[261]

76. Greatest of Deeds

Imām al-Ṣādiq ﷺ has said: "Whoever recites Sūrah al-Ikhlāṣ, Sūrah al-Qadr and Āyatul Kursī in every *rakʿat* of one's recommended prayers will indeed find Allāh, the Glorified and

---

[261] *Biḥār al-Anwār*, vol. 73, p. 320.

Mighty, record the greatest of deeds of all human beings (in the person's book of deeds)."[262]

77. Closest Angels and Deputed Prophets Supplicate

The Noble Messenger ﷺ has said: "Indeed Āyatul Kursī has been written on a special tablet [in the presence of Allāh] with green emeralds, and a special pen. I swear by Allāh that there is not a single Friday which comes except that the tablet makes [the angel] Isrāfīl tremble, and when he shakes, he beings to recite the *tasbīḥ* [glorification of Allāh] by saying:

سُبْحَانَ مَنْ لاَ يَنْبَغِي التَّسْبِيحَ إِلاَّ لَهُ وَ لاَ الْعِبَادَةَ وَ الْخُضُوعَ
إِلاَّ لِوَجْهِهِ ذٰلِكَ اللّٰهُ الْقَدِيرُ الْوَاحِدُ الْعَزِيزُ

> Glory be to the One who other than Him, none are worth glorifying and [who other than Him] none are worthy of being worshipped or shown humility to. That is Allāh – the All-Powerful, the One, the Grand.

When the angel recites this glorification of Allāh, all of the angels in the heavens proclaim the praise and glory (of Allāh). Then, when the inhabitants of the heavens and the earth hear their glorification, they too begin to venerate Allāh and there is not a single close angel and deputed prophet except that they do this for every single individual who recited Āyatul Kursī on this day."[263]

78. Supplication of the Angels

ʿAbdullāh b. Hasan said: "My mother Fāṭima, the daughter of Imām al-Ḥusayn ؑ said: 'I saw the Messenger of Allāh in my sleep and he told me: 'O my daughter! I do not see any harm coming to the scale of balance of your good deeds because of your recitation of Āyatul Kursī.' Therefore, there is not a single

---

[262] Ibid., vol. 82, p. 36.

[263] Ibid., vol. 86, p. 355.

person who is from me that recites this, except that the heavens and the earth are filled with (their respective angels) who sing the glorification, praise, adoration and acclaimation of Allāh - through which the person is spiritually cleansed, and it is at this time that the angels make supplications for that person who just recited Āyatul Kursī and for which Allāh forgives all of their sins and overlooks all of their slips and errors.'"[264]

---

[264] Ibid.

Section 7

Frequently Referenced Quranic Passages

Sūrah al-Fātiḥa (1)

بِسْمِ اللهِ ٱلرَّحْمَـٰنِ ٱلرَّحِيمِ ۝١ ٱلْحَمْدُ لِلَّهِ رَبِّ ٱلْعَالَمِينَ ۝٢ ٱلرَّحْمَـٰنِ
ٱلرَّحِيمِ ۝٣ مَـٰلِكِ يَوْمِ ٱلدِّينِ ۝٤ إِيَّاكَ نَعْبُدُ وإِيَّاكَ نَسْتَعِينُ ۝٥
ٱهْدِنَا ٱلصِّرَاطَ ٱلْمُسْتَقِيمَ ۝٦ صِرَاطَ ٱلَّذِينَ أَنْعَمْتَ عَلَيْهِمْ
غَيْرِ ٱلْمَغْضُوبِ عَلَيْهِمْ وَلاَ ٱلضَّآلِّينَ ۝٧

《1》 In the Name of Allāh, the Beneficent, the Merciful. 《2》 All praise belongs to Allāh, Lord of the Worlds. 《3》 The Beneficent, the Merciful. 《4》 Master of the Day of Judgement. 《5》 You alone do we worship and from You alone do we seek assistance. 《6》 Keep us on the right path. 《7》 The path of those to whom You have granted blessings, those who are neither subject to Your anger nor have gone astray.

Āyatul Kursī (2), verses 255-257

بِسْمِ اللهِ ٱلرَّحْمَـٰنِ ٱلرَّحِيمِ

ٱللَّهُ لَآ إِلَـٰهَ إِلَّا هُوَ ٱلْحَىُّ ٱلْقَيُّومُ لَا تَأْخُذُهُۥ سِنَةٌ وَلَا نَوْمٌ لَّهُۥ مَا
فِى ٱلسَّمَـٰوَٰتِ وَمَا فِى ٱلْأَرْضِ مَن ذَا ٱلَّذِى يَشْفَعُ عِندَهُۥٓ إِلَّا بِإِذْنِهِۦ
يَعْلَمُ مَا بَيْنَ أَيْدِيهِمْ وَمَا خَلْفَهُمْ وَلَا يُحِيطُونَ بِشَىْءٍ مِّنْ
عِلْمِهِۦٓ إِلَّا بِمَا شَآءَ وَسِعَ كُرْسِيُّهُ ٱلسَّمَـٰوَٰتِ وَٱلْأَرْضَ وَلَا يَـُٔودُهُۥ
حِفْظُهُمَا وَهُوَ ٱلْعَلِىُّ ٱلْعَظِيمُ ﴿٢٥٥﴾ لَآ إِكْرَاهَ فِى ٱلدِّينِ قَد تَّبَيَّنَ
ٱلرُّشْدُ مِنَ ٱلْغَىِّ فَمَن يَكْفُرْ بِٱلطَّـٰغُوتِ وَيُؤْمِنۢ بِٱللَّهِ فَقَدِ
ٱسْتَمْسَكَ بِٱلْعُرْوَةِ ٱلْوُثْقَىٰ لَا ٱنفِصَامَ لَهَا وَٱللَّهُ سَمِيعٌ عَلِيمٌ
﴿٢٥٦﴾ ٱللَّهُ وَلِىُّ ٱلَّذِينَ ءَامَنُوا۟ يُخْرِجُهُم مِّنَ ٱلظُّلُمَـٰتِ إِلَى ٱلنُّورِ
وَٱلَّذِينَ كَفَرُوٓا۟ أَوْلِيَآؤُهُمُ ٱلطَّـٰغُوتُ يُخْرِجُونَهُم مِّنَ ٱلنُّورِ إِلَى
ٱلظُّلُمَـٰتِ أُو۟لَـٰٓئِكَ أَصْحَـٰبُ ٱلنَّارِ هُمْ فِيهَا خَـٰلِدُونَ ﴿٢٥٧﴾

In the Name of Allāh, the Beneficent, the Merciful. ﴾255﴿ Allāh - there is no god except Him – He is the Ever-Living, the All-Sustainer. Neither drowsiness befalls Him nor sleep. To Him belongs whatever is in the heavens and whatever is on the earth. Who is it that may intercede with Him except by His permission? He knows that which is before them and that which is behind them, and they do not comprehend anything of His knowledge except what He wishes. His Throne embraces the heavens and the earth, and He is not wearied by their preservation, and He is the All-Exalted, the All-Supreme. ﴾256﴿ There is no compulsion in religion:

rectitude has become distinct from error. So one who disavows the rebels and has faith in Allāh has held fast to the firmest handle for which there is no breaking; and Allāh is All-Hearing, All-Knowing. ﴿257﴾ Allāh is the Master of the faithful: He brings them out of the darknesses into the light. And as for the faithless, their patrons are the rebels, who drive them out of the light into the darknesses. They shall be the inmates of the Fire, in it they shall remain [forever].

Sūrah Āle ʿImrān (3), verses 190-200

﴿إِنَّ فِي خَلْقِ ٱلسَّمَٰوَٰتِ وَٱلْأَرْضِ وَٱخْتِلَٰفِ ٱلَّيْلِ وَٱلنَّهَارِ
لَأَيَٰتٍ لِّأُوْلِي ٱلْأَلْبَٰبِ ﴿١٩٠﴾ ٱلَّذِينَ يَذْكُرُونَ ٱللَّهَ قِيَٰمًا وَقُعُودًا
وَعَلَىٰ جُنُوبِهِمْ وَيَتَفَكَّرُونَ فِي خَلْقِ ٱلسَّمَٰوَٰتِ وَٱلْأَرْضِ رَبَّنَا مَا
خَلَقْتَ هَٰذَا بَٰطِلًا سُبْحَٰنَكَ فَقِنَا عَذَابَ ٱلنَّارِ ﴿١٩١﴾ رَبَّنَآ
إِنَّكَ مَن تُدْخِلِ ٱلنَّارَ فَقَدْ أَخْزَيْتَهُۥ ۖ وَمَا لِلظَّٰلِمِينَ مِنْ
أَنصَارٍ ﴿١٩٢﴾ رَّبَّنَآ إِنَّنَا سَمِعْنَا مُنَادِيًا يُنَادِي لِلْإِيمَٰنِ أَنْ ءَامِنُواْ
بِرَبِّكُمْ فَـَٔامَنَّا ۚ رَبَّنَا فَٱغْفِرْ لَنَا ذُنُوبَنَا وَكَفِّرْ عَنَّا سَيِّـَٔاتِنَا
وَتَوَفَّنَا مَعَ ٱلْأَبْرَارِ ﴿١٩٣﴾ رَبَّنَا وَءَاتِنَا مَا وَعَدتَّنَا عَلَىٰ رُسُلِكَ وَلَا
تُخْزِنَا يَوْمَ ٱلْقِيَٰمَةِ ۗ إِنَّكَ لَا تُخْلِفُ ٱلْمِيعَادَ ﴿١٩٤﴾ فَٱسْتَجَابَ لَهُمْ
رَبُّهُمْ أَنِّي لَآ أُضِيعُ عَمَلَ عَٰمِلٍ مِّنكُم مِّن ذَكَرٍ أَوْ أُنثَىٰ ۖ
بَعْضُكُم مِّنۢ بَعْضٍ ۖ فَٱلَّذِينَ هَاجَرُواْ وَأُخْرِجُواْ مِن دِيَٰرِهِمْ
وَأُوذُواْ فِي سَبِيلِي وَقَٰتَلُواْ وَقُتِلُواْ لَأُكَفِّرَنَّ عَنْهُمْ سَيِّـَٔاتِهِمْ
وَلَأُدْخِلَنَّهُمْ جَنَّٰتٍ تَجْرِي مِن تَحْتِهَا ٱلْأَنْهَٰرُ ثَوَابًا مِّنْ عِندِ

ٱللَّهِ ۚ وَٱللَّهُ عِندَهُۥ حُسْنُ ٱلثَّوَابِ ﴿١٩٥﴾ لَا يَغُرَّنَّكَ تَقَلُّبُ ٱلَّذِينَ
كَفَرُوا۟ فِى ٱلْبِلَـٰدِ ﴿١٩٦﴾ مَتَـٰعٌ قَلِيلٌ ثُمَّ مَأْوَىٰهُمْ جَهَنَّمُ ۖ وَبِئْسَ
ٱلْمِهَادُ ﴿١٩٧﴾ لَـٰكِنِ ٱلَّذِينَ ٱتَّقَوْا۟ رَبَّهُمْ لَهُمْ جَنَّـٰتٌ تَجْرِى مِن
تَحْتِهَا ٱلْأَنْهَـٰرُ خَـٰلِدِينَ فِيهَا نُزُلًا مِّنْ عِندِ ٱللَّهِ ۗ وَمَا عِندَ
ٱللَّهِ خَيْرٌ لِّلْأَبْرَارِ ﴿١٩٨﴾ وَإِنَّ مِنْ أَهْلِ ٱلْكِتَـٰبِ لَمَن يُؤْمِنُ بِٱللَّهِ
وَمَآ أُنزِلَ إِلَيْكُمْ وَمَآ أُنزِلَ إِلَيْهِمْ خَـٰشِعِينَ لِلَّهِ لَا يَشْتَرُونَ
بِـَٔايَـٰتِ ٱللَّهِ ثَمَنًا قَلِيلًا ۚ أُو۟لَـٰٓئِكَ لَهُمْ أَجْرُهُمْ عِندَ رَبِّهِمْ ۗ إِنَّ
ٱللَّهَ سَرِيعُ ٱلْحِسَابِ ﴿١٩٩﴾ يَـٰٓأَيُّهَا ٱلَّذِينَ ءَامَنُوا۟ ٱصْبِرُوا۟ وَصَابِرُوا۟
وَرَابِطُوا۟ وَٱتَّقُوا۟ ٱللَّهَ لَعَلَّكُمْ تُفْلِحُونَ ﴿٢٠٠﴾ »

《190》 Surely, in the creation of the heavens and the earth and (in) the alternation of the night and the day there are many signs for people of pure and clear understanding. 《191》 These are the people who remember Allāh standing, and sitting and (lying) on their sides and reflect upon the creation of the heavens and the earth (and say,) 'Our Lord! You have not created (all) this in vain. Glory be to You, save us from the punishment of the Fire. 《192》 Our Lord! Whomsoever You cause to enter the Fire, You have truly disgraced him, and there will be none to help these unjust. 《193》 Our Lord! Certainly, we heard a crier calling to the Faith, saying, "Believe in your Lord," and so we have believed. Our Lord! Protect us against our sins and rid us of our evils and cause us to die (and after death count us) with the virtuous. 《194》 Our Lord! Grant us what You have promised us through Your messengers and do not disgrace us on the Day of Resurrection. Surely, You do not break Your promise.' ﴾195﴿ Their Lord then, accepted their prayer for them (saying), 'I will not, most certainly suffer the deed of any doer (of good) from among you, whether male or female, to be lost; the one of you being as the other. Hence those who have emigrated, and have been driven out of their homes, and have been persecuted in My cause, and who have fought and been killed, surely I will absolve them of their evils and will, of course, admit them into Gardens served with running streams, a reward from Allāh. And Allāh, with Him is the fairest reward (to offer). ﴾196﴿ Do not let the moving about in the land, of those who have disbelieved, deceive you. ﴾197﴿ (It is) a brief provision, then the fire of hell shall be their abode. What an evil place of rest! ﴾198﴿ But those who took their Lord as a shield shall have Gardens served with running streams, therein shall they live for ever, an entertainment from Allāh Himself; and that which is with Allāh is better still for the virtuous. ﴾199﴿ There are some among the people of the Scripture who believe in Allāh and in that which has been revealed to you and in that which has been revealed to them, humbling themselves before Allāh, they barter not the Messages of Allāh for a paltry price, it is these whose reward is due with their Lord. Indeed, Allāh is Swift in reckoning. ﴾200﴿ O you who believe! Be patiently persevering and strive to excel (the disbelievers) in being patiently persevering and guard (the frontiers) and ward off evil, keep your duty to Allāh so that you may attain your goal.﴿

Sūrah al-Mulk (67)

بِسْمِ اللهِ ٱلرَّحْمَـٰنِ ٱلرَّحِيمِ

﴿تَبَـٰرَكَ ٱلَّذِى بِيَدِهِ ٱلْمُلْكُ وَهُوَ عَلَىٰ كُلِّ شَىْءٍ قَدِيرٌ ١ ٱلَّذِى

خَلَقَ ٱلْمَوْتَ وَٱلْحَيَاةَ لِيَبْلُوَكُمْ أَيُّكُمْ أَحْسَنُ عَمَلاً وَهُوَ
ٱلْعَزِيزُ ٱلْغَفُورُ ﴿٢﴾ ٱلَّذِى خَلَقَ سَبْعَ سَمَاوَاتٍ طِبَاقاً مَّا تَرَىٰ
فِى خَلْقِ ٱلرَّحْمَـٰنِ مِن تَفَاوُتٍ فَٱرْجِعِ ٱلْبَصَرَ هَلْ تَرَىٰ مِن
فُطُورٍ ﴿٣﴾ ثُمَّ ارجِعِ البَصَرَ كَرَّتَيْنِ يَنْقَلِبْ إِلَيْكَ البَصَرُ
خَاسِئاً وَهُوَ حَسِيرٌ ﴿٤﴾ وَلَقَدْ زَيَّنَّا ٱلسَّمَآءَ ٱلدُّنْيَا بِمَصَابِيحَ
وَجَعَلْنَاهَا رُجُوماً لِّلشَّيَاطِينِ وَأَعْتَدْنَا لَهُمْ عَذَابَ ٱلسَّعِيرِ ﴿٥﴾
وَلِلَّذِينَ كَفَرُواْ بِرَبِّهِمْ عَذَابُ جَهَنَّمَ وَبِئْسَ ٱلْمَصِيرُ ﴿٦﴾ إِذَآ
أُلْقُواْ فِيهَا سَمِعُواْ لَهَا شَهِيقاً وَهِىَ تَفُورُ ﴿٧﴾ تَكَادُ تَمَيَّزُ مِنَ
ٱلغَيْظِ كُلَّمَا أُلْقِىَ فِيهَا فَوْجٌ سَأَلَهُمْ خَزَنَتُهَآ أَلَمْ يَأْتِكُمْ
نَذِيرٌ ﴿٨﴾ قَالُواْ بَلَىٰ قَدْ جَآءَنَا نَذِيرٌ فَكَذَّبْنَا وَقُلْنَا مَا نَزَّلَ
اللهُ مِن شَىْءٍ إِنْ أَنتُمْ إِلاَّ فِى ضَلاَلٍ كَبِيرٍ ﴿٩﴾ وَقَالُواْ لَوْ كُنَّا
نَسْمَعُ أَوْ نَعْقِلُ مَا كُنَّا فِىۤ أَصْحَابِ ٱلسَّعِيرِ ﴿١٠﴾ فَٱعْتَرَفُواْ
بِذَنبِهِمْ فَسُحْقاً لِأَصْحَابِ ٱلسَّعِيرِ ﴿١١﴾ إِنَّ ٱلَّذِينَ يَخْشَوْنَ
رَبَّهُم بِٱلْغَيْبِ لَهُم مَّغْفِرَةٌ وَأَجْرٌ كَبِيرٌ ﴿١٢﴾ وَأَسِرُّواْ قَوْلَكُمْ
أَوِ ٱجْهَرُواْ بِهِ إِنَّهُ عَلِيمٌ بِذَاتِ ٱلصُّدُورِ ﴿١٣﴾ أَلاَ يَعْلَمُ مَنْ
خَلَقَ وَهُوَ ٱللَّطِيفُ ٱلْخَبِيرُ ﴿١٤﴾ هُوَ ٱلَّذِى جَعَلَ لَكُمُ ٱلأَرْضَ
ذَلُولاً فَٱمْشُواْ فِى مَنَاكِبِهَا وَكُلُواْ مِن رِّزْقِهِ وَإِلَيْهِ ٱلنُّشُورُ
﴿١٥﴾ ءَأَمِنتُمْ مَّن فِى ٱلسَّمَآءِ أَن يَخْسِفَ بِكُمُ ٱلأَرْضَ فَإِذَا هِىَ
تَمُورُ ﴿١٦﴾ أَمْ أَمِنتُمْ مَّن فِى ٱلسَّمَآءِ أَن يُرْسِلَ عَلَيْكُمْ حَاصِباً

فَسَتَعْلَمُونَ كَيْفَ نَذِيرِ ﴿١٧﴾ وَلَقَدْ كَذَّبَ ٱلَّذِينَ مِن قَبْلِهِمْ
فَكَيْفَ كَانَ نَكِيرِ ﴿١٨﴾ أَوَلَمْ يَرَوْا إِلَى ٱلطَّيْرِ فَوْقَهُمْ صَافَّاتٍ
وَيَقْبِضْنَ مَا يُمْسِكُهُنَّ إِلاَّ ٱلرَّحْمَـٰنُ إِنَّهُ بِكُلِّ شَيْءٍ بَصِيرٌ ﴿١٩﴾
أَمَّنْ هَـٰذَا ٱلَّذِي هُوَ جُندٌ لَّكُمْ يَنصُرُكُم مِّن دُونِ ٱلرَّحْمَـٰنِ
إِنِ ٱلْكَافِرُونَ إِلاَّ فِي غُرُورٍ ﴿٢٠﴾ أَمَّنْ هَـٰذَا ٱلَّذِي يَرْزُقُكُمْ إِنْ
أَمْسَكَ رِزْقَهُ بَل لَّجُّوا فِي عُتُوٍّ وَنُفُورٍ ﴿٢١﴾ أَفَمَن يَمْشِي مُكِبًّا
عَلَىٰ وَجْهِهِ أَهْدَىٰ أَمَّن يَمْشِي سَوِيًّا عَلَىٰ صِرَاطٍ مُّسْتَقِيمٍ ﴿٢٢﴾
قُلْ هُوَ ٱلَّذِي أَنشَأَكُمْ وَجَعَلَ لَكُمُ ٱلسَّمْعَ وَٱلْأَبْصَارَ
وَٱلْأَفْئِدَةَ قَلِيلاً مَّا تَشْكُرُونَ ﴿٢٣﴾ قُلْ هُوَ ٱلَّذِي ذَرَأَكُمْ فِي
ٱلْأَرْضِ وَإِلَيْهِ تُحْشَرُونَ ﴿٢٤﴾ وَيَقُولُونَ مَتَىٰ هَـٰذَا ٱلْوَعْدُ إِن كُنتُمْ
صَادِقِينَ ﴿٢٥﴾ قُلْ إِنَّمَا ٱلْعِلْمُ عِندَ ٱللَّهِ وَإِنَّمَا أَنَا نَذِيرٌ مُّبِينٌ
﴿٢٦﴾ فَلَمَّا رَأَوْهُ زُلْفَةً سِيئَتْ وُجُوهُ ٱلَّذِينَ كَفَرُوا وَقِيلَ هَـٰذَا
ٱلَّذِي كُنتُم بِهِ تَدَّعُونَ ﴿٢٧﴾ قُلْ أَرَأَيْتُمْ إِنْ أَهْلَكَنِيَ ٱللَّهُ وَمَن
مَّعِيَ أَوْ رَحِمَنَا فَمَن يُجِيرُ ٱلْكَافِرِينَ مِنْ عَذَابٍ أَلِيمٍ ﴿٢٨﴾ قُلْ
هُوَ ٱلرَّحْمَـٰنُ آمَنَّا بِهِ وَعَلَيْهِ تَوَكَّلْنَا فَسَتَعْلَمُونَ مَنْ هُوَ فِي
ضَلاَلٍ مُّبِينٍ ﴿٢٩﴾ قُلْ أَرَأَيْتُمْ إِنْ أَصْبَحَ مَاؤُكُمْ غَوْراً فَمَن
يَأْتِيكُم بِمَاءٍ مَّعِينٍ ﴿٣٠﴾ »

In the Name of Allāh, the Beneficent, the Merciful. ⟪1⟫ Blessed is He in whose hands is the Kingdom and who has power over all things. ⟪2⟫ It is He who has created death and life to put you to the test and see which of you is most virtuous in your deeds. He is Majestic and All-Forgiving. ﴾3﴿ It is He who has created seven heavens, one above the other. You can see no flaw in the creation of the Beneficent God. Look again. Can you see faults? ﴾4﴿ Look twice (and keep on looking), your eyes will only become dull and tired. ﴾5﴿ We have decked the lowest heavens with torches. With these torches We have stoned the devils and We have prepared for them the torment of hell. ﴾6﴿ For those who have disbelieved in their Lord, We have prepared the torment of hell, the most terrible place to return. ﴾7﴿ When they are thrown into hell, they will hear its roaring while it boils. ﴾8﴿ It almost explodes in rage. Whenever a group is thrown into it, its keepers will ask them, "Did no one come to warn you?" ﴾9﴿ They will say, "Yes, someone did come to warn us, but we rejected him saying, 'God has revealed nothing. You are in great error.'" ﴾10﴿ They will also say, "Had We listened or used our minds, we would not have become the dwellers of hell." ﴾11﴿ They will confess to their sins, but the dwellers of hell will be far away from God's (mercy). ﴾12﴿ Those who fear their Lord in secret will receive forgiveness and a great reward. ﴾13﴿ Whether you conceal what you say or reveal it, God knows best all that the hearts contain. ﴾14﴿ Does the One Who is Subtle, All-Aware, and Who created all things not know all about them? ﴾15﴿ It is He who has made the earth subservient to you. You walk through its vast valleys and eat of its sustenance. Before Him you will all be resurrected. ﴾16﴿ Do you feel secure that the One in the heavens will not cause you to sink into the earth when it is violently shaking? ﴾17﴿ Do you feel secure that the One in the heavens will not strike you with a sandstorm? You will soon know, with the coming of the torment, how serious Our warning was. ﴾18﴿ Those who lived before them had also rejected Our warning, and how terrible was Our retribution! ﴾19﴿ Did they not see the birds above them, stretching out, and flapping their wings. No one keeps them up in the sky except the Beneficent God. He certainly watches over all things. ﴾20﴿ Do you have any armies who will help you against the Beneficent God? The disbelievers are certainly deceived (by Satan). ﴾21﴿ Is there anyone who will provide you with sustenance if God were to deny you sustenance? In fact, they obstinately persist in their transgression and hatred. ﴾22﴿ Can one who walks with his head hanging down be better guided that one who walks with his head upright? ﴾23﴿ (Muḥammad), say, "It is God who has brought you into being and made ears, eyes, and hearts for you, but you give very little thanks." ﴾24﴿ Say, "It is God who has settled you on the earth and to Him you will be resurrected." ﴾25﴿ They say, "When will this torment take place if what you say is true?" ﴾26﴿ Say, "God knows best. I am only one who gives warning." ﴾27﴿ When they see the torment approaching, the faces of the disbelievers will blacken and they will be told, "This is what you wanted to (experience)." ﴾28﴿ (Muḥammad), say, "Have you not considered that regardless whether God forgives me and my followers or grants us mercy, but who will protect the disbelievers from a painful torment? ﴾29﴿ Say, "He is the Beneficent One in whom we have faith and trust. You will soon know who is in manifest error." ﴾30﴿ Say, "Have you not thought that if your water was to dry up, who would bring you water from the spring?"

Sūrah al-Qadr (97)

بِسْمِ اللهِ ٱلرَّحْمَـٰنِ ٱلرَّحِيمِ

إِنَّا أَنزَلْنَاهُ فِى لَيْلَةِ ٱلْقَدْرِ ﴿١﴾ وَمَآ أَدْرَاكَ مَا لَيْلَةُ ٱلْقَدْرِ ﴿٢﴾
لَيْلَةُ ٱلْقَدْرِ خَيْرٌ مِّنْ أَلْفِ شَهْرٍ ﴿٣﴾ تَنَزَّلُ ٱلْمَلاَئِكَةُ وَٱلرُّوحُ
فِيهَا بِإِذْنِ رَبِّهِم مِّن كُلِّ أَمْرٍ ﴿٤﴾ سَلاَمٌ هِىَ حَتَّىٰ مَطْلَعِ
ٱلْفَجْرِ ﴿٥﴾

In the Name of Allāh, the Beneficent, the Merciful. ⟪1⟫ We revealed it [the Quran] on the Night of Destiny. ⟪2⟫ Would that you knew what the Night of Destiny is! ⟪3⟫ The Night of Destiny is better than 1,000 months. ⟪4⟫ On this Night, the angels and the spirit descend by the permission of their Lord with His Decree (to determine everyone's destiny). ⟪5⟫ This Night is all peace until the break of dawn.

Sūrah al-Zilzāl (99)

بِسْمِ اللهِ ٱلرَّحْمَـٰنِ ٱلرَّحِيمِ

إِذَا زُلْزِلَتِ ٱلأَرْضُ زِلْزَالَهَا ﴿١﴾ وَأَخْرَجَتِ ٱلأَرْضُ أَثْقَالَهَا ﴿٢﴾
وَقَالَ ٱلإِنسَانُ مَا لَهَا ﴿٣﴾ يَوْمَئِذٍ تُحَدِّثُ أَخْبَارَهَا ﴿٤﴾ بِأَنَّ رَبَّكَ
أَوْحَىٰ لَهَا ﴿٥﴾ يَوْمَئِذٍ يَصْدُرُ ٱلنَّاسُ أَشْتَاتاً لِّيُرَوْاْ أَعْمَالَهُمْ ﴿٦﴾
فَمَن يَعْمَلْ مِثْقَالَ ذَرَّةٍ خَيْراً يَرَهُ ﴿٧﴾ وَمَن يَعْمَلْ مِثْقَالَ ذَرَّةٍ
شَرّاً يَرَهُ ﴿٨﴾

In the Name of Allāh, the Beneficent, the Merciful. ⟪1⟫ When the earth is shaken by a terrible quake ❨2❩ And it throws out its burden, ❨3❩ The human being will say (in horror), "What is happening to it?" ❨4❩ On that day the earth will declare all (the activities of the human being) which have taken place on it, ❨5❩ Having been inspired by your Lord. ❨6❩ On that day, people will come out of their graves in different groups to see (the results of) their own deeds. ❨7❩ Whoever has done an atom's weight of good, will see it. ❨8❩ And whoever has done an atom's weight of evil, will also see it.

Sūrah al-Kāfirūn (109)

بِسْمِ اللهِ ٱلرَّحْمَـٰنِ ٱلرَّحِيمِ

قُلْ يَٰٓأَيُّهَا ٱلْكَٰفِرُونَ ۝١ لَآ أَعْبُدُ مَا تَعْبُدُونَ ۝٢ وَلَآ أَنتُمْ عَٰبِدُونَ مَآ أَعْبُدُ ۝٣ وَلَآ أَنَا۠ عَابِدٌ مَّا عَبَدتُّمْ ۝٤ وَلَآ أَنتُمْ عَٰبِدُونَ مَآ أَعْبُدُ ۝٥ لَكُمْ دِينُكُمْ وَلِىَ دِينِ ۝٦

In the Name of Allāh, the Beneficent, the Merciful. ❨1❩ Say (O Muḥammad): O you the disbelievers, ❨2❩ I do not worship what you worship, ❨3❩ Nor do you worship what I worship ❨4❩ I have not been worshipping what you worshipped, ❨5❩ Nor will you ever worship what I worship. ❨6❩ You follow your religion and way of life and I follow mine.

Sūrah al-Ikhlāṣ (112)

بِسْمِ اللهِ ٱلرَّحْمَـٰنِ ٱلرَّحِيمِ

قُلْ هُوَ اللهُ أَحَدٌ ۝١ ٱللهُ ٱلصَّمَدُ ۝٢ لَمْ يَلِدْ وَلَمْ يُولَدْ ۝٣ وَلَمْ يَكُن لَّهُۥ كُفُوًا أَحَدٌۢ ۝٤

In the Name of Allāh, the Beneficent, the Merciful. ❬1❭ (Muḥammad), say, "He is the only God. ❬2❭ God is Absolute. ❬3❭ He neither begets nor was He begotten. ❬4❭ There is no one equal to Him.

Sūrah al-Falaq (113)

بِسْمِ اللهِ ٱلرَّحْمَٰنِ ٱلرَّحِيمِ

قُلْ أَعُوذُ بِرَبِّ ٱلْفَلَقِ ﴿١﴾ مِن شَرِّ مَا خَلَقَ ﴿٢﴾ وَمِن شَرِّ
غَاسِقٍ إِذَا وَقَبَ ﴿٣﴾ وَمِن شَرِّ ٱلنَّفَّاثَاتِ فِى ٱلْعُقَدِ ﴿٤﴾ وَمِن شَرِّ
حَاسِدٍ إِذَا حَسَدَ ﴿٥﴾

In the Name of Allāh, the Beneficent, the Merciful. ❬1❭ (Muḥammad), say, "I seek protection from the Lord of the Dawn. ❬2❭ Against the evil of whatever He has created. ❬3❭ I seek His protection against the evil of the invading darkness, ❬4❭ from the evil of those who practice witchcraft ❬5❭ and from the evil of the envious ones.

Sūrah al-Nās (114)

بِسْمِ اللهِ ٱلرَّحْمَٰنِ ٱلرَّحِيمِ

قُلْ أَعُوذُ بِرَبِّ ٱلنَّاسِ ﴿١﴾ مَلِكِ ٱلنَّاسِ ﴿٢﴾ إِلَٰهِ ٱلنَّاسِ ﴿٣﴾
مِن شَرِّ ٱلْوَسْوَاسِ ٱلْخَنَّاسِ ﴿٤﴾ ٱلَّذِى يُوَسْوِسُ فِى صُدُورِ ٱلنَّاسِ
﴿٥﴾ مِنَ ٱلْجِنَّةِ وَٱلنَّاسِ ﴿٦﴾

In the Name of Allāh, the Beneficent, the Merciful. ❬1❭ (Muḥammad), say, "I seek protection from the Cherisher of mankind, ❬2❭ The King of mankind, ❬3❭ The Lord of mankind

﴾4﴿ Against the evil of the temptations of the satans, ﴾5﴿ Who induce temptation into the hearts of mankind. ﴾6﴿ From among the jinn and the human beings.

Other Writings and Translations from Saleem Bhimji and Publications from the Islamic Publishing House[265]

1. 40 Aḥādīth: Completion of Islām – Ghadīr written by Mahmud Sharifi and translated by Saleem Bhimji[3]
2. 40 Aḥādīth: Qur'an written by Sayyid Majid Adili and translated by Arifa Hudda and Saleem Bhimji[3 and 4]
3. 40 Aḥādīth: The Saviour of Humanity – the 12th Imām in the Eyes of the Ahl al-Bayt written by Nasir Karimi and translated by Saleem Bhimji[3]
4. 40 Aḥādīth: The Spiritual Journey – Ḥajj written by Mahmud

---

265 Note of publishers:

1 = *Islamic Humanitarian Service* (Canada) – www.al-haqq.com

2 = *Al-Fath Al-Mubin Publications* (Canada) – www.al-mubin.org

3 = *World Federation of KSIMC* (UK) – www.world-federation.org

4 = *Islamic Publishing House* (Canada) – www.iph.org

5 = Various publishers

6 = Not available in print [either an eBook] or out of print

7 = *Jaffari Propagation Centre* (India) – www.jpconline.org

1. Most of the above books and hundreds of other articles can be read for free at **www.al-mubin.org** or **www.al-islam.org**

Mahdipur and translated by Saleem Bhimji[3]

5. A Biography of the Marjaʿ Taqlid of the Shiʿa World: Ayatullah al-Uzma Sayyid ʿAli al-Husayni al-Sistani translated by Saleem Bhimji[5]
6. A Code of Ethics for Muslim Men and Women written by Sayyid Masʿud Maʿsumi and translated by Arifa Hudda and Saleem Bhimji[1]
7. A Mother's Prayer compiled and translated by Saleem Bhimji and Arifa Hudda[1 and 2]
8. A Summary of the Rulings of Ṣalātul Jamāʿat according to the edicts of Ayatullah al-Uzma Sayyid ʿAli al-Husayni al-Sistani compiled and translated by Saleem Bhimji[1]
9. Alif, Baa, Taa of Kerbala written by Saleem Bhimji and Arifa Hudda[4]
10. Arbāʿīn of Imām Husayn compiled and translated by Saleem Bhimji[6]
11. Deficient? A Review of Sermon 80 from Nahj al-Balāgha by Ayatullah al-Uzma Shaykh Nasir Makarim Shirazi and translated by Saleem Bhimji[6]
12. Ethical Discourses – Volume 1 written by Ayatullah al-Uzma Shaykh Nasir Makarim Shirazi and translated by Saleem Bhimji (not printed)
13. Ethical Discourses – Volume 2 written by Ayatullah al-Uzma Shaykh Nasir Makarim Shirazi and translated by Saleem Bhimji (not printed)
14. Exegesis of the 29th Juz of the Qurʾān – a Translation of Tafsīr-i Nemuneh by Ayatullah al-Uzma Shaykh Nasir Makarim Shirazi and translated by Saleem Bhimji[1 and 4]
15. Fountain of Paradise – Fāṭima az-Zahrāʾ in the Noble Quran written by Ayatullah al-Uzma Shaykh Nasir Makarim Shirazi compiled and translated by Saleem Bhimji[4, 5 and 7]
16. Guiding the Youth of the New Generation written by Ayatullah Shaykh Murtadha Mutahhari and translated by

Saleem Bhimji[2 and 3]

17. History Behind Masjid Jamkarān along with Selected Supplications to the 12th Imām and translated by Saleem Bhimji[1]
18. House of Sorrows written by Shaykh ʿAbbas al-Qummi and translated by Aejaz Ali Turab Husayn Hussayni[4]
19. Introduction to Islām written by Saleem Bhimji[1]
20. Introduction to the Science of Tafsīr of the Quran written by Shaykh Jaʿfar Subhani and translated by Saleem Bhimji[3]
21. Islam and Religious Pluralism by Ayatullah Shaykh Murtadha Mutahhari and translated by Sayyid Sulayman Ali Hasan[3]
22. Islāmic Edicts on Family Planning by the UNFPA with the Ministry of Health of the Islamic Republic of Iran and translated by Saleem Bhimji[5]
23. Istikhāra: Seeking the Best from Allāh written by Muhammad Baqir Hayderi and translated by Saleem Bhimji[1]
24. Journey to Eternity – A Handbook of Supplications for the Soul compiled and translated by Saleem Bhimji and Arifa Hudda[4 and 7]
25. Khums: The Islāmic Tax written by Ayatullah al-Uzma Shaykh Nasir Makarim Shirazi and translated by Saleem Bhimji (not printed)
26. Love and Hate for Allah's Sake by Mujtaba Saburi translated by Saleem Bhimji[4, 5 and 7]
27. Love for the Family compiled and translated by Yasin T. Al-Jibouri, Saleem Bhimji and others[4, 5 and 7]
28. Manifestation of the Divine Light – A Glimpse into the Ziyārah of Fāṭimah az-Zahrāʾ by Shaykh ʿAli Saʿadat Parwar translated by Saleem Bhimji[4]
29. Meʿrāj: The Night Ascension written by Mullah Muhammad Faydh al-Kashani and translated by Saleem Bhimji[1]
30. Message of the Quran a translation of Payām-e-Quran –

Volume 1 – A Thematic Exegesis of the Noble Quran written by Ayatullah al-Uzma Shaykh Nasir Makarim Shirazi and translated by Saleem Bhimji[3]

31. Method of Ṣalāt written by Muhammad Qadhi and translated by Saleem Bhimji[5]
32. Moral Management written by ʿAbbas Rahimi and translated by Saleem Bhimji[4 and 7]
33. Morals of the Masumeen written by Arifa Hudda[4]
34. On the Shore of Contemplation - Authority of the Jurist – Compiled by the office of Ayatullah Ja'far Subhani and translated by Saleem Bhimji[4]
35. Prayers of the Final Prophet – A collection of supplications of Prophet Muhammad written by ʿAllamah Sayyid Muhammad Husayn Tabatabai and translated by Tahir Ridha-Jaffer[4 and 7]
36. Ramaḍhān Reflections compiled by A Group of Muslim Scholars and translated by Saleem Bhimji[4 and 7]
37. Rules Relating to the Deceased: Condensed Version according to the edicts of Ayatullah al-Uzma Sayyid ʿAli al-Husayni al-Sistani translated by Saleem Bhimji[1]
38. Rules Relating to the Deceased: Philosophy and Ahkam according to the edicts of Ayatullah al-Uzma Sayyid ʿAli al-Husayni al-Sistani and translated by Saleem Bhimji[1]
39. Salat al-Ayat written by Saleem Bhimji[1 and 4]
40. Ṣalāt al-Ghufaylah written by Saleem Bhimji[4 and 7]
41. Secrets of the Ḥajj written by Ayatullah al-Uzma Shaykh Husayn Mazaheri and translated by Saleem Bhimji[2 and 4]
42. Simplified Islāmic Laws for Youth and Young Adults according to the edicts of Ayatullah al-Uzma Sayyid ʿAli al-Husayni al-Sistani and translated by Saleem Bhimji[1]
43. Simplified Islāmic Laws for Youth and Young Adults according to the edicts of Ayatullah al-Uzma Shaykh Lutfullah Safi Gulpaygani and translated by Saleem Bhimji[5]

44. Sunan al-Nabī written by ʿAllamah Sayyid Muhammad Husayn Tabatabai and translated by Tahir Ridha-Jaffer[4]
45. Tafsir of Sūratul Jinn by Ayatullah al-Uzma Shaykh Nasir Makarim Shirazi and translated by Saleem Bhimji[1 and 3]
46. Taʿqībāt: The Daily Prayers compiled and translated by Saleem Bhimji and Arifa Hudda[1,4 and 7]
47. The Firmest Armament: Commentary on Āyatul Kursī [The Verse of the Throne] written by Sayyid Nasrullah Burujerdi and translated by Saleem Bhimji[4]
48. The Islāmic Moral System: A Commentary of Sūratul Ḥujurāt written by Ayatulalh Jaʿfar Subhani and translated by Saleem Bhimji[1 and 3]
49. The Last Luminary and Ways to Delve into the Light written by Sayyid Muhammad Ridha Husayni Mutlaq and translated by Saleem Bhimji[4 and 7]
50. The Light of the Family of the Prophet – A Colouring Book with Ḥadīth for Young Muslim Children translated by Saleem Bhimji[1]
51. The Tasbīḥ of Fāṭima al-Zahrāʾ written by ʿAbbas Azizi and translated by Arifa Hudda and Saleem Bhimji[1]
52. The Torch of Perpetual Guidance - A Commentary on Ziyārat al-ʿĀshūrāʾ written by ʿAbbas Azizi and translated by Saleem Bhimji[4 and 7]
53. Weapon of the Believer written by ʿAllamah Muhammad Baqir Majlisi and translated by Saleem Bhimji[4 and 7]
54. Ziyārah: History, Philosophy and Etiquette compiled and translated by Saleem Bhimji[4]

To be published, Inshā-Allāh (God Willing):

1. A Year with Prophet Muḥammad ﷺ written by Saleem Bhimji, Arifa Hudda and Muhadditha Fatema Saleem
2. People of the Frontiers - Commentary on the Supplication

for the People of the Frontiers by Imām ʿAlī ibn al-Ḥusayn Zayn al-ʿĀbidīn ﷺ written by Shaykh Ḥusayn Anṣāriyān and translated by Saleem Bhimji

3. The Ninth Day – The Day of ʿArafah compiled and translated by Saleem Bhimji and Arifa Hudda
4. Young Muslims' Daily Devotions - Volumes 1, 2, 3 - compiled and translated by Saleem Bhimji and Arifa Hudda

...and more to come, Insha-Allāh (God Willing)

ABOUT THE ISLAMIC PUBLISHING HOUSE

عَـنْ أَبِي عَبْـدِ اللّٰـهِ عَـنْ آبَائِـهِ ﷺ: قَـالَ جَـاءَ رَجُـلٌ إِلىٰ رَسُـولِ اللّٰـهِ ﷺ فَقَـالَ يَـا رَسُـولَ اللّٰـهِ مَـا الْعِلْـمُ؟ قَـالَ أَلإِنْصَـاتُ. قَـالَ ثُـمَّ مَـهْ؟ قَـالَ أَلإِسْـتِمَاعُ. قَـالَ ثُـمَّ مَـهْ؟ قَـالَ أَلْحِفْـظُ. قَـالَ ثُـمَّ مَـهْ؟ قَـالَ أَلْعَمَـلُ بِـهِ. قَـالَ ثُـمَّ مَـهْ يَـا رَسُـولَ اللّٰـهِ؟ قَـالَ: نَـشْرُهُ.

Abū ʿAbdillāh narrates from his ancestors ﷺ who said the following: "A man once came to the Messenger of Allāh ﷺ and said, 'O' Messenger of Allāh, what is knowledge?' The Prophet replied, **'It is silence.'** The man then asked, 'Then what?' The Prophet said, **'It is listening.'** The man asked, 'Then what?' The Prophet replied, **'Then it is remembering.'** The man asked, 'Then what?' The Prophet said, **'Then it is to practice (according to what has been learnt).'** The man then asked, 'Then what O' Messenger of Allāh?' The Prophet replied, **'Then it is to disseminate (what one has learned).'**"

[Ref: *Al-Kāfī*, vol. 1, p. 48, trad. 4.]

Established in early 2001, gaining inspiration from the above quoted statement from Prophet Muḥammad ﷺ, the *Islamic Publishing House* has developed into Canada's premier publisher of high quality Islamic literature for Muslims of all ages. Our mission is to ensure that the authentic teachings of normative Islam — in all aspects of life — as exemplified by Prophet Muḥammad ﷺ and his immaculate family, the Ahlul Bayt ؑ, are made available for everyone in a clear and easy to understand language.

Over the past several years, we have been fortunate to publish **20 full length texts** which have been distributed throughout the world in print; released **7 ePublications;** and authored hundreds of articles - all thanks to the blessings of Allāh ﷻ, the grace of the Prophet ﷺ and the Ahlul Bayt ؑ and the continued material support from donors all around the world.

With the ever changing landscape of how and where we consume information, we have embarked upon the creation of what we term, '***Visualations***' in which we fuse together audio, video and the written word to develop a unique educational experience – videos which are uploaded to our YouTube channel and also on the station at Shia TV – garnishing tens of thousands of viewers.

Our publications and video productions are all financially supported by generous donations of individuals and non-Profit institutions in North America and Europe, for whom we are eternally grateful.

As we continue to produce English publications and unique and original video content, we continually appeal to all of those people who have a passion for the spread of the faith of Islam as taught by the family of the Prophet ؑ to assist us in any way possible in promoting the teachings of Islam as taught by Prophet Muḥammad ﷺ and the Ahlul Bayt ؑ.

HOW CAN YOU GET INVOLVED?

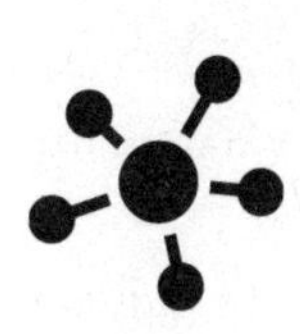

PROMOTE our content – books, videos, etc... with your contacts on social media and within your local communities in addition to your circle of family and friends.

VOLUNTEER your time and talents to assist us with our print publications or our video content and help us to expand our global reach via social media.

SUPPORT our work by generously donating financially towards content creation and the costs associated with publications, video production and future initiatives.

SUGGEST content which you feel is needed for Muslims to better understand their faith or to educate non-Believers which is not already available in print or video.

HELP us by making du'a – supplication – to Allah for our guidance and success in our efforts to spread the teachings of Islam to others and educate them.

To support us in any of the ways mentioned above, please contact us at iph@iph.ca